JOHN BUNYAN'S
GRACE ABOUNDING
and
THE PILGRIM'S PROGRESS

GARLAND REFERENCE LIBRARY
OF THE HUMANITIES
(VOL. 773)

JOHN BUNYAN'S
GRACE ABOUNDING
and
THE PILGRIM'S PROGRESS

An Overview of Literary Studies 1960–1987

Beatrice Batson

GARLAND PUBLISHING, INC. • NEW YORK & LONDON
1988

© 1988 Beatrice Batson
All rights reserved

Library of Congress Cataloging-in-Publication Data
Batson, E. Beatrice.
John Bunyan's Grace abounding and the Pilgrim's progress.

(Garland reference library of the humanities ; vol. 773)
Includes index.
1. Bunyan, John, 1628–1688—Criticism and interpretation—History. 2. Bunyan, John, 1628–1688. Grace abounding to the chief of sinners. 3. Bunyan, John, 1628–1688. Pilgrim's progress. 4. Bunyan, John, 1628–1688—Bibliography. 5. Christian literature, English—History and criticism. I. Title. II. Series.
PR3332.B36 1988   828'.407   87-35684
ISBN 0-8240-6630 (alk. paper)

Printed on acid-free, 250-year-life paper
Manufactured in the United State of America

To
Lois and Yvonne
Nancy, Mark, and Jane

ACKNOWLEDGEMENTS

I should like to express special thanks to Johns Hopkins University Press for permission to include Wolfgang Iser's essay from The Implied Reader and for permission to quote excerpts from Felicity Nussbaum's essay, "By These Words I was Sustained: Bunyan's Grace Abounding" and from Robert Bell's "Metamorphoses of Spiritual Autobiography." Full citation is given at the end of each essay.

Special thanks also go to the University of North Carolina Press, which holds the copyright to John Knott's "Bunyan and the Holy Community," SP, LXXX, no. 2 (Spring 1983), 200-25 and to Dayton Haskin's essay, "The Burden of Interpretation in The Pilgrim's Progress," SP, 79 (1982), 256-78, for granting permission to reprint Professor Knott's essay in its entirety and to reprint a brief section from Professor Haskin's article. I also express my gratitude to Anne Hawkins and the Philological Quarterly for permission to reprint sections of "The Double-Conversion in Bunyan's Grace Abounding," Philological Quarterly, LXI, no.3 (Summer 1982), and to the Editor of SEL for permission to reprint Rebecca Beal's essay "Grace Abounding to the Chief of Sinners: John Bunyan's Pauline Epistle," SEL 21 (1961), 147-60. To the Editor of English Literary Renaissance and again to Professor John Knott, I owe a debt of gratitude for permission to include portions of Professor Knott's essay, "Bunyan's Gospel Day: A Reading of The Pilgrim's Progress," ELR, 3, (1973), 443-46. The Editor of Journal of Narrative Technique also gave permission to include under "Viewpoints" a few paragraphs from James F. Forrest's splendid essay.

By permission of Oxford University Press, I am also including sections from N.H. Keeble's Introduction to his edition of The Pilgrim's Progress (World Classic's paperback, 1984). The Oxford Press also gave permission to use the Wharey-Sharrock edition of The Pilgrim's Progress for a few lines from Bunyan.

To each author, editor and to all presses

which hold copyrights, I deeply appreciate permission to include their excellent works in this book.

CONTENTS

Preface	xi
Introduction	xiii
Bunyan Studies Since 1960	3
Selected Examples of Critical Studies	63
Annotated Bibliography	175
Index	240

PREFACE

The purpose of this book is to present an overview of literary studies since 1960 on John Bunyan's Grace Abounding and The Pilgrim's Progress (Part One and Part Two). A brief introduction focuses on John Bunyan, and on what might be called Bunyan's literary theory, and then shows the direction critical studies on Bunyan's three well-known works have taken since 1960. A summary of studies of Bunyan prior to 1960 is briefly sketched. How modern scholars read, analyze, and interpret Grace Abounding and The Pilgrim's Progress (Part One and Part Two) is undoubtedly primarily due to their theories of literature and as the study will show, Bunyan's relgious writings become a testing ground for the notions of leading modern critics.

Various critical assessments will become obvious from a chapter devoted to a discussion of trends in the scholarship. Some of the journal articles, chapters in books, and entire books are thoroughly examined; some are treated less thoroughly, but in each work, I have attempted to show the core of the argument without offering my own agreement or disagreement with the author's stance. At times, I have quoted rather heavily in order to give the scholar-critic a fair hearing. The next chapter brings together complete essays by scholars as well as selected viewpoints from the writings of other scholar-critics. The complete essays and viewpoints from important writings are chosen not because they happen to pertain to the three works under consideration but because they show the focus of modern studies and assist readers in understanding the trends of modern scholarship on these three Bunyan works. A final chapter is an annotated bibliography, primarily devoted to various readings and interpretations of the works. To my knowledge this phase of the bibliography is thorough. A few annotations include essays on particular episodes and topics within the selected Bunyan works; still fewer focus on the influences of John Bunyan on other writers. Some attention is given to writings on autobiography and allegory as literary genres. The bibliography includes books, chapters in books, journal articles, and unpublished doctoral dissertations. I have not discussed editions, but I should hope that all Bunyan scholars are aware of the excellent work by the Oxford University Press in its preparation of a new and complete edition of all Bunyan's writings.

In the preparation of this book, I owe gratitude to many individuals, particularly to the authors of the various essays as well as to the editors of journals and books in which the essays included in my second chapter originally appeared. I deeply appreciate their permission to reprint their studies in the book. I am also grateful to the Clarendon Press for permission to quote from the Wharey-Sharrock edition of The Pilgrim's Progress. To numerous members of library staffs in this country and abroad I express my deep appreciation for their assistance in locating essays not readily accessible. Mark Atterbury and Jane Yarhouse, two excellent majors in English Literature at Wheaton College, gave unstintingly of their time and energy in assisting with bibliographical materials and with other features entailed in the long preparation of the manuscript, and to them I owe a special debt. To Yvonne B. Robery, secretary of Wheaton's Department of English, I express my most sincere thanks for her careful work with the word processor in order to offer this manuscript in orderly condition to Garland, and for her thoughtful help in ways far too varied to include here and which goes beyond her mastery of a word processor, I shall always be deeply grateful.

INTRODUCTION

"He is as individual as Shakespeare, as Dr. Johnson; like them he is of our English institutions: like Shakespeare he is more--he belongs to humanity," Gwilym O. Griffith (John Bunyan, London, 1927) glowingly states of John Bunyan. Whether one views Griffith's statement as a mere exaggeration or a valid fact, it is indisputable that Bunyan's writings, especially Grace Abounding and The Pilgrim's Progress, have had a profound impact on readers for three centuries. The greater part of the writing about Bunyan's works prior to the middle of the twentieth century was primarily in the nature of religious commentary and moral exhortations. Early critics of the works tended either to dwell on the way the works exemplified the Puritan tradition or on the uniqueness of The Pilgrim's Progress, particularly in its attempt to disguise the Puritan source of the allegory. Critics of Grace Abounding focused on the interior struggle of Bunyan, who like other Puritans, wrote of a consuming sense of guilt and of a deep need for knowing beyond question the free grace of Christ. What fed the thinking of early critics, who bothered at all with Grace Abounding, was the pathological intensity of Bunyan's experiences and the manner in which fearful dreams and visions tormented each step of his existence. To say that such an emphasis is no longer the concern of the critic is without foundation; to see the tendency of the modern critic to explore other facets of the autobiography will be part of our discovery in this study. It is of interest, at this point, to remind ourselves that James Sutherland in English Literature of the Late Seventeenth Century (Oxford, 1969) recognizes in Grace Abounding, the "odd vagaries of the human mind and the psychological eccentricities of individual experience." He refuses, however, to leave his comments with

xiii

this observation and goes on to declare: "Indeed, there is as much knowledge of the human heart and the human mind in Bunyan as we meet with in the whole body of Restoration drama" (p. 326). What Bunyan does is to narrate his own absorbing drama of the struggle between the forces of good and evil for his own soul, and that dramatic narrative embodies numerous features of drama as a literary genre.

When Bunyan wrote The Pilgrim's Progress in 1678, and despite its almost instant popularity with readers, literary scholars practically ignored it, but it is probably not too far removed from the truth to say that Bunyan became his own critic. Although what Bunyan had to say in his allegory was not new, his method of saying it was unpopular with scores of readers who had previously thought that imaginative literature was in Sutherland's words "almost wholly in the hand of the literary sons of Belial."

Bunyan's central idea of the life of the Christian on earth as a long and difficult pilgrimage was a well-known theme of devotional writers, but many of his friends apparently preferred straightforward exhortation found in the various treatises of the era, including those written by Bunyan. This new book, which seemed to happen without warning to the author, lacked solidity. It was "dark, feigned"--not true, according to the thinking of some of his friends who wanted Bunyan to say clearly what he had to say, and to declare these important matters without disguise. In the rhymed preface to his allegory, Bunyan shapes his own theory of literature in that he finds in the distinctive characters of The Pilgrim's Progress a crucible to test his views of the nature of imaginative literature.

Whatever Bunyan wrote he did so with a specific purpose in mind, or as James Sutherland states " ... his whole endeavor was to use words so that they did God's work" (p. 315). Even though Sutherland contends that "the perfection of his [Bunyan's] prose style is to be found in the extent to which his words are the incarnation of his thoughts; and its tremendous impact on the reader is largely due to his utter devotion to the spiritual business in hand," he admits that one can still discuss Bunyan's "prose style, his command of narrative, his keen sense of character, his skill in reproducing colloquial speech, and much else ... " (p. 316). That Bunyan himself shows concern for the "much else" or for literary art is undeniable; that he also believes in the hortatory nature of his writings is equally true. What appears to contradict such a position may be partially due to Bunyan's own statements. When he declares in the Preface to Grace Abounding that had he chosen to do so, he could have written in a style much higher than that of the plain and simple discourse of his autobiography, he perhaps leaves himself open to criticism for his indifference to literary merit. Yet a careful scrutiny of the narrative graphically shows the traditional features of a spiritual autobiography: a focusing on a particular self and the relation of that self to God, the recapturing of a past, the unfolding of incidents as part of one process, the examination of the inner landscape and its relation to external activities, and a sudden perception of reality through reliving it in the imagination.

What may also seem to be convincing proof that he had interest only in preaching a message in his writings is yet another quotation from Bunyan himself. In the rhymed preface to The Pilgrim's Progress, he compares himself to a fisherman who "ingageth all his Wits; /Also Snares, Lines, Angles, Hooks and Nets" and to a fowler, who seeks "to catch his Game, by divers means ... /His Gun, his Nets, his Lime-twigs, light and bell ... " (p. 3) to accomplish his goals. Again, Bunyan seems preoccupied with the urgency to clarify his purpose for writing any word, and that purpose appears to be exclusively to evangelize or to ensnare his readers. That Bunyan writes from a theological thrust is incontrovertible; that he also believes in the wonder and power of language is equally unquestionable. To him, art and truth are not incongruous; in numerous passages from his own writings he gives his views on literary art. These passages bring into focus aspects of his own literary theory.

In the rhymed preface to The Pilgrim's Progress and, paradoxically, in lines closer to doggerel than to poetry, Bunyan pinpoints characteristic qualities of literary art, especially in his insistence upon the truth of metaphor, upon art as incarnation, and upon the transforming power of the imagination. To explain that art is no enemy of truth, he summons the authority of the Bible and insists:

> The Prophets used much by Metaphors
> To set forth Truth; Yes, who so considers
> Christ, his Apostles too, shall plainly see,
> That Truths to this day in such Mantles be
> (p. 4).

What he perceives is that the Bible is an artistic book filled with metaphors; thus, he not only has the highest authority for writing metaphorically, but he further believes that metaphors embody truth. Unlike those who criticize without understanding the nature of metaphorical language, Bunyan discerns the multi-dimensional power of metaphor to generate new meaning by making words suggest more than they ordinarily mean.

From the Book he knows best, Bunyan sees that familiar and commonplace words like pearls, wine skins, seeds, a clay lamp, a city on a hill, a lost coin, a barren fig tree, a lost sheep, and other ordinary terms become suggestive of reality beyond themselves and embody spiritual truth. Convinced that metaphorical language tells us something about God as well as something about ourselves and that one gets at the "something" through metaphor and not through extricating abstract statements, Bunyan argues without apology that "base things usher in divine." He would probably be the last individual to negate the significance of conceptual language, but for the literal-minded message hunters, who desire only direct proposition and exclusively expository interpretations, Bunyan still declares that metaphor, too, embodies truth and in language that is not finally paraphrasable or translatable. To show resemblances, to depict connections, to express more than the familiar, and to unite the ordinary and mundane with the transcendent and mysterious are the ways of metaphor, and for Bunyan a writer's work is no less true if written in metaphorical language.

It is through the central metaphor of a journey that John Bunyan writes of the stages of a Christian pilgrim from the City of Destruction to the Celestial City. The metaphorical journey takes Pilgrim into numerous conflicts with the world, and yet he goes beyond and ultimately out of it. No words with specialized and technical meanings are in his narrative; there are, however, many words that mean more than usual and many that "call for one thing to set forth another" (p. 6).

If he recognizes that literary art suggests far more than it actually says, that it shows by indirection, and that metaphor embraces the transcendent and the immediate, Bunyan further suggests that the method of God in revealing the Word is also the method of the writer.

In the Incarnate God, Holy Truth, are hid all treasures of wisdom and knowledge. The Divine is clothed in flesh; the Infinite dwells in the finite. This is the central paradox of the Incarnation; it is also the paradox of Bunyan's literary art. As Christ, the Word, is the physical embodiment of the Divine so the written word is capable of capturing the profoundly transcendent in the immediate. In an obvious reference to the scriptual passage, "And she brought forth her firstborn son, and wrapped him in swaddling clothes, and laid him in a manger," Bunyan declares, "Truth, although in swadling-clouts, I find" (p. 5). Holy Truth in swaddling clothes does not come among men in catalogued discourse but rather dwells in human form. As a Christian writer, Bunyan perceives that he must incarnate the spiritual and transcendent in terms of the physical and immediate. For, he says, the "Truth in Swadling-clouts":

> Informs the Judgement, rectifies the Mind,
> Pleases the Understanding, makes the Will
> Submit; the Memory too it doth fill
> With what doth our Imagination please ...
> (p. 5).

In only a few lines, Bunyan captures his arduous task: to find the language that will image forth a perception of reality in a manner that not only embodies truth but penetrates the judgment, the mind, the understanding, the will, indeed the entirety of the human being, in a fresh, imaginative way. The writer makes, says Bunyan, "base things usher in divine." Art as incarnation is at the center of his view of literary art.

If it is true that metaphorical language embodies truth and that the writer must seek to incarnate the spiritual in concrete terms, it is equally true that creative qualities come through an act of the imagination. While believing the Bible to be the inspired Word of God, Bunyan also knows that it is an artistic book; consequently, he lacks no justification for his imaginative, dream vision of man on a journey from gracelessness to rebirth; from earth to heaven. Unabashedly he can say:

>   ... would'st thou see
> A man i' the Clouds, and hear him speak to thee?
> Would'st thou be in a Dream, and yet not sleep?
> Or would'st thou in a moment Laugh and Weep?
> Wouldest thou loose thy self, and catch no harm?
> And find thy self again without a charm? (p. 7)

Bunyan delineates his understanding of the nature of imaginative literature--its illusory quality, its nexus of meaning, its tragi-comic essence, and its power to evoke response. Equally important is his obvious belief in the imaginative faculty to show something significant and to show it by embodying shaped and interpreted experiences in an imagined yet real world. The pattern of Bunyan's great allegory is to take man <u>through dream</u> to an understanding of his human situation and bring him <u>in dream</u> to a transformed condition. Significantly, the final turn in Bunyan's best known, imaginative allegory is a <u>return</u> to the actual world of men. The dreamer sees the gates of the Celestial City open, but only in dream vision; he wishes himself among those in the beautiful city, but he has to awaken from the dream to the reality of Bedford jail. If he awakens, so also must the reader, but the paradox implicit in the imaginative but realistic image of the dream vision still provokes the reader. The burden of proof is now upon the dream-reader, and that is exactly where Bunyan wants it.

Bunyan, in his defense of imaginative literature, has also suggested a rather remarkably thorough depiction of a Logos-centered theory of literature. It seems accurate to state that Bunyan himself tested a literary theory of his own work to a degree far more intensive than that of any seventeenth-century scholar. The literal fact is that in the era, literary scholars neglected to study Bunyan's works as literary writings.

As particularly stated in one essay in the next chapter, throughout the eighteenth century Bunyan received little attention of a positive nature. Joseph Addison perhaps was as generous an any author when he cited Bunyan as proof that even despicable writers had their admirers.

Writers of the nineteenth century began to consider Bunyan as an imaginative writer and to study his allegory as an artistic work. Coleridge, for instance, contended that The Pilgrim's Progress was one of the few books that might be read repeatedly with always a new and different pleasure. The vigorous, rhythmic style of Bunyan appealed to George Eliot, another nineteenth-century author. Attention to sources of Bunyan's imaginative writings, particularly his allegory, was also a prominent concern of nineteenth-century scholarship.

It is the twentieth-century academician who has gone beyond treating Bunyan as an isolated Puritan author, capable of writing a reputable autobiography and a unique allegory. Key studies include Henri A. Talon's John Bunyan, l'homme et l'oeuvre (Paris, 1948; translated into English by Barbara Wall, London, 1951) and Roger Sharrock's John Bunyan (London, 1954, 1968) and the short study of The Pilgrim's Progress (London, 1966). In his careful studies on the writings of Bunyan, including Grace Abounding and The Pilgrim's Progress, Sharrock's contributions to Bunyan scholarship are evident even from the various essays and books mentioned in this study.

Richard L. Greaves and James F. Forrest,

whose scholarly works illuminate from many angles the writing of Bunyan, are not only familiar with Puritan theology and Bunyan's appreciation of it, but they also understand Bunyan as literary artist.

What is apparent in Bunyan studies today is that the writer who was once scorned by the scholar is now primarily studied by university and college professors and their students. As the overview and the annotated bibliography will show, Bunyan's writings, particularly <u>Grace Abounding</u> and <u>The Pilgrim's Progress</u>, have a prominent place in the thinking of critics such as Stanley Fish, Wolfgang Iser, Maureen Quilligan and many others. Numerous critics see in Bunyan's works splendid bases for a discussion of their views on narrative, on the involvement of the reader in the reading process, on radical play with langauge, on the relation of reading convention to textual interpretation, and on the "affective" nature of literary art. Whatever the critical approach, the thrust focuses primarily on narrative art. U. Milo Kaufmann, for example, in <u>The Pilgrim's Progress and Traditions in Puritan Meditation</u> (New Haven, 1966) examines the narrative art of <u>The Pilgrim's Progress</u> in terms of the conflict of Bunyan's theological tradition and his literary art. Kaufmann's work leads to subsequent and subtle discussions on the narrative mode, some agreeing with Kaufmann's view, others elaborating upon it, and others vilifying it.

The overview of works, included in this study, attempts to show honestly the opinions of numerous modern scholars and critics, and to demonstrate clearly that Bunyan's writings lend themselves to a variety of theoretical approaches.

JOHN BUNYAN'S

GRACE ABOUNDING

and

THE PILGRIM'S PROGRESS

GRACE ABOUNDING

and

THE PILGRIM'S PROGRESS
(Parts One and Two)

Studies since 1960 on Grace Abounding show interest in the pattern of the work as a spiritual autobiography; some few scholars still explore the artistic nature and purpose of the work, but the primary focus of the modern scholar is on the narrative art of the work. Various scholars explore the narrative, as one expects, from major theoretical positions adopted by contemporary critics. The latter thrust particularly entails various aspects of reader-response criticism, a term not considered to be a conceptually unified critical position. To borrow a phrase from M.H. Abrams, "How to do things with Texts" also becomes an all-consuming concern. To show an overview of the trends, it seems wise to begin not with a chronological ordering of the various essays but rather with a study that gives attention to Grace Abounding within the autobiographical tradition.

Robert Bell ("Metamorphosis of Spiritual Autobiography," ELH, 44, 1977) believes that Grace Abounding, "in its broad contours" belongs to the Augustinian model. Conversion remains, in Bell's judgment, "the formal principle of organization, determining the selection of details and development of plot." Like Augustine, Bunyan selects from various and random experiences and depicts unexceptional action which takes on spiritual implications. Also like Augustine, he begins the autobiography with his "own natural life" at the time he was "without God and in the world."

Bunyan is different, however, from Augustine in that he employs greater realistic detail and gives much more attention to his perspective at a given time in his experience. Perhaps the most telling departure from Augustinian narrative, in Bell's judgment, is that Bunyan is much less "confident of his present authority." Following statements in which he conceives of experience as moments for gluttony and games, Bunyan will, in turn, conclude an episode with a defense of his integrity, which would be beneath "Augustine's eminent dignity."

The essay also considers other autobiographers such as Franklin and Defoe. Franklin produces a "secular version of spiritual autobiography" through his "ascetic self-denial" and "famous scheme for moral regeneration." Defoe accomplished "as defiant an assertion of the primacy of individual experience in the novel as Descartes' 'cogito ergo sum' did in philosophy."

Bell's entire essay is a substantial study of the literary history of autobiography, showing clearly where Grace Abounding stands in the tradition.

Dayton Haskin ("Bunyan, Luther, and the Struggle with Belatedness in Grace Abounding," UTE, 50 no. 3, 1981) continues a discussion of models for spiritual autobiography and contends that Luther held up his life, and that of the Apostle Paul's, as a model for the true Christian experience. Bunyan then borrowed a paradigm of Christian experience from Luther, who in turn borrowed it from Paul. Haskin further holds that Luther cannot be accorded all the credit for creating the introspective conscience which Bunyan inherited. The introspective strain had received its definitive formulation in Augustine's Confessions; Luther simply rescued a "suppressed tendency in Western spirituality." For Haskin, Luther's influence upon the writing of autobiographies as well as his impact upon his followers' religious experiences derives from his categories of two "times": the "time" of the Law and the "time" of the Gospel. These "times," Luther finds, in the Scriptures; and the Scriptures provide the starting-point for spiritual autobiography. That Luther was conforming his experience to a biblical original did not render him derivative, according to Haskin, in that "originality consists, rather precisely in that conformity, inasmuch as it has been achieved through personal inward experience." If Haskin's statement is true of Luther and his originality, so also does the same statement refute the charges that Bunyan is merely derivative.

Anne Hawkins has little concern for the tradition of the spiritual autobiography or the place of Grace Abounding in literary history. In her article "The Double Conversion in Grace Abounding," (Philological Quarterly 61, 1982), she approaches the work as a narrative which lacks structure due to the nature of Bunyan's conversion--"a kind of conversion which is by definition diffuse, repetitive, and cumulative." She declares as her intent to look at Grace Abounding as a narrative which derives its thematic properties and structural unity from Bunyan's personal experience of conversion--an experience which is itself derivative of existing models in the theology and cultural milieu of seventeenth-century England" (p. 259). What Hawkins assumes is that types of conversion can be treated as morphological categories, whether gradual or sudden. Adapting terminology from William James' Varieties of Religious Experience, she describes conversion in terms of James' analogy between spiritual and physical healing: lysis and crisis, one gradual, the other abrupt.

Early in her study, Hawkins thoughtfully observes that the temptations which Bunyan endures are orthodox Calvinist issues; "but that these doctrinaire problems have their correlatives in the non-formulaic truths of the heart is not always so evident" (p. 261). In Calvinist theology, however, conversion is a lifelong process, on a lysis model. She then defines the lysis conversion as a "gradual process of spiritual maturation" which follows a dyadic structure. In Grace Abounding, this means that Bunyan's conversion is represented as a process which unfolds gradually over a long period of time, but also that there are two specific transitional nodes in this gradual process; in other words, that there are two conversion events" (p. 264). What Haw-

AN OVERVIEW

kins has in mind regarding the two conversion events is the first event when Bunyan receives evidence of his election and the second is the later episode when the "two opposing forces of salvation (represented by the New Testament passage about the sufficiency of Grace) and of damnation (represented by the Old Testament story of Esau) meet together on the battlefield of the heart ..." (p. 264). The latter event is actually the "dyadic nature" of conversion. What this dyad suggests in theological terms is justification and sanctification.

Hawkins finds the dyadic nature of conversion clearly articulated by William Ames, whose work precedes Bunyan's by some forty years. Ames defines conversion as twofold: The "relative" change, freeing the believer from guilt, and the "real" change, purifying the believer himself. First, Bunyan turns from nature to grace, receiving the sign of election ("relative" change). Then he turns from grace to glory, learning the sufficiency of grace (the "real" change).

The autobiography of the Baptist Anne Trapnel manifests the same dyadic structure, and Hawkins less convincingly argues that the spiritual autobiography of James Fraser (1670) and that of John Bunyan clearly correspond. It is clear that there are many striking similarities between the two autobiographies, and Hawkins helpfully maps these out by setting an outline of Fraser's synopsis--a synopsis Fraser sets forth in a preface to his spiritual autobiography--side by side with an outline of Grace Abounding.

After arguing that Bunyan's experience is that of the lysis conversion, Hawkins observes that one should expect to find that pattern in his allegories as well. In The Pilgrim's Progress, Christian and Great-heart in a sense represent "two developmental facets of John Bunyan": the Bunyan who has undergone justification and the Bunyan who has experienced sanctification. There are correspondingly two types of clothing in The Pilgrim's Progress: the "Raggs" and a "Broidered Coat."

Returning to Grace Abounding, Hawkins declares that the autobiography may appear structurally diffuse because one expects a crisis conversion, but actually its structure is "the literary counterpart to the theological anxiety which underlies lysis conversion." Thus, Hawkins, finds in the nature of Bunyan's conversion the structure of the autobiography, thereby explaining her early statement that "there appears to be little sense of structure at all in Grace Abounding," the latter, of course, being unavoidable if one refuses to see her "double-conversion" pattern. What she clearly contends is that the "structural diffuseness which we find in the autobiography is not a product of faulty craftsmanship but a literary counterpart to the theological anxiety which underlies lysis conversion--where salvation is not perceived in birth imagery as the simultaneous death of the old man and rebirth of the new, but in the language and metaphor of education, as a gradual process of error and relearning, or fall and recovery, or wrong-doing and punishment whereby the soul matures into a regenerative state" (p. 271). Hawkins believes that the principle of "dyadic repetition" is a recognizable "structural element" in the seventeenth century which acts "both on the conversion experience itself and also on the autobiographical reconstruction of the conversion" (p. 273).

Without referring to the terminology of lysis and crisis, Melvin Watson ("The Drama of Grace Abounding," ES 46, 1965) agrees with Hawkins that Bunyan's conversion was not an instantaneous event. Believing that Bunyan's "salvation was not achieved in the twinkling of an eye" and that his "conversion at times seemed to stretch out to the crack of doom," Watson's focus is not exclusively on gradual conversion experience but rather it is primarily on the way Bunyan uses time in Grace Abounding. He contends that Bunyan treats time impressionistically; the reader feels "the drama of time." In this examination of Bunyan's handling of time, Watson attempts to counteract some of the more vitriolic criticism of Bunyan's Grace Abounding. Watson sees this "drama of time," not through a "dyadic" structure but rather through the formal ordering of the autobiography, especially through paragaph

AN OVERVIEW

264, "that would please the fussiest neoclassicist." What concerns Watson is not merely Bunyan's gradual conversion experience but rather that he writes an autobiogaphy which is a work of art. Watson sees Grace Abounding as an artistic work particularly in the way in which the body of the autobiography falls into four sections, each of which leads up to a climax.

Watson recognizes that some of the modern approaches, which emphasize a "sensitive personality reacting violently to the workings of a strong conscience in a supercharged religious milieu," may be valid, but equally valid, however, is an examination of Grace Abounding as a work of art. Approaching it in the latter manner causes the critical reader to see it as a carefully constructed dramatic work of art which comes to a powerful climax and thence to a long-delayed resolution.

Barret J. Mandel ("Bunyan and the Autobiographer's Artistic Purpose," Criticism 10, 1968) dismisses Watson's treatment of time in that he holds Bunyan's treatment of time (and space) to be the one aspect of Grace Abounding which tends to separate it from other spiritual autobiographies, but immediately contends that Bunyan's handling of setting is hardly sufficient to give his work uniqueness as a whole. Mandel's primary thrust is two-fold: Bunyan has a governing principle, which defines the artistic end toward which his spiritual autobiography moves; and in a number of ways Bunyan's autobiography is not all original. The governing principle is a didactic purpose for the encouragement primarily of his Puritan flock. He admits that occasionaly Bunyan does write for the unbeliever as well as for the believer. Mandel presses his view of the lack of originality in Grace Abounding. He argues: "Even the title of Bunyan's autobiography strikes uninitiated modern ears as a bold original phrase. But not only do all Puritans long to compete for the distinction of being the most despicable of vermin, but also most of them will not be happy unless they are literally the chief of sinners" (p.237). It is of interest, however, that of the five examples to support his statement about "all

Puritans," one refers to a Methodist, Rebekah Benner, another to a Quaker, John Crook. Although he insists on Bunyan's lack of originality, Mandel suggests that perhaps Bunyan demonstrates a degree of originality in his exclusive concentration on the inner life and his relative silence on outward, historical events. What is further evident, however, is Mandel's somewhat restricted view of Bunyan's work. He analyzes it basically as case history, and describes Bunyan's sense of choice as "controlled by his spiritual fantasy world" in connection with an "absolutism in the interpretaion of Biblical passages" (p. 239).

Felicity A. Nussbaum ("'By These Words I was Sustained': Bunyan's Grace Abounding," ELH 49, 1982), calls into question the traditional pattern of spiritual autobiography as a satisfying description of the narrative structure of Grace Abounding. She seeks to explore the way in which Bunyan's autobiographical self-presentation sets two impulses--one toward the "universal allegorical ideal" and the other toward the particularized individual--in continual conflict. In order to show that the two ways of conceptualizing the self both compete with and complement each other in the text, Nussbaum holds that Bunyan alters the "traditional pattern" of autobiography. What immediately suggests the approach she takes is her statement: "We may be better able to understand the altered form Bunyan uses if we examine the complexity of his relationship to the divine patriarchal authority, as he substitutes his own personal authority for God's" (p. 19). What further provides a complication in the structure of the text is that "Bunyan moves swiftly to his apparent conversion in thirty-seven paragraphs, only to reiterate the process of temptation for another two hundred paragraphs" (p. 20). The act of conversion that Bunyan states early on in the text provides for Nussbaum "a glimpse of an idealized self, a self in harmony with Providence, and the remaining sections of the autobiography explore the narrator's attitude toward the protagonist" (p. 20). She then asserts that the autobiographical process is "the action of the straining toward an idealized state. He moves from the child who pines after his birthright to the more mature self who claims the goal, the birthright, through establishing his own words as both the complementary and the competing authority" (pp. 20-21). Furthermore, to Nussbaum, Bunyan capitalizes on the early conversion to create "a temporal and spatial arena for the exploration of a series of possible selves which tests the patriarchal authority" (p. 24). As Bunyan explores the possibilities of rebellion against God, he actually investigates, at the same time, the possibilities of rebellion "of Bunyan the father rather than God the father" and thus, "the autobiographical text begins to compete for authority with the Scriptural texts" (p. 21). Following the early conversion, he then tests the limits of his own new found authority and the autobiography, the text, becomes a validation for Bunyan that the temptations will not have to occur again, and the text, like Scripture, is a text of authority for the reader" (p.21).

Nussbaum, "deconstructs" the allegedly supernatural character of Bunyan's spiritual temptations into a psychological striving between the author's "universal allegorical ideal" and his realization of himself as a "particularized individual." Her reading of Grace Abounding leads her to conclude that perhaps the number of revisions suggest that "Bunyan began to suspect that Grace Abounding created a self in continual process that was not quite real, not quite conventional, while the work itself, the text of the autobiographical account, asserted a self that proselytized and witnessed for his God, but also more subtly, competed with the Scriptures for authority" (pp. 32-33). To Nussbaum, the self which Bunyan described becomes "a center in a way the charismatic authority of God had been the center for Augustine and others in the spiritual autobiography tradition" (p. 32).

If Felicity A. Nussbaum attempts to deconstruct Bunyan's work, it is Peter J. Carlton ("Bunyan: Language, Convention, Authority," ELH 51 no. 1, Spring 1984) who attempts to "demythologize" both Bunyan and his critics. According to Carlton, critics have thus far made the error, on one hand, of interpreting Bunyan's revelatory events in Freudian terms while on the other hand, preserving a silent respect for the "divine Other" which Bunyan claimed to know. However, Freudian psychology assumes the active character of the psyche; and Bunyan "when he narrates the violent incursions of biblical texts upon his soul," says Carlton, "represents himself as a passive locus for the activity of alien agents, a battleground where God and the Devil enact their eternal warfare" (p. 18). For Carlton, critics, prior to his reading of Grace Abounding, have been unable to say what Bunyan is really doing when he makes statements regarding a particular scriptual text like "that sentence fell with weight upon my spirit." He acknowledges that "one appreciates the sympathetic effort of these critics to convey Bunyan's own belief that it is God Himself, dwelling in His holy Word, who imprints these texts on his mind," but the same critics, to Carlton, offer explanations that "prove no less magical than Bunyan's own statements--they secularize them, but they fail to demythologize them" (pp. 18-19).

So then, Peter J. Carlton demythologizes Bunyan and prior critics. What is taking place when Bunyan writes statements like, "that Scripture fell upon me"? "Quite simply," says Carlton, "he is narrating his own action as if it has happened to him" (p. 19). What Carlton maintains is that Bunyan's experiences of "falling and bolting" Scriptures were not really experiences but actions. Since, then, these experiences are mental events, Carlton contends that "we have no choice but to regard them as actions Bunyan performs, however unconsciously" (p. 19).

Now that Carlton knows what Bunyan did, he turns to the question of why he did it. Bunyan and other Puritans of the era felt an anxiety over the loss of an objective religious authority when Protestant reformers broke with the Church of Rome and the Church of England; consequently, "disclaiming locutions" became "conventional for Puritan autobiographies because they filled the void left by the loss." Furthermore, Carlton argues: "By constituting certain thoughts and feelings as happenings, such statements transformed mental events into direct communications from God, making them implicity authoritative" (p. 20). Thus, Bunyan and other Puritans used "disclaiming locutions" to transform their own thoughts "into authoritative utterance from God;" unfortunately, however, they deceived themselves into believing that they had retained Scripture as an objective authority, but in fact they had "completely subjectivized it."

For Carlton, "disclaiming locutions" not only contest authority or compensate for its absence, "but conform to authority as well--the authority of convention" (p. 27). Puritans talked frequently of their experiences and recounted in detail the 'events'--the "disclaimed actions" of their inner lives, but says Carlton, they were not free to cast these in any form but rather the "stages of conversion were mapped out by Calvinist doctrine and reinforced by Puritan preaching" (pp. 26-27). The pattern for the Puritan experience is so strong to Carlton that he declares: "The pattern they were taught, they sought for, the pattern they sought, they experienced; the pattern they experienced, they narrated to those who taught it to them, so that they might be accepted and teach the pattern to others in their turn" (p. 29). Such "lockstep conformism" seems a far cry from the Bunyan which some readers see in Grace Abounding, who on the strength of an inner Voice and on an inspired Scriptural authority (in which he passionately believed) would ascend to the heights of ecstasy or plunge to the pit of despair. Yet, Carlton believes that one can reconcile what he calls "lockstep conformism" with the claims of inspiration that one finds in Bunyan's autobiography. The essence of his stance is that "in a subjective, experience-based religion such as Bunyan's, obedience to convention is, paradoxically, precisely the mark of inspiration," and the single criterion "by which Bunyan and his coreligionists could decide whether an utterance was inspired was if it sounded like other 'inspired' utterances" (p. 29).

Near the end of his essay, Carlton admits

that conventions that prevail in a given community of discourse have been established for compelling reasons, but he contends that "communal sanctions" raise an important question: "what does the rigorous conventionality of Puritan autobiography reveal about the nature of convention itself?" He succintly responds to his own query: "Where convention is, authority and punishment, power and submission are too" (p. 30). Only a few sentences from the conclusion of his own discourse, Carlton offers the reader a telling statement: "It remains true, nevertheless, that the enforcement of convention is always an exercise of power by the appropriate authorities, whether they be Puritans enforcing certain narrative conventions or English professors perpetuating the conventions of a given literary critical discourse" (p. 31).

The first essay in this survey is a discussion of Grace Abounding in its "broad contours" as a spiritual autobiography and the place of Bunyan's work in the tradition. It seems wise to conclude with a study which rejects the long-assumed belief that Grace Abounding is actually a spiritual autobiography at all.

Rebecca S. Beal ("Grace Abounding to the Chief of Sinners: John Bunyan's Pauline Epistle," SEL, 1981) thoroughly and interestingly demonstrates the similarity between Bunyan's Grace Abounding and the Pauline Epistle. In a footnote, she alludes to E.D. Hirsh's work, Validity in Interpretation (1967; rpt. New Haven: Yale University Press, 1976), which discloses his concept of "intrinsic genre" and "extrinsic genre," arguing that the genre of autobiography is "extrinsic" to Grace Abounding because it does not "explain the meaning of the work in its entirety." She bases this conclusion on a preconception (which she introduces on the first page) that autobiography yields its kernel of meaning through psychological analysis. Beal admits that if the work is indeed autobiographical "an analysis of its psychological revelations and 'narrative texture' may be primary keys to interpretation of the text" (p. 147). What concerns Beal, however, is that the more salient features of the work--"its title, address, form" must not be overlooked, and when "the book's contents and form are assessed in the context of social and theological milieu, it may be seen that <u>Grace Abounding to the Chief of Sinners</u> is more accurately defined as a seventeenth-century version of the Pauline epistle" (p. 148).

According to Beal the title of the work reflects "the major emphasis of Pauline epistles: salvation by grace alone," and if one understands the Pauline allusions in the title--various combinations of 'abound' and 'grace'--'Abundant grace'--and if one is aware of Bunyan's imprisonment, his readers would understand the title as an explanation of Bunyan's own suffering" (pp. 148-49). Consciously Pauline, the title bears, for Beal, "theological, epistolary, rather than psychological, autobiographical significance" (p. 149). The didactic meaning implicit in his phrase "Chief of Sinners" is clear to Beal; indeed, the sinner "thinks himself 'the biggest sinner' when confronted by the holiness of God" ... and consciousness of his sins "engenders despair, but awareness of the meaning of grace, abounding grace, leads the sinner to an understanding of justification and of the redemptive work of Christ" (p. 149).

Rebecca Beal further contends that Bunyan makes clear that "his theology of law and grace, as well as his work's genre, depends on sources which are closely tied to the Pauline tradition but not directly associated with Puritan thought" (p. 149). Her belief is that Bunyan learned his theology of law and grace not from Calvin but from Martin Luther, particularly Luther's <u>Comment on the Galatians</u>. Holding that Bunyan presents Luther's teaching "experientially rather than abstractly;" there is, "in Paul's writing, especially as the commentators of the seventeenth century understood it, a close connnection between experience, autobiographical detail, and didactic matter" (p. 150).

Continuing her argument for the identification of <u>Grace Abounding</u> with Paul's epistles, Beal offers convincing evidence of the ways in which the structure of the work follows that of the Pauline epistle and further shows that the "organization of his "Matter," which had baffled or frustrated many a critic, follows Paul's practice of didactic digression" (p. 151). She also gives attention to the relation between the nature of Bunyan's vocation and the Apostle Paul's ministry. Unlike some critics, she sees a rejection of the devotional books from his wife's dowry and declares that neither Arthur Dent's The Plain Man's Path-way to Heaven nor Lewis Bayly's The Practice of Piety are likely models for the genre of Grace Abounding. Furthermore, Paul's epistles, "directly or through the medium of Luther's Comment, take priority in Bunyan's emphasis on the importance of Scripture in the life of the Christian," and in addition, "the Pauline letter proves necessary in each stage of Bunyan's spiritual life" (p. 157).

To Beal, Bunyan attempts in his work "to bring his readers to a clear vision of Christ; autobiographical criticism has striven mightily to analyze 'the chief of sinners'"(p. 160). She closely argues for a clarification of Bunyan's aims and the form (a pastoral letter following the pattern of the Pauline epistle) he appropriates to accomplish his purposes.

Critical attention to allegory as well as to Bunyan as an allegorist has increased in the modern era. As suggested in the Introduction, studies focus on analyses of the narrative art of The Pilgrim's Progress as well as on various theories of reading allegory in general and of reading Bunyan's allegory in particular.

U. Milo Kaufmann (The Pilgrim's Progress and Traditions in Puritan Meditation, New Haven, 1966) explores the relation of Bunyan's imaginative realism to the Puritan aesthetic with which it is in obvious tension. As he suggests, "The Pilgrim's Progress presents a conspicious superimposition of stasis and linear movement," and later states that the "modern reader can perhaps be forgiven for his impression that in a pilgrimage that is in large measure the exfoliation of a Word once and for all delivered, events only seem to be happening" (pp. 107, 112). Although the

AN OVERVIEW

"peculiar dynamics" of Bunyan's narrative is indebted to the "Puritan conception of reading the Word as static system," the author is capable of qualifying Puritan hermeneutics "in his handling of scriptural event and metaphor" (pp. 112-13). By analyzing this tension between mythos and logos and searching through the fictive narrative and edifying doctrine, Kaufmann discovers that Bunyan's complex art is both true to the Puritan ethos and also foreign to that ethos in the way it appropriates the imagination. He finds in the tradition of "heavenly meditation," first developed by Richard Sibbes, a provenance for the imaginative approach to the Word as mythos. In this tradition, Kaufmann discovers an approach that counters what he considers to be "the characteristically Puritan disposition" toward a rational and doctrinal view of logos, which has its source in the works of Joseph Hall. The Puritan practice of "heavenly meditation," which recognizes the importance of imagination, qualifies and moderates Bunyan's view of the Word and his personal experience as sources of imagery and action.

To show the impact of Puritan meditation on The Pilgrim's Progress, Kaufmann gives a careful analysis of particular episodes such as the Interpreter's House and House Beautiful and contends that these episodes cannot be adequately appreciated without knowledge of Puritan meditation. His close examination of the Valley of the Shadow of Death and of the Land of Beulah shows how meditative technique encourages Bunyan to exploit biblical metaphor and other sources of imagery and thus assists him in making concrete abstract and doctrinal thought.

What a reader must understand, however, is that in The Pilgrim's Progress it is impossible to disengage Word from Way, especially "when the focus" says Kaufmann, "is the coherence of the entire work." He thinks of the way Christian goes as a canonization of Puritan religious experience, and "its unity is the historically refined wholeness of that experience. If to be a Christian is to travel the way, it is equally true that the Way names the course which the Christian takes" (pp. 114-15). Christian's way, therefore, is the way in which the Puritan pilgrim must go. While it is true that he helps inscribe in the landscape the road he walks, and the unity of the way is humanly achieved; it is equally true, for Kaufmann, that "we can scarcely avoid speaking of Christian the pilgrim as one of God's elect, whose willing must sooner or later be related to the fact of prevenient and sustaining grace." But, he further avers that "prevenient grace, like prevenient knowledge, if too evident in the springs of narrative, is likely to destroy the illusion of a dynamic career" (p. 116). In Kaufmann's judgment Bunyan is completely aware of this possibility and consequently directs the reader's attention away from the "problematic dynamics" of the narrative (pp. 107, 116).

Unlike Kaufmann, Stanley Fish ("Progress in The Pilgrim's Progress," ELR 1 no. 3, 1971, reprinted nearly whole in Self-Consuming Artifacts, Berkeley and Los Angles, 1972) sees an author completely unaware of problems his narrative creates. Furthermore, Fish declares that Bunyan makes no move to draw the "reader's attention away from the 'problematic dynamics' of the narrative," and the proper focus of analytical study is not the work, but the reader.

One of Fish's earliest comments is that Christian's initial error--and the reader's error--is to "take seriously and literally the title of his story," and according to Fish, this is an error the pilgrim himself "censured" in the episode of Formalist and Hypocrisy. Christian censures Formalist and Hypocrisy for "climbing up some other way" and for not coming in at the Wicket Gate, but the other two travellers see no reason for quibbling, after all they are in the same place as Christian, or so they think. Fish contends that the "assessment" Formalist and Hypocrisy make of their place in the way "is based on the physical and available evidence ... which defines the boundaries of their belief." They believe only in what they see, and since it is what they see, they believe in themselves" (p. 228). On the other hand, Christian walks by the "rule" of his "master." For Fish, the rule is

AN OVERVIEW

nowhere stated but scriptural allusions definitely point to Christ's statement in John 14.6. "I am the way...." He adds that the statement "I am the way" is an "absolute and unqualified assertion which defines both the obligations and dangers of the pilgrimage" (p. 229). The various temptations are "essentially one, the temptation to substitute for the way of Christ the way of self, either by presuming to come alone, without His intercession, or by presuming to come by an external way, and not by the inner way of belief ... " (p. 229).

What Fish, then, contends is that these same "presumptions" are inherent in the title of the allegory, The Pilgrim's Progress, and in the allegory which carries us through the story" (p. 229). To Fish, this suggests that the form of The Pilgrim's Progress, "because it spatializes and trivializes the way, is as great a danger as any the pilgrims meet within its confines." If a reader is to "read the work correctly," that reader must "resist the pressure of its temporal-spatial lines of cause and effect." To read correctly, the reader must be aware that there is only an illusion of progress; in fact, The Pilgrim's Progress is "anti-progressive, both as a narrative and as a reading experience" (p. 229).

Even though the experiences of "the way" vary for the pilgrims, there is no progression; the way is "static in its variety, since each traveler meets himself, over and over again," asserts Fish. He further contends that the only "consistent spatial pattern Christian's actions trace out are cyclical" (p. 232). To support his view, he argues that in every temptation which Christian faces to repeat a previous sin, he never fails to fall. Again, the pattern is cyclical; there is no progress, and this "refusal to trace out a program frustrates the reader's desire to follow one" (p. 233). What one learns from various episodes, whether in the footrace when Christian overtakes Faithful and then glorying in accomplishment stumbles and falls, or whether in the Formalist and Hypocrisy episode or on the occasion after the Christian-Apollyon battle when "an hand" appears or whatever the episode, these provide one major instruction for

Stanley Fish: how not to read The Pilgrim's Progress. In brief, Fish holds that one must not read it "as a progress," or "a sequence of causally related events, for the true agency can at any time reverse the direction generated by a sequence," and one must not read the allegory "in the way that every reader will certainly be tempted (a word precisely intended) to read it." (p.236).

To one who questions why Bunyan subverts his major figure or why he "makes the journey the vehicle of his narrative" and then asks the reader "to turn away from the interpretative direction it affords," Fish has a reply. The answer lies, he says, "in the correspondence between reading and wayfaring, and the complementary obligations they confer. The truth about the world is not to be found within its own confines or configurations, but from the vantage point of a perspective that transforms it" (p. 237). Christian will face his struggle in terms of that perspective, and the reader performs "his acts of interpretation in the same way." A tendency of a reader in Fish's view is to interpret events of the narrative "as if their springs were visible and rational, as if sequence were the generator rather than simply the bearer of meaning," and this is precisely "equivalent to the tendency to every erring pilgrim to forsake the way of Christ for the rude workings of his own fancy" (p. 237). If then this means that the reader and the pilgrim who believe in the metaphor of the journey actually believe in themselves, it is equally true that Bunyan's method encourages and then disallows "this prideful self-reliance by encouraging and then disallowing the interpretative pretensions of his prose" (p. 237). What follows, in Fish's judgment, is that in this way Bunyan "makes the subversion of the 'dynamics of the narrative' the subversion of the reader's understanding."

After arguing that there is a pattern of the subversion of the interpretative direction and that causal influences come from an invisible power; indeed the things seen are discredited in favor of the "inner light of faith," he discovers a pattern that subsumes all others, and that is the theme of memory. It is memory that enables a reader to "impose the correcting perspective of what is distant on what is near" (p. 250).

Stanley Fish's argument finally leads him to conclude that The Pilgrim's Progress ends not once, but five times and "with each successive ending much of the satisfaction we experience at the first is taken away" (p. 260). So, the reader is the object of analysis. What is at the heart of Fish's argument is that the reader's self is consumed in responding to the author's narrative, just as the work itself is destroyed in the process of achieving that end. In brief, The Pilgrim's Progress is "the ultimate self-consuming artifact, for the insights it yields are inseparable from the demonstration of the inadequacy of its own forms, which are also the forms of the reader's understanding" (p. 264).

If Stanley Fish opposes Kaufmann, John R. Knott, Jr. (Bunyan's Gospel Day: A Reading of The Pilgrim's Progress," ELR no. 3, 1973) opposes Fish and extends Kaufmann's argument. Rather than subverting the central image of the journey as Fish holds, Bunyan instead exploits it, Knott believes, as a means of showing that the individual Christian's way of faith varies and there is only one true way to the Celestial City. In brief, he uses the metaphor in two basic senses: the way is the path for all Christians "through the wilderness of this world," and simultaneously, the inner way of faith of the individual believer. What Fish pictures as deceptive "linear form" is for Knott the "sustaining metaphor of Puritan spiritual life" in seventeenth-century England. "To devalue this metaphor by considering it in purely formal terms," says Knott, "is to explain away the reason for the extraordinary power of The Pilgrim's Progress over the imaginations of actual readers for several centuries" (p. 444). He contends that Bunyan knows that he speaks no less truly for speaking "metaphorically and that the metaphor, which he saw as embodying God's promise that his saints would succeed in making their way through the wilderness to the 'land of promise' is the key to his conception of

The Pilrim's Progress and to the appeal of the work for his Puritan readers" (p. 446). The readers believed in progress; in fact, that "ground of their faith was a belief in the possibility of progress from this world to the next" and furthermore, The Pilgrim's Progress offered Puritan readers "the hope that an ordinary believer, not without weaknesses might attain the New Jerusalem" (p. 446).

The journey Christian takes and his actions along the way describe a progression through the stages of spiritual life. Knott admits that the progression is clearer in some places than in others, but he declares that his "point is simply that one can and should talk about stages in the journey that correspond to mileposts in the development of spiritual vitality" (p. 449). He also agrees with Kaufmann's view that Christian helps "to define the road to be walked" and prepares the way for Christiana and the family, but he believes too that one "could take Kaufmann's argument a step further and say that by elaborating the metaphor of the way Bunyan ordered and explained the potentially chaotic events of the spiritual life for his readers" (p. 449).

In the early stages of the journey, testings and temptations are frequently the lot of Christian, but changes in the nature of temptations mark changes in the nature of the pilgrim's growth. There are also way stations along the journey for resting, learning and growing, and the joys of Beulah and the New Jerusalem consummate the promised delights of the end of the way. Knott says that the "emotional intensity of Bunyan's narrative, as it rises to a series of peaks leading up to the moment of Christian's and Hopeful's reception into the New Jerusalem, registers in unmistakable fashion his own estimation of how far his pilgrims have progressed" (p. 460). "The climactic episodes of The Pilgrim's Progress," he states, "bring the reader all the way from the "carnal" world in which the narrative began up to the contemplation of a transcendant world whose reality is validated by the Word" (p. 461). The pilgrim does progress, and the progress is no illusion.

AN OVERVIEW

Nick Shrimpton ("Bunyan's Military Metaphor," The Pilgrim's Progress, Critical and Historical Views. Edited by Vincent Newey, 1980) also enters the Kaufmann-Fish-Knott discussion by reminding the reader that Kaufmann argues that "prevenient grace" and the immovable surety of the word cancel out any urgency for progress. Fish conversely holds that Bunyan deliberately undercuts the reader's expectation of progress. Neither Kaufmann nor Fish pause "to consider the relationship between the untrustworthy metaphor of pilgrimage and the book's other predominant image, warfare" (p. 207). Shrimpton believes that the allegory is indeed static and the progress painfully slow until Christian is fully "armed" at the House Beautiful. Following the "arming" at the House Beautiful, Christian lives as a changed man, and his exploits resemble those of St. George in The Seven Champions of Christendom. What is especially significant to observe is that the dominant image of the allegory now changes, and a reader should give as much attention to the imagery of a book as to its title. Thus, prior to the House Beautiful episode, Christian is indeed a pilgrim; after House Beautiful, he is a Christian warrior. "Progress gives way to knight-errancy, to a military perambulation" (p.222). The progress, therefore, is the transition from pilgrim to warrior, and this apparent paradox necessitates no need for the reader to abandon early expectations of a pilgrim's progress.

Philip Edwards ("The Journey in The Pilgrim's Progress," Critical and Historical Views. Edited by Vincent Newey, 1980) also finds disagreement with Fish. He holds that Fish assumes that the word, "progress," has its modern sense of improvement, but in fact, Edwards contends that "Bunyan's 'progress' correctly quoted by the Oxford English Dictionary under sense I, means, quite neutrally, travelling, a movement from one place to another, how Christian got from this world to the world which is to come" (p. 111). Since travelling has more applications than that of achievement or improvement, Edwards recognizes that Bunyan's image commands concentrated attention. He believes that since everyone "who has ever lived has had the multiple experience of making a journey, Bunyan can rely on his readers' instinctive adjustment to each new application of the image as it is introduced" (p. 111). There are several aspects of the journey, and pilgrims do sometimes go astray. Formalist and Hypocrisy, for instance, take whatever short-cuts they can find, and Ignorance wrongly thinks he has arrived at the "heavenly destination" even though he deliberately took the wrong road. "According to Fish," says Edwards, "the mistake of these pilgrims is 'to believe too literally in the image of the journey'--a mistake the reader himself is constantly tempted to make" (p. 111). For Edwards, these pilgrims "believe too literally in one use of the image of the journey" (p. 111-12).

Initially in The Pilgrim's Progress the journey is simply an escape. Christian wants to escape his city which, he has been told, will be burned with fire. If he escapes, he wants a refuge, and very soon the idea of fleeing from a place entails going towards another place. Evangelist tells him to go towards the shining light which will lead him to the gate which he is unable to see. Thus, "when Christian reaches the gate," says Edwards, "the journey is seen as a balance between escape from and movement towards" (p. 112). The idea of journey as pilgrimage is not introduced until about "a quarter of the way through the book." By this new word another perspective is given to the journey, for the emphasis now falls not on an escape but on "journeying towards a destination" (p. 113). Christian now says that his wife and family were all of them utterly adverse to his going on pilgrimage. Nothing was actually said about pilgrimage when he left the city. Edwards contends that "the concept of pilgrimage shifts the emphasis from the departure to the destination, the phrase 'a pilgrim's life' shows how strongly the journey itself is a center of attention" (p. 113).

"Bunyan's journey," according to Edwards, "combines three distinct ideas. These are (a) the vicissitudes of a Christian's life, arising from external threat and inner disturbance, (b) obeying the strict demands of the true faith, and

AN OVERVIEW

(c) advancing in the understanding and practice of the Christian life" (p. 115). There is, however, a fourth idea which Edwards sees and that is "not only keeping to the path but keeping the right path." The final use of the journey image is "the metaphor of arrival and welcome for the union of Christian with his maker" (p. 116).

In this lucid essay, Edwards gives a word of caution, holding that this compound journey, "constantly and imperceptibly changing its meaning, raises problems when looked at closely" (p. 116). He has little anxiety over the "unsophisticated reader," but "the critic is advised to carry a proper map" (p. 116).

Although his entire work does not focus on John Bunyan, Wolfgang Iser ("Bunyan's Pilgrim's Progress: The Doctrine of Predestination and the Shaping of the Novel," The Implied Reader: Patterns of Communication from Bunyan to Beckett, Johns Hopkins Press, 1974), uses words similar to Fish--words like reader, the reading process, and response--to chart his area of investigation. He explores The Pilgrim's Progress under the assumption that reading is a process in which the reader participates to discover meaning not only in the text but also to find in the work "a new reality" that discloses limitations in the reader's own behavior as well as in pervading norms.

His study demonstrates how The Pilgrim's Progress grows out of the personal need for "certitude" or certitudo salutis in the face of the Calvinistic doctrine of predestination. Since salvation is an a priori factor (that is, a person is predestined either to have salvation or not to have it even before birth), allegory in Bunyan's treatment of it must turn inward: one must search the depths of the heart to determine whether one really is of the elect. The only escape from total passivity, according to Iser, was for the Puritan "to hunt for signs of his hoped-for salvation. The more signs he found the greater seemed his chances of salvation, but even then his certainty had inevitably to remain subjective .... " (p. 5).

Iser contends that the allegory is meant to

appeal to each individual reader, whatever his disposition, and "its aim is to lead the believer to recognize himself. Thus the idea of salvation is treated predominantly as a means of illuminating human reality and not as an end in itself" (p. 7). He also finds striking the way in which the narrative technique alternates between "omniscient narration and dialogue," and believes that "the increasing preponderance of dialogue is an indication of the increasing importance of subjectivity within an objective context" (p. 9). What Iser also suggests is that the dream narrator describes the "objective, exemplary road to salvation" and the dialogues develop the "increasing subjective certitude of salvation." The dialogues also "give rise to the whole picture of the pilgrim's empirical situation, and they reflect the Puritan reader's own inner conflicts" (pp. 9,11).

Observing that most of the dialogues are in prose, he further notes that so long "as events and reactions are the subject of the narrative, the language remains prose, but when the abstract, edifying idea behind these events is to be placed in the forefront, prose gives way to verse" (p. 12). He holds, for example, that when Christian comes to climb the Hill Difficulty, the narrative gives way to verse. The lines which Christian speaks puts emphasis on his "firm resolve to continue his quest." Furthermore, as he has "just received the first sign of grace, he is no longer put off by the difficulty of the way ... " (p. 12). The function of the verse is "to pinpoint the general significance of particular events" (p. 12).

In Iser's judgment, there are two separate groups of characters in The Pilgrim's Progress: the one purely functional and the other extending beyond mere function. He sees characters like Evangelist, Pliable, and Obstinate as functional, but members of the second groups are Christian, Hopeful and Faithful. "If the characters are purely functional," says Iser, "then it is the abstract idea of salvation that is uppermost; when the characters cease to be mere personification, emphasis is thrown on human conduct and motivation" (p. 14). The two planes are complementary, however, in that "the certitudo salutis can only be subjective, with the pilgrims extracting the signs from his own individual human experience" (p. 14).

Following a thorough examination of the significance of experience, particularly the experiences of Christian and his shared experience with Little Faith, Iser affirms that the fact "that Christian went through the same despondency as Little-faith and yet still took his place in the scheme of salvation, because he was able to transform his distress into beneficial knowledge, is what constitutes the instructional basis of Pilgrim's Progress" (p. 23). For Iser, "experience is the force that mediates between the human character and its hidden destiny" and this "withholding of certitude activates the human potential, the manifestations of which orientate the character toward the good he is striving after" (p. 24).

Wolfgang Iser's entire essay with its emphasis on the phenomenology of the reading process is included in its entirety in the next chapter.

Like Iser, Nick Davis ("The Problem of Misfortune in The Pilgrim's Progress," Critical and Historical Views. Edited by Vincent Newey, 1980) understands the need which Bunyan's central figures feel for certainty of personal salvation, certitudo salutis. Yet, Davis contends that in the course of this quest for certainty, the central characters are exposed to a vast variety of persecutors whose main design appears to be the undermining of certainty. This plight, however, "is understood to be a trial imposed by Providence, the apparent randomness of whose operations is an illusion born of man's corrupt nature" (p. 184). Furthermore, Calvinist thought creates a tension in that while divine purposiveness pervaded everywhere, its operations are inscrutable. For Davis, Bunyan faces up to this tension in such a way as to suggest "that human agency has a place in a world controlled by an extra-human Providence, and that the providential order is not altogether masked from human experience" (p. 185). Rather than believing that allegory must turn inward as Iser suggests, Davis holds that Bunyan writes an allegory within a largely secular artistic tradition. The Pilgrim's Progress has some indebtedness, as Davis also suggests, to romance literature, and certain parts of the allegory resemble folktales of that time or a popularization of early chivalric romance. The five consequences of the popularization are : 1) Wish-fulfillment assumes a greater prominence, 2) popular romances are less unified, 3) interest in a particular hero guides the reader through the narrative and becomes a hook on which to hang a series of adventures which separate him from his fellowmen, 4) the hero becomes a more homely figure, especially in his needs, 5) fate becomes a greater force in shaping the hero's adventure.

Having made these assertions on the popularization of the romance, Davis further contends that a response must be found to the question of why so few pilgrims make a successful journey to the Celestial City while others, who apparently wish the same prize, fail in their objective. Theology can supply an external solution, but for Davis, "this is not the interpretation which the patterning of the narrative keeps uppermost in the reader's mind" (p. 192). He also clearly states that it is impossible "to accept Stanley Fish's argument that Bunyan does everything in his power to subvert the metaphor of 'progress' which informs the entire work" (p. 192). What Davis believes is that Bunyan displaces "the unequal fortune from a position where it blocks the development of narrative; while it remains, implicitly, a theological problem, it also becomes a problem mediated through recourse to an artistic strategy ..." (p. 192).

The folktale helps to provide this "artistic strategy" for Davis. The allegory is unlike a folktale, however, "in so far as it offers to supply a final interpretation of the events which compose it by reference to this external authority" (p. 194). On the other hand, the allegory is like a folktale "in so far as it hints at the existence of a general 'interpretability' which just eludes the human agents involved" (p. 194). By and large, Nick Davis believes that Bunyan sustains this tension in Christian's journey, but tips the balance "somewhat in the direction of overt commentary when he comes to deal with the journey of Christiana" (pp. 194-95). He further holds that language "assumes something of the status of an imperative in the narrative" and later asserts that the "existence of a domain of order and sense lying just beyond the reach of ordinary discourse is suggested in Part I ... through the frequence of the pilgrims' encounter with riddles" (pp. 194-95). Furthermore, the pilgrims solve the verbal riddles by turning to a higher level of discourse represented by Scriptural language. The pilgrims' encounter "with 'scripture language' and its riddles are, however, an augury of hope, a sign that language participates in the Providential ordering of things" (p. 198).

If Nick Davis sees the significance of the language of a text, Maureen Quilligan (The Language of Allegory, Ithaca and London, 1979) contends that all allegorical narrative emerges from a play with language. Her book is important in modern criticism and commands a lengthy treatment.

Challenging traditional definitions of allegory, she defines the genre in terms of the text, the pretext, the context, and the reader. Her view of these various aspects leads Quilligan to take issue with beliefs held by numerous critics that allegory says one thing and means another. Furthermore, a reader is not necessarily a critic or at least, the reader's view of allegory is dissimilar to that of the critic. The reader, she believes, is drawn inside the text and within the text performs not only an aesthetic reading or interpretation but an ethical action. In brief she cogently argues in her last chapter, "The Reader," that "the final focus of any allegory is its reader, and the real 'action' of any allegory is the reader's learning to read the text properly" (p. 24). She further holds that after one reads an allegory, "we only realize what kind of readers we are, and what kind we must become in order to interpret our significance in the cosmos" (p. 24).

To understand more clearly how her central position pertains to The Pilgrim's Progress, one must attempt, first of all, to state succinctly her view of text, pretext, and context. Before she proceeds, however, to a discussion of these three features, she states: "Other genres appeal to readers as human beings; allegory appeals to readers as readers of a system of signs" (p. 24). She does add that "this may be only to say that allegory appeals to readers in terms of their most distinguishing human characteristic, as readers of, and therefore as creatures finally shaped by their language" (p. 24).

What Quilligan sees as "the truly literal meaning of 'literal' is, in fact, not 'actual,' 'real,' or 'lifelike,' but 'letteral'--having to do with letters and with the reading of letters grouped into words ..." (p. 67). In her judgment, reading on the literal level in the traditional view is actually not reading on the literal but the metaphorical level. Readers must learn to look carefully at words, and "the letters used to spell them," and consciously determine the process by which words signify and "signifying not only the action, but the meaning of that action" (p. 68).

In her study of "pretext," Quilligan immediately asserts that the Bible is the original "pretext," but also holds that the protagonists of allegory frequently "find themselves in scenes which simply reenact the details of that other book, the first text ..." (p. 97). What she contends is that allegories "do not state but discover the nature of that book, and the process of discovery begins on the pretext (or pretense) that the narrative the reader reads is an original story in its own right--not simply another commentary on the Bible" (p. 97). In brief, Quilligan is underscoring the "letteral" text or the language of the literal text and what the words of that text signify. She asserts: "By pretext I mean the source that always stands outside the narrative (unlike the threshold text, which stands within it at the beginning); the pretext is the text that the narrative comments on by reenacting, as well as the claim the narrative makes to be a fiction not built upon another text" (pp. 97-98). It must be kept in mind, however, that Quilligan insists that the language of the pretext is the most important factor in guiding the interpretation of the allegory. She strongly declares that if the language of the pretext "can name truth, then the language of the allegorical narrative will be able to. If its language is not felt to have special powers for revealing reality, then the language of the allegory will have a corresponding difficulty in articulating the truth of the human condition" (p. 98).

If allegory is always a text, predicated on the existence of a pretext, so also is it "always fundamentally about language and the ways in which language itself can reveal to man his highest spiritual purpose within the cosmos" (p.156). In order for allegory to be written and to be read intelligently, there must be a cultural context which grants to language a "potentially sacralizing power" and "a significance beyond that belonging to a merely arbitrary system of signs" (p. 156). The cultural conditions that foster allegory include the existence of what Quilligan calls a "suprarealist" attitude toward language. In fact, allegory will never exist as a "viable genre" unless there is this "suprarealist" attitude toward words. What this entails is that "abstract nouns themselves are perceived to be as real and as powerful as the things named" (p. 156). Before the allegorist can even begin language "must be felt to have a potency as solidly meaningful as physical fact ..." and "out of language sensed in terms of a nearly physical presence--the allegorist's narrative comes, peopled by words moving about an intricately re-echoing landscape of language" (p. 156). If and when this "suprarealist" attitude toward language prevails in a culture, then allegory is either the "dominant form of literature" or "a possible alternative."

In light of her definition, Quilligan finds The Pilgrim's Progress lacking in qualities that she deems essential to allegorical narrative. An early concern of hers is that the language of the pretext is so privileged in Bunyan's treatment that it threatens any antonomy of the text to the narrative itself. Rather than discovering the nature of the text, "Bunyan's narrative," says Quilligan, "investigates the practical application of the reading of scripture to life in the world" (p. 122). Furthermore, Bunyan implies that to speak the truth in one's own words is impossible. When U. Milo Kaufmann explains that "prevenient grace, like prevenient knowledge, if too evident in the springs of narrative, is likely to destroy the illusion of a dynamic career," Quilligan's reply is: "The status of the pretext is likely to destroy the narrative of the text" (p. 123). She explains further that the beginning of the allegory "signals the pretext so clearly that it risks making no claim whatsoever for the story as an independent narrative" (p. 123). Kaufmann believes that Bunyan himself was aware of this danger but simply directed his readers' attention from the problem by providing rich realistic details.

When she refers to Stanley Fish's handling of the problem and suggesting that "the illusory nature of the pilgrim's progress is a large part of Bunyan's point, and the reader's awareness of the problematics of the narrative is essential to his intention, which is nothing less than the disqualification of his work as a vehicle of the insight it pretends to convey," Quilligan appears more willing to agree with him than Kaufmann. Indeed, "Bunyan's narrative is the ultimate self-consuming artifact;" furthermore, Fish's view is perhaps "to say no more than what Christian had said when he explained that it was easier to conceive of the pilgrimage in his mind than to speak of it with his tongue" (p. 124). Quilligan believes that Bunyan's resolution to this apparent problem is to have Christian use language "as close as possible to the words in the book he reads." Again, she sees the privileged pretext undercutting the language of the text.

The narrating of travelers on a journey "through the words of the Bible" is not without a great deal of wit, Quilligan suggests. The confrontation of Christian with Formalist and Hypocrisy, for example, in their discussion over being "in the way" shows the play between the theological and the colloquial meanings of the term. Formalist and Hypocrisy argue, of course, that it doesn't matter which way they got in; if they "are in," they "are in." It's true that they are in by "tumbling over the wall" and Christian is "in the way" by coming in "at the gate." Yet, why argue over how they got "in"?

Quilligan finds in the play with the phrase "in the way" a suggestion that Formalist thinks of Christian as being "'in his way,ptra' that is, an obstacle to further progress" (p. 124). In her thinking, the literal position of the three individuals within the allegorical landscape fails to distinguish among them. It is true "that their point of origin in the landscape can be said to distinguish them, but "this distinction," says Quilligan, "disappears to the external eye as they all three stand together in the road" (p. 125). Christian does not agree with Formalist and Hypocrisy that some "external sign" is perhaps the distinguishing quality, and when he declares that it is the mark on his forehead and the reading of his scroll that make the distinction, Quilligan remarks that "it is not finally the way he came to be in the way, but his reading that distinguishes him from them" (p. 125). Bunyan's methods for "making allegory's usual distinctions" is to appeal to the pretext and to offer the "external act of reading to clinch the matter." To Quilligan, his constant appeal to the pretext actually means that "he does not trust the reader to make the distinctions unaided by explicit indications that the pretext is the key to interpretation" (p. 126).

In her discussions of Bunyan's characters, Quilligan sees them as individuals who are not "incarnate by personifying but rather exemplify qualities," and the difference between "an incarnation" and "an exemplification is profound." Quilligan thinks of Old Honest as an example of one who expresses this difference, and at the same time, she thinks of Honest as "more alive" than Guyon, for instance, and "more realistic" than Shamefastnesse, and other characters in The Faerie Queene, but Spenser's poem "delivers the moral and philosophical truth to be found in words, while Bunyan's work offers us the attributes of individual characters, dramatically conceived" (p. 128). Honest is an examplar of such a character, and Mercy is perhaps an even clearer example of Bunyan's personifications. Quilligan holds that Mercy's name "could as easily have been Jane or Sally," for the play with her name "derives from the fact that Bunyan has reversed the normal process of personifying abstract qualities. She does not personify God's grace itself, but represents the lowly object of his grace" (p. 129). Quilligan sees Bunyan's personifications coinciding with his use of pretext: rather than "setting his characters out across a landscape of words to discover simultaneously the truths of their psyches and of scripture," he sets out "more or less real people who discover in their journeys the difficulties of behaving according to scripture" (p. 129). Quilligan further believes that Bunyan's characters function in a landscape that has no "final authoritative statement to make about their 'progress.'"

With all of her various comments on Bunyan's work, Quilligan emphatically states that "Bunyan's book is therefore at once an allegory, yet also something different" (p. 130). What she sees as the "something different" is the novelistic tendency of the work. Yet, the "novelistic tendencies" do not distinguish Bunyan as an allegorist from the allegorists before him, but he "does not assume that language can do as much" as, for example, Spenser or Langland "trusted to it." He has--or appears to have--a low opinion of the power of his own text, unaided by the pretext, and this attitude is at the heart of Quilligan's concern.

When she discusses her views of "the context," or of her conviction that a "suprarealist" attitude toward words must exist if allegory is to be a viable genre, Quilligan focuses briefly on Bunyan. It is wise to recognize that she believes that the realist attitude toward language gives way at the end of the seventeenth century "before a vast epistemological shift" and "words lost the battle to 'things' and language disappeared as a potent force for shaping man's sense of his cosmos" (p. 157). Among religious groups and authors, Quilligan argues that the suprarealist attitude toward language is "something we associate more readily with what has been called the 'Metaphysical' (or 'Anglican' or 'Ciceronian') style of sermon--as in John Donne's puns, or Lancelot Andrewes' elegant etymologizing-- than with the plain and Ramist methodology of the logical Puritan sermon" (p. 182). Consequently, she admits that there is something "inexplicable in Bunyan's decision to write narrative allegory at all." She also reiterates that the epistemology of the culture shifted away from the suprarealist attitude. But, what of Bunyan and his allegory?

Quilligan turns now to a positive contribution of the Puritan imagination. She reminds the reader that if, as Foucault has suggested, "in the seventeenth century language had been 'withdrawn from the midst of beings themselves and ... entered a period of transparency and neutrality,' then the Puritan imagination ... paradoxically reintroduced a context for allegory by reconstituting the union between human history and scripture" (pp. 184-5). The Puritans did this by declaring a transcendent God who intervened in every affair of life, which to Quilligan, "then constituted an elaborate system of signs." Therefore, if man's language were an "unacceptable guide to the truth," then there was still the language of one book "whose words were assumed to be coherently at one with current human history" (p. 185). Bunyan believes in this one book, he has a suprarealist attitude, and he writes an allegory of enduring art. Yet, "the components of that art," says Quilligan, "are of a piece with the Puritan aesthetic which suspects the abilities of man's own language, unaided by scripture, to speak the truth." Readers of Bunyan's allegory, like readers of any allegory, read it "by learning how to read it," and the experience of reading allegory "always operates by the gradual revelation to a reader who, acknowledging that he does not already know the answers, discovers them, usually by a process of relearning them" (p. 227). To Quilligan, Bunyan primarily places the effect of his allegory in his forthright promise to the reader to "make a traveller of thee."

Another view of the allegorical mode and of Bunyan's allegory in particular may be seen in Leopold Damrosch, Jr. ("Experience and Allegory in Bunyan," God's Plot and Man's Story, Chicago, 1985). He studies The Pilgrim's Progress for some twenty-one packed pages in his lengthier chapter on Bunyan.

He admits early in his study that "modern thinking about allegory has taken two main forms, emphasizing either the ability of its images to denote universal truths, or else insisting on their arbitrary nature" (p. 50). To Damrosch the latter position is to some extent espoused by theorists "like Paul de Man who stress the paradox that allegory looks like vivid representation but concerns precisely those ideas and intuitions that cannot be represented ..." (p. 150). This arbitrary invention of signs is contrasted with the "grandiose claims of the Romantics (who despised 'mere' allegory) to reproduce ultimate reality in symbolic form" (p. 150). To Damrosch it is almost impossible simply to distinguish between an older and newer way of discussing allegory, for critics usually stress both aspects-- "veracity and arbitrariness." Yet, Damrosch agrees that the interest in semiotics and hermeneutics has contributed to the rehabilitation of allegory, "which instead of being despised as merely arbitrary is now celebrated as supremely arbitrary" (pp. 150-51). To support this "supremely arbitrary" nature, he quotes from Quilligan's The Language of Allegory and observes: "Maureen Quilligan somewhat chillingly declares, 'Other genres appeal to readers as human beings; allegory appeals to readers as readers of a system of signs" (p. 151).

For Damrosch, however, if one thinks of allegory from the point of view of Puritan theory, any "distinction between sign systems and human life is illusory." In fact, he says that the "two are identical, since all persons, whether they ponder literary narrative or the divinely ordered narrative of their own lives, are compelled to interpret signs" (p. 151). For this reason, The Pilgrim's Progress "ignores or abolishes the gap which critics postulate between literal sense and allegorical meaning. Life it-

AN OVERVIEW

self is for Bunyan continuously allegorical ..." (p. 151).

Damrosch next turns to a study of Bunyan's special kind of dream and his particular view of the words of the Bible, as "a collection of one-sentence texts." "Every sentence in the Bible has a direct and specific meaning," Damrosch declares, and "the chief goal of The Pilgrim's Progress is to exhibit those meanings in narrative guise" (p. 154). The author then asserts that Bunyan expresses the essential purpose of his allegory in the final lines of the introductory poem to the reader. Bunyan asks:

Wouldest thou lose thyself, and catch no harm
And find thyself again without a charm? /Would'st
read thyself, and read thou knowest not what
And yet know whether thou art blest or not,
By reading the same lines? O then come hither,
And lay my book, thy head and heart together.

(As quoted by Damrosch (pp. 154-55) from Sharrock edition of The Pilgrim's Progress, p. 37)

What is especially important for Damrosch is that Bunyan not only discloses his essential purpose but also embodies in the quotation the view that the "reader loses himself (or herself) by surrendering to a convincing fictive universe, but since it is built up of scriptural texts it is also the real universe, and so there is no need to suspend disbelief" (p. 155). Thus, the reader "finds himself by learning to read himself," and as Damrosch later shows, what Bunyan ultimately desires is to lead the reader out of his book into the permanent truths that it conveys. He has no interest in escaping from dogma, but "allegorical imagery that gives the dogma intelligible shape" is the contribution of The Pilgrim's Progress. Thus, to hold to particular dogma and yet move toward a goal is the supreme purpose of the Christian pilgrims. Perhaps this in part causes Damrosch to say: "So the tone of the book is finely suspended between two attitudes which might seem contradictory but in Puritan experience were both deeply felt: the conviction of election which no power can possibly repeal, and the duty to avoid complacency and engage in unending struggle" (p. 161).

In his handling of The Pilgrim's Progress, Damrosch gives some attention to the way in which critics have regarded the allegory as a "kind of proto-novel." This label raises questions for him. He says, for example, that Iser does not inspire confidence with his breezy claim that "mere allegory is surpassed through the sheer aliveness of the characters" or "It is through this inner self that the character outstrips the allegory." After all, "the characters seem at many points programmatic rather than sheerly alive ..." and, Damrosch continues, "the interiority of the work applies to the experience of all men and women, not of novelistic individuals" (p. 170). Yet, he holds that The Pilgrim's Progress does have affinities with the novel. After careful argument, Damrosch concludes that "what makes The Pilgrim's Progress look forward to the novel is the way in which it displays characters in action" (p. 177). The most significant affinity between The Pilgrim's Progress and later novels, however, is "its recognition of the differentness of different persons" (p. 179).

In tending toward the novel, Damrosch believes that "Part II of The Pilgrim's Progress sacrifices much of what makes the first part immortal: its psychological intensity" (p. 184). The great point of Part I was that "the Bible is mediated through symbols that have to be lived before they can be understood, and cannot furnish a map to be infalliby followed at every specific turning-point" (p. 184). Above all, "The Pilgrim's Progress is powerful because it compels the reader to share in the pilgrimage" (p. 185).

Another critic of the allegory with an obvious interest in semiotics is Brian Nellist ("The Pilgrim's Progress and Allegory," Critical and Historical Views. Edited by Vincent Newey, 1980). For him, The Pilgrim's Progress is closer to post-allegorical works like Kafka's Castle than to traditional allegory. Whereas, traditional allegory involves the assumption of some great typifying roles, there stands, on the contrary, at the center of The Pilgrim's Progress, "not a coherent body of thought or a process of developing reflection ... but a consciousness" (p. 133). Bunyan's apprehensions are "objects and locations which suggest more than they specify"; the "only continuous relationship in the book," in Nellist's judgment, is not with another person but with a thing, the road, and our concern is with an inner process of attentiveness" (pp. 133-34).

At the same time, the characters and figures of Bunyan's allegory do not relate to one another in a structured hierarchy, but they relate solely to Christian. Bunyan focuses on the inner features of his central character, a practice different from early allegorists; moreover, he "restricts the large resonances of his symbolic places, even Vanity Fair and the two dreadful Valleys. Mythic associations would imply a centre of truth outside the consciousness of the hero himself" (p. 137). So, Nellist informs the reader that Bunyan writes a secondary form of allegory "whose value is both to disguise and then to show forth the radical individualism of his position" (p. 137). Even if the reader brings to The Pilgrim's Progress "the reading habits appropriate to allegory," Nellist opines, "he is surprised to discover that he cannot compose the images into a coherent order in themselves. They always carry him back to the introspective self of Christian" (p. 139). Images, too, in the allegory are different from earlier writers of allegory, due not primarily to their lack of an ordering principle but to their being used "to resist a process of generalization and to restrict access to any coherent body of knowledge" (p. 145). Nellist's obvious theoretical assumptions lead to no surprises. One of his most telling conclusions is: "The inability to connect sign with sign coherently in the work, which begins as a source of alarm, ends as a release from signs altogether and an escape from allegory into a mood of trustful incertitude" (p. 146).

In yet another essay, Dayton Haskin ("The Burden of Interpretation in The Pilgrim's Progress," SP, no. 3, 1982) focuses in an interesting manner on the reader. Haskin proposes that The Pilgrim's Progress transforms the agonizing duty of searching the scriptures into a "sanctifying and reassuring pleasure." For Bunyan there is, according to Haskin, an intimate connection between guilt and Bible-reading, for in The Pilgrim's Progress the persona receives that burden on his back "by reading his Book." Perhaps in a rather extreme turn, Haskin argues that Bunyan confused book-learning with religion. In the period of "Puritan scholasticism," a new theory of inspiration arose whereby God literally dictated the words of the Bible, so that the Bible became not merely the record of revelation, but revelation itself. Hence Bunyan sought God by seeking or by reading the scripture.

Haskin further holds that the two back-breaking burdens in Puritanism were: 1) idolatry to the scriptures, and 2) predestination. Each person must interpret for himself the text on which his salvation or damnation depends.

The Pilgrim's Progress and Grace Abounding are similar in that in both works the reader acquires his burden by reading. However, with Christian the "burden of interpretation" afflicts him for only a short while; with the persona of Grace Abounding the burden lingers until he learns to interpret the Bible to his own advantage or need. Similarly, Christian loses his burden after a sojourn in the House of the Interpreter, for even before the end of the episode, he claims to be a competent interpreter himself.

Perhaps Haskin emphasizes what he considers to be cruelties of Calvinism to the exclusion of its gifts, but his essay is unusually intriguing. In brief, his conclusion is that Bunyan wrote The Pilgrim's Progress in part to relieve the reader from the "burden of interpretation" (the stark, unimaginative endeavor with a "life-and-death text") and to offer a fanciful pilgrimage to the Palace Beautiful, infused with high adventure.

Roger Sharrock ("Life and Story in The Pilgrim's Progress," Critical and Historical Views. Edited by Vincent Newey, 1980) expresses a different concern from some modern scholar-critics

AN OVERVIEW

when he recognizes that Bunyan's allegory "has suffered from the displacement of the centrality of the Bible in education just as other literature has suffered from the decline in the knowledge of the classics" (p. 49). Yet, in a provocative statement, Sharrock declares that "<u>The Pilgrim's Progress</u> both as Christian statement and as imaginative creation is still profoundly there for all those of us who would wish to contemplate the permanent outlines of one culture and make sense of the present by seeing it in relation to the past and thus not become lost in the waste land of its ephemeralities" (p. 49). Because Christian's progress is a reflection of the common human story the reader is involved.

Rejecting the Coleridgean view that Bunyan the artist triumphed over Bunyan the preacher, Sharrock insists that the religious underpinnings and structure of <u>The Pilgrim's Progress</u> make it difficult to differentiate it sharply from his other writings. In Sharrock's view we move in <u>The Pilgrim's Progress</u> "from the image of Bunyan as the author of one great isolated work of the imagination to a different image: that of an author of a large body of works of evangelical piety, arousing sermons, books on the doctrine of grace, conduct manuals and books of controversy, among which <u>The Pilgrim's Progress</u> is simply an outstanding example" (pp. 50-51). Something of the formal structure of the sermon is carried over into the allegory. The conversation among Christian and Hopeful and Ignorance, for instance, roughly follows a sermon outline. Again, in Bunyan's sermon, <u>The Barren Fig-Tree</u>, he analyzes and lists five metaphorical elements in his exposition of the parable in Luke 13:6-9 on the barren fig-tree. According to Sharrock, the listing or "numbering" of arguments extends to many of the static passages of discourse that lie between the episodes of adventure, challenge and temptation in <u>The Pilgrim's Progress</u>.

What may be close to evangelical sermonizing or what may be classified as less dramatic elements of the allegory is by no means the only feature which Sharrock emphasizes. He explicity states that he wants "to turn once more to what is permanent and powerful in the appeal of the book" (p. 55). In turning to this direction, Sharrock suggests that Bunyan's critics "have sometimes done him a disservice by inviting us to look backwards or forwards when regarding him, back to the Middle Ages or forward to the modern realistic novel" (p. 55). For Sharrock, The Pilgrim's Progress has the features of that very old but long-lasting form, the story, "something growing out of oral narrative like the fairy--or folk tale" (p. 56). What is so significant is that the story speaks of shared human experience, and the experience is communicable. Never denying that "the stages of a soul's progress as charted by three generations of Puritan psychologists are there ... conviction of sin, legality, justification, sanctification, and growth in grace" (p. 65), Sharrock shows a greater concern with those parts of the narrative "where Bunyan indicates a surprising tendency to throw away his fiction, to turn up his own metaphors, without leaving it to the reader, or to break with the wholeness of his fable entirely in order to bring out the myth of its meaning" (p. 65). And this concern, Sharrock commendably develops in his essay.

If narrative technique and the reading process have captured the attention of the Bunyan critic, so also have particular topics or specific features of the narrative. The emblem becomes an important subject for study for David J. Alpaugh ("Emblem and Interpretation in The Pilgrim's Progress, ELH 33, 1966). His thesis that through "the art of emblem interpretation Christian learns" is in a large sense the art that all aspiring pilgrims must learn before they can enter the Celestial City. For Alpaugh, Bunyan insists that our intellectual concepts be grounded in empirical experience, and hence he places emphasis on rightly interpreting the visual emblem.

The essay classifies the emblem which Christian encounters into two general types: emblems of brightness and emblems of darkness. Bunyan portrays the Celestial City through imagery of gold. Alpaugh suggests that in Bunyan's treatment of the imagery of gold, he thinks of it "in its alchemical sense, as the fifth essence, the elixir, the final purity and reality that remains after the dross of the world had been refined away." Against this emblem associated with brightness, Bunyan places the emblems of darkness: The Valley of the Shadow of Death, the Doubting-Castle, the black-skinned Flatterer, and the cave in the side of the hill. That the dark emblems will ultimately fall away and prove illusory is obvious when Christian and Hopeful reach Beulah.

Alpaugh also sees The Pilgrim's Progress as a progression. It traces Christian's growth from ignorance to wisdom. Christian begins as "little more than an archetypal emblem of conviction of sin," but after he accumulates more and more emblematic experience, he becomes "a more reliable interpreter." For Alpaugh, the dream is the final emblem of the work, and he exhorts that like Christian, we must become shrewd interpreters and discover the correct meaning behind the emblem.

Not only is the emblem of importance in interpretation of The Pilgrim's Progress, for dialogue and debate are equally important to David Seed ("Dialogue and Debate in The Pilgrim's Progress," Critical and Historical Views. Edited by Vincent Newey, 1980). For Seed, The Pilgrim's Progress consists mostly of dialogue, and Bunyan is particularly adept at capturing different levels of discourse which correspond to certain characters. He was not mere tinker, but rather his art distills the essence of genuine regional dialects. "In his pacing and arrangement of dialogue he shows," says Seed, "a fine sense of psychology in both speaker and listener" (p. 69).

Bunyan also has a gift for externalizing inner struggle through the use of dialogue. For Seed, dialogue is a "means of dramatizing self-examination as well as presenting confrontations with hostile agencies" (p. 73).

The characters whom Christian meets in his pilgrimage fall into two categories: the tempters and instructors. Part One has a main rhythm in that after every trial of temptation there follows a "brief explanatory interlude." Near the beginning Christian is either tested or taught. Later he participates more actively in self-analysis and grows in his ability to distinguish between a tempter and an instructor. Seed also holds that the diction of dialogue often follows the particular tone of the episode. As Hopeful, for example, is explaining the perils of despair to Christian in Doubting Castle, his language becomes less colloquial and more formal with involved syntax.

One certain indicator of Christian's spiritual progress is his ability to debate. The better he can counter the arguments of tempters, the stronger he is morally. Since so much is at stake in these debates, there is "frequently more drama in the dialogues than their surface might suggest" (p. 81). Seed also reminds the reader that apart from particular devices of dialogue, Bunyan "shows his skill at combining moral purpose with characterization in his depiction of styles of speech" (p. 82). Talkative's verbosity, for example, becomes obvious by Bunyan's "careful and sophisticated play of vocabulary against syntax in his speech" (p. 83). "Tone, texture, and order, says Seed, "all perform crucial functions in the play of character against character in Part I" (p. 84). A perceptive study of Part Two of the allegory shows Bunyan attempting to combine the two narrative modes of the dream and dialogue.

Elizabeth Adeney ("Bunyan: A Unified Vision?" Critical Review, Melbourne, 1974) finds Bunyan's tone and "play of character against character" to be worthy of study. Her focus, however, is primarily on the frequent passages of comic writing. She readily admits that his comedy is as multifarious as are the characters that inspire it, but she also contends that it is in Bunyan's comic passages that he is most persistently himself. Some of these passages serve no purpose in the allegory, but they are there, Adeney believes, because Bunyan simply could not resist adding comedy. Examples such as the image of Christian scared half-speechless at being caught off the path by Evangelist or the "touching conjugal felicity" of Giant Despair and his wife are incidental to the main line of the story; but Bunyan is writing freely, caught up in creating a situation, and with imaginative integrity, comically showing how people interact under unfamiliar circumstances. She further argues that up to the "rather cliche-like tableau of Passion and Patience," one of the finest qualities of the prose has been its "almost surprising freedom from any off-key shrillness or vindictiveness." When Bunyan meets Talkative, he enjoys him and writes with energy and wit, and in this enjoyment, he recognizes and uses the kinds of energies generated by people such as Talkative. It is here, however, according to Adeney that "the split with Christian comes." In her thinking, Christian is incapable of recognizing, let alone using, these energies, for he sees Talkative as nothing other than a "bad man." This "split" between Bunyan and Christian grows as Christian becomes more and more intolerant, and it reaches its climax in the section on Mr. By-ends and his friends, Mr. Money-love, Mr. Save-all. and Mr. Hold-the-world. Simultaneously, the comic writing reaches a kind of peak.

What Adeney sees is a tension between Christian's narrow response to the world around him and Bunyan's far more generous but responsible feeling for it. She concludes that in The Pilgrim's Progress, Bunyan's imaginative vigor, which concentrates itself in the comic passages, establishes his feeling for life as fuller and far greater than the sum total of his Puritanism or of any religious dogma.

Rather than seeing a division between Bunyan's religious beliefs and feelings for life as Adeney does, Geoffrey Finch ("The Puritan Imagination of John Bunyan," Orita (Ibadan) 7, 1974) contends that Bunyan belongs near the end of a long medieval tradition, which places no separation between the supernatural and the natural. To Finch, Bunyan's whole outlook on life is narrow, but this narrowness seems not a handicap but a benefit in that it results in a dramatic frame of mind which helps shape his creativity. What gives strength to Finch's stance is illustrative material from several episodes in The Pilgrim's

Progress (and Grace Abounding) which, to him, demonstrate how doctrine, transformed into pictorial representation, is perceived as truth, independent of personal belief. For Finch, this lack of separation between the supernatural and the actual explains the power of Bunyan's art to captivate readers, even though some may see Christian's journey "as a pilgrimage to heaven" while others view it as a "process of becoming."

An overview of studies on The Pilgrim's Progress also demands attention to the theology embodied in the allegory. Although references have been made to the subject by several critics previously discussed, Gordon Campbell ("The Theology of The Pilgrim's Progress," Critical and Historical Views. Edited by Vincent Newey, 1980) focuses almost exclusively on the theology of the allegory--or perhaps the absence of it. Campbell holds that Bunyan was a sectarian, not a Puritan; moreover, he did not advocate the purification of the Church of England, but separation from it. His doctrine of the separated Church appears in The Pilgrim's Progress in the episode in which Christian visits the Palace Beautiful. For Campbell, the "house rules" of the Palace Beautiful are the same rules as those of The Church Book of Bunyan Meeting. An examination of that book shows that "those who desired to join the Bedford Church had to wait outside until they were called in." Yet, Campbell argues that Bunyan's theology and his own experince of salvation tend to be incidental to Christian's journey. "The doctrine of election was ... crucial to Bunyan's theology and to his own experience of salvation," says Campbell, "and yet it does not affect the Christian of The Pilgrim's Progress" (p. 257). He does not deny that various doctrines to which Bunyan subscribed are mentioned, but overtly "theological passages in the book tend to be incidental to Christian's journey, even though that journey is allegorically soterial" (p. 257). The allegory is a religious rather than a theological work. What Bunyan does in his theological writings is "to articulate divine truth; in The Pilgrim's Progress he eliminates the truths that are set in the mind of God ... and presents a theology accommodated to the experience and limited perspective of man" (p. 261).

N.H. Keeble ("<u>The Pilgrim's Progress</u>: A Puritan Fiction," <u>Baptist Quarterly</u> 28, 1980) disagrees with Campbell and attempts to show that <u>The Pilgrim's Progress</u> is a "complete Puritan masterpiece." He sees Christian's achievement of his quest in Bunyan's realistic story as "the fortunate literary consequence of a theological conviction, not the creation of an artist liberated from his theology" (p. 327). As Keeble examines the realism of Bunyan's allegory, he argues that in passages which are frequently criticized for being "dull sermonizing," one finds a story being told. Were it not for this "thoughtful reflection upon experience to which they bear witness," Keeble says, "there never would have been a story" (p. 330). There are two main reasons for Keeble's views: Bunyan's realistic observations came from his faculty "actively encouraged to develop by the insistence of his religious tradition that the true Christian is one who constantly scrutinizes his experience" and more significant, "these passages <u>are</u> the story in that it is here real progress occurs" (p. 330). What is also important to remember is that in these passages, Christian has the "limited understanding of what happens to him which is common to all of us in our lives" (p. 330). Bunyan, on the other hand, "gives the reader the privilege of an over-view, and he can detect more surely than Christian, a developing maturity in the pilgrim's awareness and understanding of human experience" (p. 330). The author sees the failures of his pilgrim, but he also perceives the growing firmness of his judgment as he goes from event to event. In themselves, Bunyan does not believe that these events "constitute any moral or artistic sense: it is the human mind which, by fathoming them, on the one hand perceives their divine significance, and on the other creates story, that is, a coherent and meaningful sequence of incidents" (p. 330).

Keeble further discusses the way in which Bunyan embodies various facets of Puritan beliefs and teachings in the <u>The Pilgrim's Progress</u>. To complete more fully his stance, Keeble directs attention to "the narrative nature of the Puritan vision of experience," especially reflected in the allegory, thus the artistic creation and the theological beliefs are an integrated whole in that Bunyan's theology informs his allegory.

If exploration of his narrative, his handling of the metaphor of the journey or the pilgrimage, his understanding of allegory, as well as his treatment (or lack of it) of Puritan and Calvinist theology are of interest to modern scholars, so also is Bunyan's depiction of various characters. Perhaps Ignorance is more of an enigma to critics, but Flatterer too has not escaped critical attention.

In a closely argued essay, James F. Forrest ("Bunyan's Ignorance and The Flatterer: A Study in the Literary Art of Damnation," SP LX no.1, 1963) shows a causal relation between the brief episode of the Flatterer and the final rejection of Ignorance. After demonstrating his thorough understanding of various views held by scholars on Bunyan's character, Ignorance, Forrest believes that without exception they sell Bunyan short "by ignoring or obfuscating the original art he has lavished on his portrayal of a doomed sinner...." For Forrest, there is no reason to hold any view on the author's handling of Ignorance other than that Bunyan has carefully "laid the ground ... by imposing a significant pattern on prior events." The chief prior event is the episode involving the Flatterer, whom Forrest suggest initially to be taken as a type of hypocrisy or Pharisaism. In the course of the journey, the Shepherds of the Delectable Mountains caution Christian and Hopeful about the Flatterer, for they are aware that contentment might easily pass into complacency.

Forrest carefully shows a sequence of events which suggests that Flatterer underscores Bunyan's theme of the falsity of self-achieved righteousness. To see this emphasis is also to understand the author's conception of Ignorance, whose sin is willful unbelief. "Ignorance is ultimately the personification of mulish Unbelief," says Forrest, "whose ignorance being willful is irrevocable, hence unforgivable." Ignorance and Flatterer reinforce the allegory's basic thrust that each individual is personally responsible for asking for God's grace if he is to know salvation, and Forrest holds that Ignorance is just "as responsible for his condition as Christian is for his."

As Forrest suggested in his splendid essay, some see in Ignorance "testimony to Bunyan's abhorrence for the Quaker faith...." Richard F. Hardin ("Bunyan, Mr. Ignorance, and the Quakers," Studies in Philology 69 no.4, 1972) further demonstrates the accuracy of Forrest's statement which was made nine years earlier. Hardin depicts Ignorance as representative of the Quakers with whom Bunyan debated, believing them to be ignorant of their own inner selves and ignorant interpreters of the Bible. To understand how seriously Bunyan regarded Quaker teaching one has only to observe the plight of Bunyan's Ignorance, especially near the close of The Pilgrim's Progress.

If critics show interest in characters, they also demonstrate some concern with particular places mentioned by Bunyan. Elmo Howell ("Bunyan's Two Valleys: A Note on the Ecumenic Element in Pilgrim's Progress." Tennessee Studies in Literature 19, 1974) believes that although Bunyan is personally partisan, his intense vision, especially depicted in the Valley of Humilation and the Valley of the Shadow of Death, enables him to write a work characterized by it ecumenicity. What Howell contends is that the two valleys indicate spiritual trials known not only to Bunyan in his own experience but also trials similar to those described in The Dark Night of the Soul by St. John of the Cross.

James Turner ("Bunyan's Sense of Place," Critical and Historical Views. Edited by Vincent Newey, 1980) combines individuals and places in his socio-economic approach. Asserting that there are contradictions in Bunyan's topography, he states that the road is actually not as straight as it first seems, and prominent obstacles are absolutely hidden at a distance, due to the strictly symbolic nature of the dream-land. "Bunyan's places are related to a generalized concept of 'the World,'" says Turner, and "he conceived the world in political and economic terms, as a hostile hierarchy of wealth and power founded on place--social position and landed estates" (p. 97). Turner further asserts that the elements of Bunyan's "topography have social implications, and the inner states of the pilgrims are caused by ... social pressures" (p. 97). To Turner, Apollyon resembles some powerful employee, and his threat is economic. Even the Giant Despair episode is simply a "reconstruction of a country estate as it is experienced by those excluded from it." "Despair is less an abstract or existential inner state," says Turner, "than the emotional response of the poor Christian to repression and social contempt" (p. 100). Furthermore, two sorts "of landownership are thus opposed: carnal, in which the pilgrims are treated as outcasts, and spiritual, in which they 'possess the brave country alone' ..." (p. 101). This is the reason why Bunyan's landscape is so inconsistent: it is constructed of two incompatible kinds of land. The pilgrim's "use of space while on the road is vocational--a single furrow--but in the palaces and vineyards prepared for their comfort it is recreational" (p. 104). Although Turner is careful to say that property is used as metaphor, he sees this metaphor as an economic signifier.

Since N.H. Keeble also focuses on Puritan narrative and understands the place of the experience of a reader, and includes some emphasis on particular topics, places, and characters, it is perhaps fitting to conclude the overview of studies basically focusing on Part One with yet another essay by N.H. Keeble. His essay, "The Way and the Ways of Puritan Story: Biblical Patterns in Bunyan and his Contemporaries," (English 1984), also refers, at least indirectly to some of the preceding critical positions.

Beginning his article with the opening words of The Pilgrim's Progress: "As I walk'd through the wilderness of this world, I lighted on a certain place, where was a Denn," Keeble asserts that immediately the reader of the allegory is transported into an apparently improbable landscape. Yet, Bunyan is deliberately and purposefully walking there. As Keeble states: "To walk <u>through</u> a wilderness is to be going somewhere, and to <u>walk</u> through it is to be going unhurriedly but steadily" (p. 209). What one also quickly knows is that the marginal gloss "Gaol" upon "Denn" reminds the reader of the horrors and dangers associated with dens. Bunyan writes in the preface of <u>Grace Abounding</u> (1666) from the "Lions Dens", and "lurking lions" in the wilderness of Biblical story inhabit dens.

In light of the figurative meaning of the word "den," Keeble contends that the single monosyllable tells a good deal about "the plight of nonconformists during the 'Great Restoration' and of Bunyan's relationship to the authorities of the Restoration, but his wilderness is not merely that created by Charles II ... and the Cavalier Parliament" (p. 209). What Keeble wants the reader to see is that Bunyan's words recall the "geography of a far distant place" and by so doing, places "his own and his readers' experiences in that larger Biblical perspective Puritan writing habitually adopted." This perspective in large part "determined the Puritan story" (p. 209).

For Keeble, then, the two traditions of Israel's origins in the Abraham legend and the Exodus saga embody a pattern, the pattern of "decision to leave, journey under divine guidance, testing in the wilderness and covenant," and this pattern underlies Puritan story. To the Puritan mind, Israel's history makes intelligible personal and national history and offers, at the same time, "not only an interpretative key but a narrative model." He further believes that in these Old Testament stories, the Puritan imagination finds a "spiritual geography, a symbolic vocabulary, and a structure by means of which not only to apprehend but to recount both 'what the Lord hath done for my soul' (Ps. 66.16) and the 'great and mighty signs and wonders' of God (Dan. 4.3)"(p. 210). This focus on personal experience by grace and the works of Providence, "twin preoccupations" of the Puritans gives "to Puritan narratives their distinctive resonance." Within this "unified structure created by the image of the journey," Keeble sees varying "levels of significance," and "many journeys to forward at once." The Pilgrim's Progress is, consequently, "about" Christian and Bunyan; it is also a "reworking of Grace Abounding " about England and Old Testament resolution of Israel's earlier and England's later history (p. 210). What Keeble calls the "mode of Puritan story" is "at once realistic, allegorical in the old medieval sense, picturing forth theological abstractions, and symbolic in the manner of modern subjectivism, investing particular experiences with figurative significance" (p. 210).

Although the influence of the Bible was strikingly significant on Puritan story, the Puritan writers derive "the common structure and recurrent motifs" from only a few Biblical episodes. Keeble contends that these are: "(I) the emigration of Abraham; (II) the image of the way in the prophets and wisdom literature and its late application by Christ; (III) the Exodus from Egypt and Israel's desert wanderings; (IV) the oracle of the exilic prophets; (V) the interpretation of these Old Testament events in the Epistle to the Hebrews" (p. 211).

To leave what is known and to venture into an unknown land such as Abraham decides to do is exactly the decision of the man with a burden on his back at the beginning of The Pilgrim's Progress. The decision is firm, bold, decisive. "'Play the man,'" says Keeble, "echoes like a refrain through The Pilgrim's Progress: it is by rehearsing the dangers he will encounter that Valiant-for-truth's family seeks to dissuade him from pilgrimage, and that Mr. Worldly-wiseman would turn Christian himself from the way" (p. 214). Furthermore, the Puritan protagonist dares to risk, resolves to venture, and determines to traverse the wilderness of this world.

If the protagonist decides to leave, there is also a "setting out," and the only way to set out is through the gate--"the strait gate." This gate is the beginning, not the end of the journey, and through the gate is the Way he must go.

There is no tarrying inside the gate, the pilgrim must press onward and continue to go forward. "What marks out Bunyan's pilgrims," says Keeble, "is less any remarkable degree of grace than that they keep on going" (p. 219).

Pressing on in the way might mean numerous difficulties, and just how perilous forsaking the way might be, a pilgrim would find in the Exodus saga. Less than total commitment leads to disaster. There is no place in the way for arbitrary or complacent living.

Just as the prophets of the exile offered consolation to suffering people in their trials, so also does Bunyan dramatically show that not only does the pilgrim experience trials but also there is purpose in each of these. In Keeble's opinion, the plot of Puritan story invites study and analysis in Aristotelian terms. "Its beginning is no random point," he says, "no mere accident of the protagonist's birth or upbringing, but the genuine beginning of the 'new birth,' which, since it is the unprompted operations of grace, 'is not necessarily after anything else'" (p. 224). It does have something, however, that follows: "the sustained testing of that beginning in the middle section" and upon "the protagonist's performance during this middle section of trial depends the ending" (p. 224). And this ending emphatically constitutes "a final and irrevocable climax after which there is no more story to tell." Keeble declares that the "apparently slippery notion of 'progress,' which has much exercised critics of Bunyan, may be so understood in these terms" (p. 224). He then underscores his statement with the fact that Christian learns the "significance of proceeding along the way, and the whole of the way, in the direction Evangelist sends him; but for the unregenerate there is no progress of any kind, neither beginning nor middle to their stories, only a picaresque wandering ... " (p. 224). There is also a consolation for this Puritan hero--this fallible, anxious, fearful--human being, and something of consolation is evident in the varieties of pilgrims, for example, who compose the entourage of Christiana, for it included the young, the old, the crippled--indeed the "curiously unheroic."

Keeble closes his comprehensive essay with brief comments on the interpretation of Old Testament events in the Epistle to the Hebrews. The interpretation of the Old Testament by the author of the Epistle informs the attempt of "Puritan story to present 'the visible world of ordinary experience in the metaphoric terms established by the Word.'" When the author of the Epistle notes that God is said to deny the erring Israelites not Canaan but 'my rest,' he further suggests that the way in the wilderness is not merely "to a homeland but to an eternal salvation." The Puritan protagonist perceives himself as a pilgrim led like the Israelites through a wilderness--the wilderness of this world. Bunyan's use of "similitudes" permits the reader to comprehend the hazards as well as the glories of the way. In his incisive realism, perhaps Bunyan "may anticipate the novel, but that realism is an incidental means, not an end: the Puritan's only business with the world was to understand through it, as through a glass darkly (I Cor. 13.12), God's will towards him" (p. 229). Sections of The Pilgrim's Progress, such as Prudence's answers to Matthew's "emblematic catechism" of Part Two as well as the emblems of the Interpreter's House, illustrate this "'spiritualization' of the world." Keeble further contends that the Puritan faith both "perceived and created the wilderness, sought, indeed, to perceive it by creating it in its literary representation of experience and history, and to create it in readers' lives by the persuasiveness of the representation: The Pilgrim's Progress would 'make a Travailer of thee'" (p. 229).

Thus far the overview of the trends in the literary studies on The Pilgrim's Progress has primarily focused on Part One, but Part Two is not without critical attention. Some essays, of course, show critical concern for both parts. N.H. Keeble ("Christiana's Key: The Unity of The Pilgrim's Progress," Critical and Historical Views. Edited by Vincent Newey, 1980) cautions against focusing on the differences between Part One and Part Two, and this is perhaps an essential thrust with which to begin discussion.

In the nineteenth century, critics typically regarded Part Two of The Pilgrim's Progress as dramatically and stylistically inferior to Part One. Critics of the twentieth century have taken a different stance: Part Two is different from, not inferior to Part One. For E.M.W. Tillyard Part One is "epic"; Part Two is "emblematical" and "exemplary." Henri Talon regards Part One as a "novel in character or action;" Part Two as a "novel of manners."

Keeble, however, encourages readers and critics to treat Part One and Part Two as a single unit instead of merely accentuating the differences. In fact, he holds that one is unable to understand Part Two apart from Part One. The topography and episodes of the journeys remain largely the same. Familiar characters reappear. In writing Part Two, Bunyan probably intends nothing more than to reinforce and expand Part One. Christian's experience is universal, and now the task is to draw out its full implications.

The Pilgrim's Progress is more than a fictional narrative with two autonomous units. For Keeble, the fiction is only an "expository device" to portray a model of the Christian life. Part One is, of course, the individual's journey; Part Two is the corporate journey, yet the latter travellers achieve the quest as surely as Christian. Bunyan deliberately associates Part Two with Part One.

James F. Forrest ("Vision, Form, and the Imagination in the Second Part of The Pilgrim's Progress (1684)," Journal of Narrative Technique 13, 1983) offers another provocative insight. He holds that Christiana's zeal for the journey is no less real than Christian's, "but that it does not flare with the same blowtorch intensity." He further suggests the state of Christiana's soul is not so minutely studied, and the "effectual call" provokes far less perturbation of mind because it is received as a vision in the night.

Forrest also believes that the second part demonstrates the growing appreciation Bunyan had for art. In his use of vision in the work,

Forrest sees Bunyan asserting that "imaginative insight" is of tremendous value. Within the story, vision is important to the characters in order to spur them to action. Bunyan's vision is also a mirror for readers, for he, like Shakespeare and Milton, does not deny to his public "the power to see into the heart of things; the attitude of each is rather let him see and hear who can." The visions of these artists "search and investigate us: the dream is, as it were, the mirror that gives us back the image of ourselves." In this context, Bunyan practices his art; and in Forrest's judgment, Bunyan writes in the Second Part "his testament to the truth and beauty of that divinely-ordered world of the imagination."

If the prominent scholars, Keeble and Forrest, have uncovered fresh insights on the Second Part of The Pilgrim's Progress, so also has the equally eminent critic, John R. Knott, Jr. ("Bunyan and the Holy Community," SP, LXXX no. 2, 1983). Through many allusions to the text, this comprehensive essay builds an orderly description of the ideal separatist community. In showing Bunyan's concern with the nature and importance of the Christian community, Knott does, however, emphasize contrasts between the two parts. "One key difference between Christian and those who follow him," says Knott, "is the greater certainty of the latter. Valiant-for-Truth, Christiana and others seems less vulnerable to doubt than did Christian." He further holds that in the second part "the Bible functions more characteristically as a guide than as a weapon." Yet, Knott's primary concern is with the "holy community" of Part Two.

The particular features are clearly evident: the exhortation of fellowship, the trial of faith, the nurture of the Scriptures, the singing of the group, the communal meals, dignity in death, as well as the overall impression of the whole: a rich and complete portrait of a Puritan community. (Knott's essay is included in its entirety in the following chapter.)

Several critics refer to Part Two even

though the major part of their essays focuses on Part One. In David Seed's study "Dialogue and Debate in The Pilgrim's Progress," he suggests with John Knott that the emphasis is on the communal life of converts. For Seed, this emphasis is clear in the proliferation of characters in Part Two; the landscape is filled with people. "Because the notion of responsibility has been broadened beyond the individual," says Seed, "the narrative can take on more of a social texture" (p. 85). The use of verbal styles characterizes Part One as well as Part Two, but the typical rhythm of each episode is different in Part Two. Here the "characters pose no threat so there is no need for debate" (p. 86). The characterization also is both more explicit and less tense. In Seed's judgment, the main emphasis focuses "on the way in which the group steadily expands and on the relations formed, usually between pairs of characters, within the group" (p. 86). Mercy and Christiana are a classic illustration of this relation between "pairs of characters."

Leopold Damrosch, Jr. ("Experience and Allegory in Bunyan") includes brief comments on The Pilgrim's Progress (Part Two) in his study of Bunyan. One of his most interesting observations is his view that "Part II proposes a series of analogies that go impressively far toward making one feel what election must be like" (p. 180). To support his stance, he refers to Interpreter's explanations to Christiana that a hen has a "special call" for her chickens, a call later identified as "special grace," and the dying sheep which suffers but takes death quietly is an example for the Christian to suffer without complaining.

To Damrosch the "great ambition of Part II is to dramatize the full internalizing of God's will, with a sense of freedom that is embodied in moral effort rather than merely received from above" (p. 180). Elaborating on the statement, he holds that the "elect may not also feel a decisive 'call';" Mercy, for example, accompanies Christiana, whose call comes from the King, but the Keeper of the gate does not refuse her entrance even though she is without a decisive call.

"When Bunyan stresses the social environment of the pilgrims in Part II," Damrosch believes that Bunyan "loses the strangeness and terror of inner experience which had been the special province of the Puritan imagination" (p. 184). The latter, Bunyan explores, of course in Part One. Damrosch suggests that the characters in Part Two in effect read rather than relive Part One," but he admits that Bunyan at his greatest finds "reading one's life" to be "inseparable from living it" (p. 184).

U. Milo Kaufmann, whose book, The Pilgrim's Progress and Traditions in Puritan Meditation, we carefully discussed in an earlier section, also has important insights on Part Two. Differing slightly with Damrosch in his view on Mercy's "call," Kaufmann holds that "Bunyan does not categorically say that Mercy came uncalled, he plainly wants to present the broadest possible construction of the divine invitation" (p. 96). To Kaufmann, Mercy exemplifies divine mercy, and this is clear not only in her entrance upon the Way, "but in all the circumstance of her perseverance ... " (p. 97). She is also among those Wayfarer Christians listed in Kaufmann's categories of pilgrims in the Way. Christian is, of course, in the same category, and his wayfaring helps to define the road to be walked by Christiana, Mercy, and other wayfarers of Part Two. Kaufmann makes an important point on the unity of the two parts of the allegory in his discussion of the Wayfarers. "To read the two parts of the allegory in close sequence," he says, "is to be convinced of the multitude of ways Christian prepares the way for his wife and family. By instructive markers, by decisive victories over besetting enemies, by the impalpable influence of reputation, he transforms the way he covers" (p. 115).

If he sees the unity of the two parts, Kaufmann also recognizes the divergence between Parts One and Two. To cite an example of this divergence, he shows that the bulk of the specific appearances of the tradition of occasional meditation is to be found in Part Two. To Kaufmann, this is no surprise: "Christiana learns, by and large, through reflection and meditation, while Christian learns, for the most part, through action" (p. 188). He admits, however, that Christian's urgent pilgrimage offers little opportunity for reflection, but Christiana, in contrast, spends a month in House Beautiful alone and has abundant opportunity to "step outside the stream of compulsive routines" and to meditate on what she hears and sees.

Differences in point of view may be seen in yet another essay discussed in relation to Part One. S.J. Newman ("Bunyan's Solidness," <u>Critical and Historical Views</u>. Edited by Vincent Newey, 1980)," asserts that in Part Two "The wilderness of the world is reinvested with the properties of human society" (p. 239). The emphasis is on a community, strong and weak alike. "In Part II," says Newman, "carnal appetites are reinstated. Sleep for instance: no discredit is implied when Honest is found asleep under and oak ... Christiana is charmingly conscious of and even obliquely receptive to the suggestions of the Ill-favoured ones ... Mercy is described as 'alluring' ... Fertility and procreation are now signs of grace ... " (p. 239-40).

Bunyan's confidence in his community is reflected in a different attitude to language; it is once again "miraculous, poetic and potential" (p. 241). To illustrate the "power of language to embrace the corporeal and spiritual, Newman selects the image of Mercy's looking glass. Yet, he cautions against any belief that in Part Two there is "a return to the medieval condition of language and society" (p. 241). He does contend, however, that Bunyan renewed and incorporated "a sacramental image of society" out of the implicit contradiction inherent in a Protestant allegory. For Newman, " ... Protestantism is elective, anti-egalitarian and potentially hostile to the catholic, collective representation of man through allegory" (p. 242). That Bunyan should have renewed a sacramental image is "his greatest achievement, and one which might have led to a further evolution of the allegoric tradition," but in the Romantic age "allegory is displaced as an imaginative mode by symbolism" (pp. 242-43).

What strikes the reader as a complement, or perhaps a contradiction to Newman, is James F. Forrest's essay "Mercy with Her Mirror," PE, LII 1, 1963) in which he explicates the prominent episode of Mercy and her mirror. Forrest traces the symbolic meaning of the mirror from medieval times to Bunyan's day, and in a most remarkable way shows how Bunyan plays on almost all of these meanings in his own treatment of the mirror. To the medievalists the mirror signified both the Virgin Mary and veritas, truth. To the Puritan of Bunyan's time, it suggested God's word and human conscience. Mercy's language in the context of this episode recalls the Annunciation; the language is "startlingly evocative."

There is yet another layer of allegorical significance for Forrest and that is Part Two "communicates an artistic self-consciousness" that is more pronounced than in Part One.

What seems to emerge as trends in modern criticism on the second part of The Pilgrim's Progress is an emphasis on: 1) the unity of the second part with Part One, 2) the differences between Part One and Part Two, 3) the emphasis on kinds of communities of individuals in Part Two rather than on the nature of individuals (as in Part One), 4) the artistic merit of the second part, 5) significance of specific episodes in context, and 6) the power of language to embrace the "corporeal and spiritual."

No study on modern studies of Bunyan's Grace Abounding and The Pilgrim's Progress can completely ignore the influence of the author on subsequent writers. That the topic continues to be discussed is subject to no debate; but the exact nature of the influence continues to be a more complex question than a surface examination of selected works suggests. A few examples will suffice.

E.E. Stokes, J. (Bernard Shaw's Debt to John Bunyan," Shaw Review 8, 1965) rather convincingly shows that Bunyan's didactic motives appealed to

AN OVERVIEW

George Bernard Shaw to the extent that he became a major influence in Shaw's artistic and intellectual development. Shaw's use of moral allegory also manifests a debt to Bunyan.

Rachel Bennett ("Punch Versus Christian in The Old Curiosity Shop," RES 22, 1971) claims that Bunyan influenced Dickens in that two opposing tendencies in Dickens' novel incorporates two antithetical motifs--The Pilgrim's Progress and Punch--which establish the tone of the two parts. The "death-directed" world of Nell and her grandfather parallels Christian's pilgrimage, although the influence is primarily on place rather than on character. Punch, on the other hand, directs the tone of the other part Quilp and his associates. Dickens selects the two motifs in the hope of reconciling his love for life with his fear of death.

Another critic who sees Bunyan's influence on Dickens is Paul Delany ("Bleak House and Doubting Castle," Dickens Studies Newsletter 3, 1972). Through internal and external evidence he claims a clear thematic relationship between Krook's house and Doubting Castle, primarily because any who come to either place fall into despair. Dickens, however, regards despair not as sin but as a disease of civilization, and the tempter is the Lord Chancellor, not Satan.

Thomas Curley ("The Spiritual Journey Moralized in Rasselas," Anglia 91, 1973) claims that there is a clear Bunyan influence on Samuel Johnson. In studying Johnson's criteria for structuring an imitation work, and by working through parallels between The Pilgrim's Progress and Rasselas, Curley finds that the allegory provides not only a "thematic blue-print" but a structural design for Rasselas.

Typical of the critics' view on the influence of Bunyan on Hawthorne is that posited by C. Robert Roulston ("Hawthorne's Use of Bunyan's Symbols in The Celestial Railroad," Kentucky Philological Association Bulletin, 1975). The Celestial Railroad manifests Hawthorne's appropriation of Bunyan's symbols to castigate Unitarianism, Transcendentalism and early nineteenth-century philosophy.

For Samuel Pickering (E.E. Cummings' Pilgrim's Progress," Christianity and Literature 28, 1978) an extensive examination of parallels between Cummings' The Enormous Room and Bunyan's The Pilgrim's Progress gives strong evidence for Bunyan's influence on Cummings, especially because of the didactic purpose in both works.

If Bunyan influenced particular works, the response to Bunyan as a literary writer was slow. In an attempt to get a succinct picture of various attitudes toward Bunyan as well as his influence on writers, it is now wise to turn to Richard L. Greaves ("Bunyan Through the Centuries: Some Reflections," ES 64, 1983). This splendid essay provides a capstone for the study of trends in Bunyan scholarship and also traces the variety of responses to Bunyan since the publication of The Pilgrim's Progress, not only since 1960. Although the allegory received instant popularity, Bunyan was repudiated in 1681 by an Anglican author "as one who believed that saints were empowered to bind sovereigns and nobles as well as to degrade ministers and ecclesiastical officials" (p. 113). The decline of Bunyan's reputation from about 1740 to 1789 was not, in Greaves' judgment, "as pronounced as is often thought." A Catholic version appeared in 1772, going through several editions, and during these decades (1740-1780), prominent figures who referred to Bunyan include Laurence Sterne, Benjamin Franklin, James Boswell, and Horace Walpole.

"Romanticism, with its renewed interest in traditional religion, the evangelical revival, and the upper classes' 'rediscovery' of popular culture," says Greaves, "intensified an already strong interest in Bunyan" (p. 114). The nineteenth century also brought the scholarly attention of Southey and Macaulay in Bunyan. Their interest combined with the evangelical commitment to him "propelled Bunyan into the Victorian Age as a writer of genius whose great

AN OVERVIEW

allegory ranked second only to the Bible as a popular religious work" (p. 115). Writers as diverse as George Eliot, Robert Browning, John Ruskin, George Bernard Shaw, and Nathaniel Hawthorne were among those who paid tribute to Bunyan. Ruskin was horrified, however, by Bunyan's <u>Grace Abounding</u>, "which he could only explain," says Greaves, "as the product of a diseased mind" (p. 116). Psychological interest in Bunyan's autobiography began to mount in the Victorian Age and studies on possible sources of influence on <u>The Pilgrim's Progress</u> preoccupied several thinkers.

As the Victorian era waned, hostile critics began to attack Bunyan with renewed scorn. A Catholic critic in 1909, for example, "deplored Bunyan's rejection of traditional medieval theology," and held that "the allegory had become a mere literary curiosity ... " (p. 117). But, in 1922, a revival of interest in Britain in Bunyan "led to a demand ... that all English teachers be required to read and teach the allegory [<u>The Pilgrim's Progress</u>] accompanied by passages from <u>Grace Abounding</u>" (p. 118).

The Tercentenary brought an enormous number of "books, articles, and addresses, most of which extolled Bunyan" (p. 118). In the academic world, Bunyan has "fared well" in the last fifty years. <u>Grace Abounding</u> is now perceived as a work "which reflects not only the pattern of conversion expected of those in the Puritan tradition but a book noted for its candor, dramatic language, and artistic merit" (p. 121). Bunyan's great allegory continues to preoccupy the critical attention of scholars whose concerns cover a wide range of interests.

A survey of the trends in modern studies lends credence to Greaves' insights and underscores the final statement of his essay: "That Bunyan excelled in rising above his environment was surely due in large measure to his decision--itself the outcome of a conflict--to give scope to his talented imagination in the espousal of his cause: 'I dreamed, and behold ... '"(p. 121).

SELECTED EXAMPLES

OF CRITICAL STUDIES

GRACE ABOUNDING TO THE CHIEF OF SINNERS:

JOHN BUNYAN'S PAULINE EPISTLE

REBECCA S. BEAL

Interpretation of Grace Abounding to the Chief of Sinners has proceeded from the assumption that "autobiography" or Puritan autobiography" serves as a broad description of the genre by which the "whole" of structure and meaning constituting the work may be construed.[1] Resulting literary approaches to the work are exemplified in David Daiches's summary and benevolent dismissal of it: "He [Bunyan] cannot provide a narrative rich enough to satisfy the reader who does not accept Bunyan's creed of the total validity of its psychological exploration of human dilemmas and states. But if there is this limiting naivete in his work, there is the compensating virtue of colloquial liveliness and the brilliant handling of the concrete image."[2] If the work is indeed autobiography an analysis of its psychological revelations and "narrative texture" may be primary keys to interpretation of the text. But when some of the work's more salient features--its title, address, form--are re-examined, and when the book's contents and form are assessed in the context of Bunyan's social and theological milieu, it may be seen that Grace Abounding to the Chief of Sinners is more accurately defined as a seventeenth-century version of the Pauline epistle.[3]
In this paper I shall explore some of the ways in which such a genre explains component parts of the text, and return to the question of the relation between autobiography and epistle in order to examine the significance of a change in critical approach necessitated by an understanding of the work's intrinsic genre.[4]

AN OVERVIEW

Bunyan's title, according to an autobiographical interpretation, points to <u>Grace Abounding's</u> uniquely Puritan context "Even the title of Bunyan's autobiography strikes uninitiated modern ears as a bold original phrase. But not only do all Puritans long to compete for the distinction of being the most despicable of vermin, but also most of them will not be happy unless they are, literally, the chief of sinners."[5] However, although the phrase is not "original" with Bunyan, its origin can be traced to Paul's epistles, a more ancient source accessible to any literate Protestant, and of course familar to Bunyan himself.[6] The title reflects a major emphasis of Pauline epistles: salvation by grace alone. Paul's letters alone among New Testament writings place repeated emphasis on grace by various combinations of "abound" and "grace"--"Abundant grace," "God is able to make all grace abound" are two of many examples. Bunyan's title seems to derive most directly from Paul's first letter to Timothy: "And I thank Jesus Christ our Lord, who hath enabled me, in that he counted me faithful, putting me into the ministry, Who as a blasphemer, and a persecutor, and injurious ... And the grace of our Lord was exceedingly abundant.... This is a faithful saying, and worthy of all acceptation, that Christ Jesus came into the world to save sinners, of whom I am chief:(I Tim. 1.12-15)." In its allusions to Paul's letter to Timothy, Bunyan's title indicates the major themes at work in <u>Grace Abounding</u>: like Paul, Bunyan will defend his pastoral vocation from prison; like Paul, Bunyan emphasizes the working of the grace of God in his own life in order to teach and console a congregation from which prison has separated him.

Paul, in the same passage, explains the grace given him as intrinsic to his ministry: "Howbeit, for this cause I obtained mercy, that in me first Jesus Christ might shew forth all long-suffering, for a pattern to them which should hereafter believe" (I Tim. 1.16). Understanding the Pauline allusions in the title, aware of Bunyan's imprisonment, his reader would understand the title[7] as an explanation of Bunyan's own suffering.

SELECTED EXAMPLES OF CRITICAL STUDIES

Consciously Pauline, Bunyan's title bears theological, epistolary, rather than psychological, autobiographical, significance. The didactic meaning implicit in the phrase "chief of sinners" is clarified by another of Bunyan's discussions: "There are then, two sorts of greatnesses in sin--greatness by reason of number; greatness by thoroughness of conviction of the horrible nature of sin. In this last sense, he that has but one sin, if such an one could be found, may, in his own eyes, find himself the biggest sinner in the world" (Offor, 1.94). The sinner thinks himself "the biggest sinner" when confronted by the holiness of God as revealed to him by his conscience and by the law. Bunyan presents the same teaching in <u>Grace Abounding</u> in the form of autobiographical anecdote; his sins are "great" for he becomes persuaded of the enormity of sin itself, by his conscience (Section 33-36), by his growing awareness of a sinful nature (83-84), and by Scripture (141, 145). Consciousness of his sin engenders despair, but awareness of the meaning of grace, abounding grace, leads the sinner to an understanding of justification and of the redemptive work of Christ.

Interestingly, Bunyan makes it clear that his theology of law and grace, as well as his work's genre, depend on sources which are closely tied to the Pauline tradition but not directly associated with Puritan thought. He has learned his theology of law and grace from Luther, not from Calvin.[8] From Luther's <u>Comment on the Galatians</u> Bunyan learns the role of the law in the process of salvation, and consequently resolves the doubts that assail him: "Besides, he [Luther] doth most gravely also, in that book debate of the rise of these temptations, namely Blasphemy, Desperation, and the like, shewing that the law of Moses, as well as the Devil, Death, and Hell, hath a very great hand therein, that which at first was very strange to me, but considering and watching, I found it so indeed" (sec. 130). Bunyan presents Luther's teaching experientially rather than abstractly; there is, in Paul's writing, especially as the commentators of the seventeenth century understood it, a close connection between experience, autobiographical detail, and didactic matter.

Before discussing such a relation, however, it is expedient to notice that Grace Abounding is not the only prison epistle Bunyan wrote, but that it is his specifically Pauline epistle. Roger Sharrock includes with his Oxford edition of Grace Abounding a companion work, A Relation of the Imprisonment of Mr. John Bunyan. Of The Relation, "a series of ... practically verbatim reports of his examination before the justices," Sharrock writes: "These must have been written in prison immediately after the events, and probably in the form of pastoral letters to console and fortify the Bedford congregation. There are five short narratives, each ending with an epistolary formula like 'Farewell'" (p. xviii). Sharrock's analysis of A Relation is of great interest because it suggests an aspect of Bunyan's pastoral work during imprisonment not often noted--his ministry through letters. In Grace Abounding the general epistolary form becomes established firmly in the tradition of Paul.

The Preface alludes to its author's imprisonment and simultaneous pastoral concern for his congregation in a language echoing Paul's own "'Children, Grace be with you,' Amen, I being taken from you in presence, and so tied up, that I cannot perform that duty that from God doth lie upon me, to you-ward, for your further edifying and building up in Faith and Holiness, &c, yet that you may see my Soul hath fatherly care and desire after your spiritual and everlasting welfare; I now once again ... do look yet after you all'" (p.1). Following the formulaic Pauline opening, "Grace be with you," Bunyan's "taken from you in Presence" and "so tied up," make explicit the resemblance to a Pauline situation suggested in the title.[9] The following lines, "for your further edifying and building up of the Faith," describe the pastoral purpose underlying the work. The beginning of the second paragraph, "'I thank God upon every remembrance of you,'" points to Paul's own epistolary address in the Epistle to the Philippians: "Paul and Timotheus, the servants of Jesus Christ, to all the saints

SELECTED EXAMPLES OF CRITICAL STUDIES

in Christ Jesus which are at Philippi.... Grace be unto you and peace, from God our Father, and from the Lord Jesus Christ. I thank God upon every remembrance of you, Always in every prayer of mine for you all making request with joy" (Phil. 4.1-4). Bunyan's second paragraph concludes with a direct reference to Paul's epistle to the Thessalonian Church: "For you are my glory and joy, (I <u>Thes</u>. 2.10)" (p.1).

Even the sub-title of the work, in which Bunyan identifies himself as author, alludes to a source in Paul, for he writes: "Written by the Author thereof, and dedicated to those whom God hath counted him worthy to beget to Faith by his Ministry in the word." Again the reader discovers allusions to the specific context to which the title itself alludes--the epistle to Timothy. "I thank Christ Jesus ... who hath enabled me, in that he counted me faithful, putting me into the ministry" (1Tim. 1.12).

The structure of the work also points to Paul's epistles as these were outlined and described by prominent commentators of the time. Theodorus Beza, a contemporary and colleague of Calvin, presenting the dominant means of understanding the organization of the epistle in his marginal gloss to the Geneva Bible, divides the Pauline epistle into three parts: a Preface or Proema, which might include a salutation, the "Matter," or Main body of the epistle, and a Conclusion. The greeting, the conclusion, or both, would contain a typically Pauline emphasis on grace: "Grace be with you." Though simple, the outline did distinguish Paul's letters from those ascribed to other New Testament writers. Commentators such as Diodati and Sclater, who do not always follow Beza's exact delineation of the divisions of Paul's epistles agree with his description of Pauline epistolic structure--Preface, Matter, and Conclusion.[10]

<u>Grace Abounding's</u> structure follows that of Paul's epistles as understood by commentators of his time. The organization of his "Matter," which has baffled or frustrated many a critic, follows Paul's practice of didactic digression. Of Paul, Beza once noted, "He addeth now confrequently according to his manner."[11] Bunyan, too,

adds "confrequently." In addition to numerous hortatory or doctrinal sequences in the original manuscript, he expands his work throughout five editions, sometimes on the basis of contemporary events, as in sections 306-17, added in the fifth edition as a defense against slander.

Seventeenth-century English commentators concentrated principally on the thematic content of Paul's Matter, and found that this content more particularly identified the works as Pauline. In non-Pauline epistles Matter was analyzed according to the doctrine and practice taught. Paul's letters, in contrast, were thought unique, in that doctrine and practice are mediated through the use of autobiographical references. All New Testament epistles present doctrines and derive practical implications from the doctrines described; in Paul's epistles, however, illustrations from the Apostle's life were thought to provide an essential integrating and motivating factor. Biography becomes the element which motivates the reader to make use of the doctrines and practice taught.

John Jewel's <u>Commentary</u> indicates the emphasis placed on the biographical material in Paul: "In these his Epistles written to the Churches of God, he is to be seene in more excellent shewe, than when he was yet in body. For here is to be seene his harte filled with the Holy Ghost, and the care which he had for al Saintes: how he did trauaile in birthe of them againe, that Christ might be formed in them."[12] Bunyan also describes his own pastoral function in terms of parenting: "<u>Yet that you may see my Soul hath fatherly care and desire after your spiritual and everlasting welfare</u> ... The father to the children shall make known the truth of God" (pp. 1-2). But whereas Jewel describes Paul's vocation in the metaphor of the mother giving birth, Bunyan describes his own in terms of pastoral care, using the metaphor of the father.

Bunyan's "father" image relates more directly to Paul's description of his life as "pattern," and to Luther's <u>Comment</u>, which Bunyan himself describes as a major influence upon his thought. The Preface to the English translation of the <u>Comment</u> sees a direct connection between

SELECTED EXAMPLES OF CRITICAL STUDIES

Luther and Paul: "Here ... thou mayest see the spirite and veine of St. Paule more liuely represented to thee.... In which, as in a myrrour or glasse, or rather as S. Stephen in the heauens being opened, thou mayest see and behold the admirable glory of the Lord ... that either thy hearte must be heuier than lead or the reading thereof will lift thee aboue thy self and gide thee to know that of Jesus Christ."[13] Here is a different pattern of conversion than that outlined by modern critics treated in Puritan Autobiography. The vision of Christ is transmitted from one believer to another: Paul sees the risen Lord in the face of the dying Stephen, shortly before his own Damascus-road conversion; Luther sees (and shows) Christ through Paul's letters; Bunyan comes to understand the working of grace in his own life through the life of Luther, presented in his commentary on Paul: "I found my condition in his experience, so largely and profoundly handled, as if his Book had been written out of my heart; this makes me marvel.... But of Particulars here I intend nothing, only this methinks I must let fall before all men, I do prefer this book of Mr. <u>Luther</u> upon the <u>Galatians</u> (excepting the Holy Bible) before all the books that ever I have seen, as most fit for a wounded Conscience" (secs. 129-30). If Bunyan's epistle is largely autobiographical, that material must be interpreted in the light of his pastoral vocation, which he expresses through a genre taken from Paul.

Bunyan's Preface shows him consciously continuing to communicate the "pattern" he learns from Paul and Luther:

<u>Wherefore this I have endeavoured to do: and not onely so, but to publish it also; that, if God will, others may be put into remembrance of what he hath done for their Souls, by reading his work upon me.... Remember also the Word, the Word, I say upon which the Lord hath caused you to hope: If you have sinned against light, if you are tempted to blaspheme, if you are down in despair, if you think God fights against you, or if heaven is hid</u>

69

from your eyes; remember 'twas thus with your father, but out of them all the Lord delivered me. (pp.2,3)

Bunyan's life, like Stephen's, Paul's, and Luther's serves a pastoral function, facilitating the spiritual birth and growth of his congregation, or of any Christian involved in conflict between law and grace. Bunyan further points to the nature of his vocation by separating and emphasizing major factors of his ministry which Paul also singles out. Sections 265-317 of the Matter of Grace Abounding are labelled "A brief Account of the Author's call to the Work of the Ministry," sections 318-39, "A brief Account of the Author's Imprisonment." Affirming the legitimacy of his vocation in the face of episcopal disapproval, Bunyan follows precedent set by Paul, who continually defended the divine nature of his apostolic calling: Bunyan's imprisonment, like Paul's, is a direct consequence of obedience to his vocation. Because of the three-fold use of biographical material--edification of the church, defense of the calling, explanation of imprisonment--the "autobiography" moves in two directions, both Pauline. Bunyan establishes the pastoral "pattern" from which his people can draw instruction for the conduct of their spiritual lives, and also, by identification with the Apostle Paul in his life and ministry, Bunyan constructs an apology for his own faith and calling.

An interpretation of Grace Abounding as a Reformation Pauline epistle necessitates a reinterpretation of Bunyan's reference to Puritan devotional material, "awakening books," in Grace Abounding. Traditionally, his early reference to two works of Puritan devotional literature has been used to signal his reliance on the autobiographical literature of his own time: "His wife's dowry brings to Bunyan the awakening books, Arthur Dent's The Plain Man's Path-way to Heaven and Lewis Bayly's The Practice of Piety; the former taught him that even a manual of instruction could employ racy colloquialisms and salt its precepts with homely proverbs" (Sharrock, p. xvii). Sharrock emphasizes the importance of

SELECTED EXAMPLES OF CRITICAL STUDIES

the awakening books as sources for Grace Abounding when he outlines it according to the four-part pattern of traditional Puritan autobiography--"Before conversion," "Conversion," "Calling," and Ministry (p. xx). Since the reference to Dent's and Bayly's books is mentioned in the first section of the work, where they seem to help bring Bunyan toward the experience of conversion, and since Bunyan does employ "racy colloquialisms" and "homely proverbs," a style which could derive from the devotional books, the analysis may seem justified.

A closer examination of Bunyan's use of the books indicates a different reason for their inclusion, however. In the development of the theological conflict between law and grace in Bunyan's life, the books do nothing more than confirm the unawakened individual in his attempts to achieve self-justification under the law: "Wherefore these books, with this relation, though they did not reach my heart to awaken it about my sad and sinful state, yet they did beget within me some desires to Religion; so that, because I knew no better, I fell in very eagerly with the Religion of the times, to wit, to go to Church twice a day, and that too with the foremost, and there should very devoutly both say and sing as others did; yet retaining my wicked life" (sec. 16). The books are spiritually soporific! Although they do indeed bring Bunyan to "religion," it is "the Religion of the times." They are incapable of inculcating an awareness of his true need for grace, or even of his true spiritual state. The "desire to Religion," so prevalent in Puritan society, for him indicates a trend toward self-justification, and points to the natural bent of man to justify himself apart from the justifying work of Christ. So Bunyan continues: "But all this while, I was not sensible of the danger and evil of sin; I kept from considering that sin would damn me, what Religion soever I followed, unless I was found in Christ: nay, I never thought of him" (sec. 19). Neither piece of "devotional literature" Bunyan mentions is a likely model for the genre of Grace Abounding; neither can accomplish his own purpose, the revelation of "abounding grace."[14]

AN OVERVIEW

In contrast to his rejection of "devotional literature" is Bunyan's continuing, dynamic interaction with Paul's epistles. During his pre-conversion dependence on "works" his inability to read Paul illustrates for Bunyan his spiritual state: "I betook me to my Bible, and began to take great pleasure in reading, but especially with the historical part thereof: for, as for Paul's Epistles, and Scriptures of that nature, I could not away with them, being as yet by ignorant either of the corruptions of my nature, or of the want and worth of Jesus Christ to save me" (sec. 29). Instead of Paul and grace, he depends at this time on Moses, and the law:

> Wherefore I fell to some outward Reformation, both in my words and life, and did set the Commandments before me for my way to Heaven: Which Commandments I also did strive to keep ... all this while, when I thought I kept this or that Commandment, or did by word or deed any thing that I thought were good, I had great peace in my Conscience, and should think with my self, God cannot chuse but be now pleased with me, yea, to relate it in mine own way, I thought no man in England could please God better than I. (secs. 30, 35)

But when he falls under conviction, his change is illustrated by his new regard for Paul's epistles: "And now, me thought, I began to look into the Bible with new eyes, and read as I never did before; and especially the Epistles of the Apostle S. Paul were sweet and pleasant to me" (sec. 46). Turning from Moses to Paul, he literally converts from a reliance on law to a dependence on grace.

After conversion, when Bunyan experiences what he later calls "the worst temptation," that is "to question the being of God, and the truth of his Gospel" (Concl., sec.1), he again turns to Paul, Apostle of Grace:

> Everyone doth think his own Religion rightest ... how if all our Faith, and Christ, and Scriptures, should be but a

SELECTED EXAMPLES OF CRITICAL STUDIES

> think-so too? Sometimes I have endeavoured to argue against these suggestions, and to set some of the Sentences of blessed <u>Paul</u> against them; but, alas! I quickly <u>felt</u> when I thus did, such arguings as these would return upon me: Though we made so great a matter of <u>Paul</u>, and of his words, yet how could I tell but that in very deed, he, being a subtle and cunning man, might give himself up to deceive with strong delusions? (secs. 97-98)

Questioning Paul, he questions the sufficiency of grace and of Christ. Paul's writings cannot corroborate his own spiritual experience, for Paul himself may be in error, or worse, consciously deluding his audience.

Accounts provided by his contemporaries are as unreliable as Paul: "I did greatly long to see some ancient Godly man's experience, who had writ some hundred years before I was born; for, for those who had writ in our days, I thought (but I desire them now to pardon me) that they had Writ only that which others felt, or else had, thorow the strengths of their Wits and Parts, studied to answer such Objections as they perceived others were perplexed with, without going down themselves into the deep" (sec. 129). Paul is suspect because his writing cannot be confirmed; Bunyan's contemporaries, on the other hand, may be addressing an exclusively cultural phenomenon in their treatments of grace. It is Luther's <u>Comment</u>, a source temporally and culturally distant from Bunyan's, which provides him with the validation he needs. For Luther's experience presented, in the <u>Comment</u> validates Bunyan's, and finally Paul's. Luther's description of the place of law and grace in the life of the Christian is such that Bunyan writes, "I found my condition ... as if his Book had been written out of my heart" (sec. 129).

Paul's epistles directly or through the medium of Luther's <u>Comment</u>, take priority in Bunyan's emphasis on the importance of Scripture in the life of the Christian. They help the convicted soul, serve as a focal point of tempta-

73

tion, and, most importantly, bring him from issues associated with Christianity to a vision of Christ:

> For by this Scripture [I Cor. 1.30] I saw that the Man Christ Jesus, as he is distinct from us, as touching his bodily presence, so he is our Righteousness and Sanctification before God: here therefore I lived, for some time, very sweetly at peace with God thorow Christ; O methought Christ! Christ! there was nothing but Christ that was before my eyes: I was not onely for looking upon this and the other benefit of Christ apart, as of his Blood, Burial, or Resurrection, but considered him as a whole Christ! As he in whom all these, and all his other Vertues, Relations, Offices, and Operations met together, and that as he sat on the right hand of God in Heaven. (sec. 231)

In this passage, the ontological center and epistemological goal of the epistle, Bunyan brings the reader to the knowledge which Luther's English translator claimed for him: "the reading thereof will lift thee above thy self and gide thee to know that of Jesus Christ." Here too is the focus of Paul's epistle: "Yea doubtless, and I count all things but loss for the excellency of the knowledge of Christ Jesus my Lord: for whom I have suffered the loss of all things and do count them but dung that I may win Christ, And be found in him, not having my own righteousness, which is of the law, but that which is through the faith of Christ, but that which is through the faith of Christ, the righteousness which is of God by faith" (Phil, 3.8-9).

Unlike the devotional books, mentioned once at the beginning of this spiritual "progress," the Pauline letter proves necessary in each stage of Bunyan's spiritual life; the use of the epistles reflects his growing awareness of his need for grace, Luther's commentary on one Pauline epistle plays a crucial role in Bunyan's understanding of the doctrine of law and grace, and Paul's writing brings Bunyan to Christ. Within

SELECTED EXAMPLES OF CRITICAL STUDIES

Grace Abounding, as in its structure, the epistle takes priority to the devotional work or "spiritual autobiography."

An interpretation of Grace Abounding as Pauline epistle explains two particular components of it which have generally been taken to illustrate the restricted quality of the "autobiography." The first is Bunyan's ostensible claim to "originality": "I never endeavoured to, nor durst make use of other men's lines, Rom. 15.18," he writes (sec. 292). But Bunyan's inclusion of scriptural reference points his scripturally literate reader to his imitation of Paul: "For I will not dare to speak of any of those things which Christ hath not wrought by me" (Rom. 15.18), writes Paul, defending his writing. Like Paul, Bunyan writes out of his own life, but his inclusion of scriptural references shows that he is identifying with Paul in purpose and method. He reemphasizes the parallel: "Yet my experience hath more interest in that text of Scripture Gal. 1.11,12 than many amongst men are aware" (sec. 292). Writes Paul: "But I certify you, brethren, that the gospel which was preached of me is not after man. For I neither received it of man, neither was I taught it, but by the revelation of Jesus Christ" (Gal. 1.11-12). In both passages the author emphasizes the nature of his message, its divine origin, and his own intent. Like Paul, Bunyan presents a doctrine not man-made, not bound to his era, but a doctrine concerning the divine revelation of God's grace, manifested in Christ, mediated by Scripture, proven in the author's own life.

Another Pauline technique is illustrated in his depiction of "a kind of Vision:"

> I saw as if they were set on the Sunny side of some high mountain, there refreshing themselves with the present beams of sun, while I was shivering and shrinking in the cold, afflicted with frost, snow, and dark clouds; methought also betwixt me and them I saw a wall that did compass about the Mountain; now, thorow this wall my soul did greatly desire to pass, concluding that if I

> could, I would goe even into the very midst of them. and there comfort myself with the heat of their Sun.
>
> (sec. 53)

Bunyan tries, in his vision, to enter the "narrow gap" in the wall, to join the company on the mountain. His description is allegorical: the mountain is the Church, the wall the Word of God, and the gap, Jesus Christ, writes Bunyan. Analyzing this dream as autobiography, Roger Sharrock tries to uncover the psychological significance. He sees the vision as an auditory hallucination, and catalogues Bunyan's forcing himself through the wall with an "obsession with violent physical activity, especially pushing or pulling" (p. 138). The gap, which the text relates to the New Testament image of the "strait gate" Sharrock also see a "widely diffused symbol of initiation into the religious life." Finally noting the "vagueness of the topography," he writes: "as a dweller in a flat, featureless countryside Bunyan had no knowledge of any more varied landscape" (p. 138).

By contrast, the essentially theological nature of the passage becomes apparent in the context of the genre of Paul's epistle. The Epistle to the Galatians, for example, contains an allegory similar to Bunyan's: "Which things are an allegory: for these are the two covenants; the one from the mount Sinai, which gendereth to bondage, which is Agar. For this Agar is mount Sinai, in Arabia, and answereth to Jerusalem which now is, and is in bondage with her children. But Jerusalem which is above is free, which is the mother of us all" (Gal. 4.24-26). Paul depicts the difference between the covenant of law—given to Moses on Mount Sinai, practiced by the Jews in the Temple at Jerusalem—and the covenant of grace—dispensed from the spiritual Jerusalem which is of Heaven. He is, through the allegory, explaining the difference between the two and urging the Galatian church not to follow the teachings of "Judaisers" who would have it return to ritual practices associated with keeping the law of Moses, "the old covenant": the church should remain firmly free of any system

SELECTED EXAMPLES OF CRITICAL STUDIES

which would offer justification by works rather than through Christ.[15] Paul's description of Judaising Galatians applies to Bunyan at the time of the vision. He has given up bell-ringing, "Cat," and dancing to please God: "[I] did see the Commandment before me for my way to Heaven" (sec. 30). His vision follows conviction of sin, when he is "mistrusting" his "condition to be naught" (sec. 39).

In the vision Bunyan looks to the "high Mountain" where alone he can experience the mercy of God, "the Sun that shone thereone, the comfortable shining of his merciful face on them that were within" (sec. 55). The contrast between the state of the people on the mountain and Bunyan, who is "shivering and shrinking in the cold," illustrates the difference between the condition of the man trying to justify himself and that of believers relying on the grace of God for justification. Bunyan's vision, of a thoroughly Pauline nature, serves the purpose of illustrating his own spiritual state at the time of the conviction, and further underlines the absolute and exclusive role of grace in conversion.

In an interpretation of this vision according to the epistolary genre, the author's psychological state had little weight. Whether or not he could describe the mountains in other than an ambiguous way is also beside the point. A knowledge of the Pauline epistle, its emphasis on the doctrine of law and grace, its use of allegory to convey such a doctrine--these are the considerations which form the basis of interpretation.

Other passages in Grace Abounding criticized as unbecoming in autobiography are important to the work as epistle.[16] Heavy doses of didacticism reflect the typical matter of Paul's writing, so of Bunyan's; his attack upon the Ranters who exploit the doctrine of grace (secs. 43-45), the passages against the Quakers who reject the authority of Scripture (secs. 123-24), both have precedent in Paul, as does the ecstatic vision which Bunyan refuses to describe (as does Paul).[17] Bunyan's epistle is, as he writes in his Preface, "a relation of grace," rather than a simple reflection of his spiritual progress; the importance of his source is evident from title to ending.

In the Conclusion, which derives precepts from the work's biographical detail, Bunyan refers to his major themes once again. Pastoral aims are brought together with his own experience of abounding grace: "[The temptations] provoke me to look up to God thorow Christ to help me, and carry me thorow this world, '<u>Amen</u>.' FINIS: (Conclusion, sec. 7). His work finished, Bunyan draws his reader to look with him beyond the doctrine of grace to Christ, the source of grace, or, as Paul would have it, "the author and finisher of our faith."

Bunyan attempts, in <u>Grace Abounding</u>, to bring his reader to a clear vision of Christ; autobiographical criticism has striven mightily to analyze "the chief of sinners." This paper has tried to clarify Bunyan's aims as well as the specific form he used to accomplish them in <u>Grace Abounding to the Chief of Sinners</u>, and so avoid Bunyan's own appraisal of future critics of the work: The Philistines understand me not" (p. 7).

SELECTED EXAMPLES OF CRITICAL STUDIES

NOTES

[1] Grace Abounding has generally been rated according to expectation of a psychological (or, more often, pseudo-psychological) nature, in accordance with a common understanding of the work as emergent autobiography. So Edmund Baldwin, in his preface to the 1910 edition of Grace Abounding (Boston: Ginn and Co.), praises Bunyan's "plain and simple" style because it reflects Bunyan's own personality: "Bunyan himself was a plain man, describing for plain people a simple, though profound religious experience" (p. viii). For a comprehensive survey of pertinent critical treatment of the work during this century see Melvin Watson, "The Drama of Grace Abounding," English Studies 46 (December 1969):471-82. Watson, who tries to counteract some of the more vitriolic criticism by examining Bunyan's use of time is in turn dismissed by Barrett J. Mandel: "What should be mentioned, however, is that Bunyan's treatment of time and space is the one aspect of Grace Abounding which tends to separate it from the other spiritual autobiographies to some degree. But it is worth emphasizing that Bunyan's handling of setting is hardly sufficient to give his work uniqueness as a whole" ("Bunyan and the Autobiographer's Artistic Purpose," Criticism 10 (Summer 1968):225-43. When Bunyan's purpose in writing is assumed to be autobiographical, and when digressive modes in it are analyzed psychologically, the work is found wanting.

[2] David Daiches, A Critical History of English Literature in Two Volumes, (New York: The Ronald Press Co., 1960), 2:587.

[3] John Bunyan, Grace Abounding to the Chief of Sinners, ed. Roger Sharrock (Oxford: The Clarendon Press, 1962). This edition is used throughout. Other references to Bunyan's works are taken from The Works of John Bunyan, ed. George

Offor (Edinburgh, 1853). The following works are mentioned in abbreviated form:
The Doctrine of Law and Grace Unfolded: Law and Grace
The Jerusalem Sinner Saved, or Good News for the Vilest of Men: Jerusalem Sinner.
The title of the work is followed by volume and page reference to Offor.

[4] The concept of "intrinsic genre" I derive from E.D. Hirsch's study Validity in Interpretation (1967; rpt. New Haven: Yale Univ. Press, 1976). To quote Hirsch, intrinsic genre is that "sense of the whole by which an interpreter can correctly understand any part in its determinacy" (p. 86). In contrast, the "extrinsic genre signifies an incorrect determination of the whole, would be used to codetermine meanings, some of which would be necessarily incorrect" (p. 88). When applied to Grace Abounding autobiography becomes "extrinsic," inadequate to explain the meaning of the work in its entirety.

[5] Mandel, p. 237. He cites five examples to support his generalization about "all Puritans": one refers to a Methodist, Rebekah Benner, another to a Quaker, John Crook.

[6] Bunyan alludes to the same passage in Paul from which he takes the title of Grace Abounding in Law and Grace:

Object:"O but I am one of the chief of sinners--."
Reply: "Why, mercy if for the chief of sinners--'Christ Jesus came into the world to save sinners of whom I am chief,' saith Paul. 1 Ti. 1.15"
(Offor, 1:565).

[7] Members of Bunyan's congregation could draw an analogy between this passage, and a similar one in Jerusalem Sinner, in which Bunyan relates the "pattern" theme of 1 Timothy 1.16 to the preceding verses and Paul's discussion of grace: "How plain are the words, 'Christ, in saving of me, has given to the world a pattern of his grace'" (Offor, 1:77).

SELECTED EXAMPLES OF CRITICAL STUDIES

[8] R.L. Greaves, "John Bunyan and Covenant Thought in the Seventeenth Century," Church History 36 (June 1967): 151-69. Concentrating Bunyan's theological emphasis, Greaves indicates that Bunyan takes a via media between moderate Calvinists and Antinomians, and that Bunyan's strong interest in the role of law and grace in salvation shows Luther's influence.

[9] The Geneva Bible includes in the introductory Argument preceding each epistle information concerning the circumstances of Paul's writing; Bunyan makes the analogy explicit.

[10] I have determined the Reformation understanding of epistolary structure by comparing Beza's notes in the epistles of the 1597 edition of the Geneva Bible. With Beza I have compared the work of Giovanni Diodati, The Pious and learned annotations upon the Holy Bible. Plainly expounding the most difficult places thereof. 3d. edn. (London: J. Flesher for N. Fussell, 1651); William Sclater, An exposition with notes upon the First and Second epistles to the Thessalonians (London: R. Thrale 1630); and the anonymous Annotations upon all the books of the Old and New Testament (London: J. Legatt and J. Raworth, 1645), which follows Beza closely in its structural analysis of the epistles. Diodati presents outlines of each epistle before his annotation; Sclater does not, and his view of the structure of the epistle must be derived from an analysis of his notes throughout. English divines might quibble over the theological or political interpretations the Genevans made of individual texts, but they gave wide, if tacit, acceptance to Beza's analysis of epistolary structure.

[11] Beza, Geneva Bible, Note on 2 Thess. 3.16.

[12] John Jewel, An exposition upon the two Epistles of the Apostle Sainct Paule to the Thessalonians (London: R. Newberie and H. Bynneman, 1583), pp. 4-5. George Herbert is alluding to this tradition in "The Windows" (1633) when he answers his own question, "how can man preach thy eternal word?":

Doctrine and life colors and light, in one
When they combine and mingle, bring
A strong regard and awe, but speech alone
Doth vanish like a flaring thing,
And in the ear, not conscience, ring.

[13] Martin Luther, <u>A Commentarie of M. Doctor Martin Luther upon the Epistle of St. Paule to the Galathians</u> (London: by T. Vautrouiller, 1575), sig.iy.

[14] The awakening books could serve as stylistic models despite their content. But Paul's epistles, too, are filled with 'homely colloquialisms' and proverbs. In fact, Pauline style was a matter of some concern to commentators such as Sclater, who wonders why the Holy Spirit, who certainly, "is not unacquainted with parts of Rhetoricks," would allow Paul those imperfect endings and transitions reproached by Origen (Sclater, p. 386). Willet excuses Paul on the grounds that his style reflects the earnestness with which the Apostle wrote. The letters contain no "affected eloquence" or "enticing speech." Paul's colloquial style, "pithy and sententious," is perfectly adapted to his matter (Andrew Willet: <u>Hexapla: that is, a six-fold commentarie upon the most divine Epistle of the holy Apostle Paul to the Romanes</u> (London: for L. Greene, 1611), pp. 8-9). Compare with Bunyan's note: "'<u>I could also have stepped into a stile much higher than this in which I have here discoursed, and could have adorned all things more then here I have seemed to do.... I may not play in my relating of them, but be plain and simple</u>'" (Preface, pp. 3-4).

[15] Bunyan's allegory also echoes a passage in the Epistle to the Hebrews a book for which some commentators argued Pauline authorship:

For ye are not come unto the mount that might be touched, and that burned with fires, nor unto blackness, and darkness.... But ye are come into mount Sion, and unto the city of the living God, the heavenly Jerusalem, and to an innumerable company of angels. To the general

assembly and church of the first-born ... and to God the judge of all, and to the spirits of just men made perfect. And to Jesus the mediator of the new covenant.
(Heb. 12.18,22-24)

The contrast between law and grace is central to this passage as it is to Paul's in Galatians, or to Bunyan's.

[16] See Gal. 3. ff. Mandel, analyzing Bunyan's narrative as case history, describes "Bunyan's sense of choice, as controlled by his spiritual fantasy world" in connection with an "absolution in the interpretation of Biblical passages" (p. 239). He does not see Bunyan's pastoral aims and misses much of the epistle.

[17] Paul records his refutation of the Apostle Peter, whom he sees leading the Gentiles into a doctrine of salvation based on works (Gal 2.11-16), and reemphasizes the importance of grace: "if righteousness come by the Law, then Christ is dead in vain" (Gal. 2.21). For Paul's "raptus" see 2 Cor. 12.

SELECTED EXAMPLES

OF CRITICAL STUDIES

BUNYAN'S PILGRIM'S PROGRESS:

THE DOCTRINE OF PREDESTINATION AND THE

SHAPING OF THE NOVEL

WOLFGANG ISER

I

John Bunyan's religious and sociological importance has long been a subject of great interest to literary critics. Herbert Schöffler,[1] for instance, used the findings of Ernst Troeltsch[2] and Max Weber[3] to show the links between sociology and literature that were apparent in the works of Bunyan and in other writings of the dissent. In his study of the social origins of writers during the early period of the Enlightenment, Schöffler also pinpointed the conditions that gave rise to the particular form of literature produced at that time. The most interesting feature of his study deals with the lower-class, Puritan originators of a new literary genre: the novel. As Schöffler's main concern was with the sociological problem of how fiction actually came into being in a Calvinist environment that was on principle hostile to literature as devil's work, he gave little or no consideration to the special form of this new genre and to the processes that shaped it. It is enough for Schöffler to maintain: "It is clear that Pilgrim's Progress takes its place in the great line of historical, narrative edifying literature," which, "however, is clearly continued in the allegorical and fictitious."[4] He uses a similar argument to explain the origins of Defoe's Robinson Crusoe: this, the first novel of the dissent, grew out of Defoe's

AN OVERVIEW

moral writings--especially the Family Instructor, which "lies directly before the beginning of Defoe's assiduous work in the field of the novel, and clearly shows the way in which forms of the novel developed out of the moral vade mecum."[5] According to Schöffler, the difference between Bunyan and Defoe lies simply in the progressive weakening of the old Calvinist orthodoxy. Puritan conduct-books led ultimately to exemplary fiction, and Defoe's literary fiction arose from moral and religious exemplarity. And so for Schöffler the link between truth and fiction is a genetic problem that can be solved in terms of secularization. "It was a significant though coincidental development that Robinson was published during the very same weeks as the inner collapse of the Old Calvinist dissent became finally obvious; and it was equally significant for the development of the mind that the first novel by a religious, lower-class citizen was written at the same time when the Enlightenment was relaxing all religious rigorism and exerting its most powerful effect on the English middle classes."[6]

Important though Schöffler's findings may be for our understanding of the sociological development of the novel, they completely ignore one very fundamental question: What exactly is a novel? Schöffler sees it as a secularized book of devotion, and for him secularization is identical with the Enlightenment. This, however, is no definition, if only for the fact that books of devotion--principally conduct-books--already contained features which, if they were not exactly fictional, were at least stylized and arose from the desire to convey the Calvinist doctrine of predestined salvation, together with the anguish of the individual soul, in such a way that the reader could actually be edified. And so it might be said that fiction descended from the idea of predestination rather than from secularization, for as "concord-fiction"[7] it had to counterbalance the fears that predestination aroused in the Puritan sects. Schöffler says that Bunyan represented "a starting-point for everything that was created by the dissent and Puritanism of the 18th century,"[8] but he does not

SELECTED EXAMPLES OF CRITICAL STUDIES

explain in what way this was so. The question of Bunyan's status is given an equally limited answer by Tillyard in his comprehensive work on the English epic.[9] Tillyard takes no account of Schöffler's arguments, and his book in fact tends to head in a completely different direction. While Schöffler considers Pilgrim's Progress to be an anticipation of eighteenth-century developments, Tillyard reverses it back into the tradition of the epic and identifies Bunyan as a Puritan epic writer. Tillyard and Schöffler in fact mark two extreme positions as regards an evaluation of Pilgrim's Progress. Schöffler sees Bunyan as a precursor of the novel, because the first novelists of the eighteenth century also sprang from the dissent; Tillyard sees him as a Puritan epic writer, because his work is concerned principally with presenting the "numinous."[10] The following analysis of Pilgrim's Progress uses these two extremes as its starting point; we shall try to gauge the part played by each and to elucidate the situation that gave rise to this landmark in literary history.

II

Ever since Coleridge, critics have been fully aware of the strange interrelation of epic and novel that constitutes the basic structure of Pilgrim's Progress. Mere allegory is surpassed through the sheer aliveness of the character, and it is this that gives the work its appeal. Talon, in his thorough and basic study of Bunyan, says: " ... ils [i.e. the characters] ont trop de chair et de sang pour être allégoriques, mais ils donnent à l'oeuvre cette vie et cette clarté qu'on y loue traditionnellement."[11] This fact alone speaks against the solely epic view of the work: the epic deliberately set out to idealize the past, and to do so it had to establish a certain distance[12] between itself and its reader's present. Distance was an integral feature. But the more alive characters are the smaller is this distance, and if characters seem genuinely to be made of flesh and blood, then their presence is immediate and not remote. And immediacy is a basic feature of the novel, not of the epic. The apology with which Bunyan introduces his book sums up the subject matter as follows:

> This Book it chalketh out before thine eyes
> The man that seeks the everlasting Prize;
> It shews you whence he comes, whither he goes,
> What he leaves undone, also what he does;
> It also shews you how he runs and runs,
> Till he unto the Gate of Glory comes.[13]

Man's quest for salvation forms the all-embracing background for the events, which are to find their culmination only in the future. Here again the work differs from the epic in that the latter presented ideal, normative conduct as something that took place in a remote past and therefore represented a goal already attained. The only epic element in this subject matter is the paradigmatic search for salvation, which loomed large in all human activities.[14] Tillyard himself drew attention to the fact that Pilgrim's Progress diverges from the medieval pattern of the pilgrimage, as shown in Deguileville's work (translated by Lydgate) Le Pélerinage de la Vie Humaine: " ... for Deguileville the pilgrimage is only partly the affair of the lonely soul, being largely the passage through the prescribed stages of an education in holiness by means of concrete religious acts."[15] And so the first 10,000 verses contain instructions for the pilgrim before he starts off on his journey.[16] Set against Deguileville's medieval allegory, Bunyan's work strikingly accentuates the importance of the individual soul, giving it precedence over means of grace, the institution, and the hierarchy. This obvious change of emphasis was conditioned by the Calvinist doctrine of predestination.[17]

This doctrine makes the goal of the pilgrimage--the attainment of the certitudo salutis--into something objectively unattainable. It excludes any active participation in the acquisition of grace. And so for Bunyan there could be no gradual education to holiness, such as there was for Deguileville, for man was either chosen or damned. If he wanted to go forth and search

SELECTED EXAMPLES OF CRITICAL STUDIES

for salvation, he would have to behave differently from the pilgrim who, by fulfilling certain set tasks, could rest assured of finding grace. While the goal for the medieval pilgrim was a gradual "education in holiness," that of the Puritan pilgrim was the urgent question of finding out whether he had been allotted to the sheep or the goats. And so instead of beginning with a list of detailed instructions, Bunyan's allegory starts off with the picture of a pilgrim in anguish and despair through the awareness of his own sinfulness.

As the Puritan believed that he was already saved or damned, his only escape from total passivity was to hunt for signs of his hoped-for salvation. And so the absence of any <u>certitudo salutis</u> led him to pay closer attention both to himself and to the world around him. The more signs he found the greater seemed his chances of salvation,[18] but even then his certainty had inevitably to remain subjective, which meant that doubt must persist right through to the end of his life--as is the case with Christian in <u>Pilgrim's Progress</u>.[19] He could only continue to look for more and more signs in his own soul and in empirical reality, thus paradoxically bringing about a revaluation of what the Calvinist doctrine has dismissed as worthless and irredeemable.[20] This search was of considerable significance for literature. "Interposed between dogmatic predestination and human inadequacy there is a mediating level of literary fiction, which promises security, orientation, and a cure for religious despair. The withholding of grace and the absolute transcendency of God give rise to the demand for a fictive, more humane cosmos of epic events."[21]

Any literary representation of the exemplary road to salvation therefore has to lay particular emphasis on the human side of the characters involved, and this means a departure from the symbolic presentation of the epic. If a gradual <u>certitudo salutis</u> can only be gauged by what happens in man's inner being, the stock figures of epic and allegory will no longer suffice, for as Lukács has pointed out, the epic character has no inner being: "for there is no exterior, no otherness for the soul. Whilst this goes off on its adventures and comes through them all unscathed, it remains unacquainted with the real torment of the search and the real danger of the find: such a soul never puts itself at risk; it is not yet aware that it can lose itself, and never thinks of having to search for itself."[22] And so the moment the soul develops an awareness of the torment of the search and the possibility of losing itself, the universality of the epic is destroyed. Once characters begin to fear for their own salvation, their humanity becomes a subject for scrutiny, and thus runs counter to any representative function, because instead of embodying salvation they adopt an attitude toward it. Thus the characters develop a striking polarity: on the one hand, they remain drawn to the goal that dominates their whole existence--salvation; on the other, their humanity, their inner world, is bound to be accentuated in order to bring out their subjective mitigation of the theocratic Calvinist doctrine. So long as the goal of salvation is binding events together, the perspective is that of the epic, for the rigid framework permits only one center of orientation; but once the characters become preoccupied with their subjective inner world, they cease to act as mouthpieces for a specific dogma and leave the realm of the epic. It is precisely those "normal human feelings,"[23] which Tillyard appears to regard as one of Bunyan's epic features, that bring <u>Pilgrim's Progress</u> out of the epic plane and onto the level of the novel.

The polarity which we have been discussing is already indicated in the prologue. Here Bunyan actually appeals to those human feelings his book is to be concerned with. After first dealing with the paradigmatic nature of all the events that are to take place along the road to salvation, the apology continues:

This Book will make a Traveller of thee,
If by its Counsel thou wilt ruled be;
It will direct thee to the Holy Land,
If thou wilt its directions understand: ....
This Book is writ in such a Dialect
As may the minds of listless men affect:

SELECTED EXAMPLES OF CRITICAL STUDIES

> It seems a novelty, and yet contains
> Nothing but sound and honest Gospel strains.
> Would'st thou divert thyself from Melancholy?
> Would'st thou be pleasant, yet be far from folly?
> Would'st thou read Riddles, and their Explanation?
> Or else be drowned in thy Contemplation?
> Dost though love picking meat? Or would'st thou see
> A man i'th'Clouds, and hear him speak to thee?
> Would'st thou be in a Dream, and yet not sleep?
> Or would'st thou in a moment laugh and weep?
> Wouldest thou lose thyself, and catch no harm,
> And find thyself again without a charm?
> Would'st read thyself, and read thou know'st not what,
> And yet know whether thou art blest or not,
> By reading the same lines? O then come hither
> Any lay my Book, thy Head and Heart together.[24]

The book is meant to appeal to each individual reader, whatever his disposition, and its aim is to lead the believer to recognize himself. Thus the idea of salvation is treated predominantly as a means of illuminating human reality and not as an end in itself. And so the gradual acquisition of <u>certitudo salutis</u> puts a subjective slant on <u>the objective events</u>. It is in fact the ultimate uncertainty of salvation that leads to closer and closer inspection of the self, for it is only through his own transformation that the believer can detect the signs he is looking for. As the idea of salvation is intangible, he can only observe its reflections and refractions in the spectrum of human conduct. The literary presentation of such observation is therefore bound to lay emphasis on the human side of the story, which continually undermines the epic or allegorical side. In <u>Pilgrim's Progress</u>, the various levels of presentation all reveal the workings of this process.[25]

III

One very striking element of <u>Pilgrim's Progress</u> is the varied narrative technique. The book is set as a dream vision, but for long sections this fact is virtually expunged by the force and immediacy of the dialogue. This shift in balance opens up two different perspectives of the events presented.

The dream vision is an old strategem of the allegory, but it is doubtful whether Bunyan deliberately wanted to fit in with the rhetorical tradition. In the Apology he emphasizes that the Bible alone can justify his "literary" venture,[26] and so if he does make use of rhetorical techniques, it is in order to serve his own particular ends and not to cultivate a literary tradition. The dream device enables him to create a vision of the exemplary road to salvation, but in Pilgrim's Progress this is not the traditional vision, allowing access to the world beyond; instead it gives us access to total knowledge of this world only. The narrator is able to see the whole of the road--unlike the pilgrim, who can see only what lies immediately before him. However, the pilgrim's view is presented just as directly as the narrator's, so that we see all events from two quite different perspectives. When the narrator is giving his account, the action is linear; events and characters are relevant only insofar as they bring out the exemplariness of the road to salvation; in their confrontation with the different vices--in Vanity Fair especially--Christian and Faithful simply embody virtues, and their characters are totally absorbed by their allegorical function. But these allegorical actions reported by the narrator are frequently interrupted and sometimes even obliterated by the dialogue of the characters, and then the all-seeing narrator gives way to the human beings caught up in the situation he has been describing; his only function then is simply to link together the situations and conversations, without offering any omniscient interpretation. In these passages the characters come alive, and we share their doubts and uncertainties as the hazards of the journey become even greater. The dream narrator knows that the pilgrim will win through, but the pilgrim himself does not know this and can only call upon his own reserves of strength and resolution to lead him forward. As Christian himself says on the way: "If I can get to the Celestial City, I am sure to

SELECTED EXAMPLES OF CRITICAL STUDIES

be in safety there. I must venture: To go back is nothing but death; to go forward is fear of death, and life everlasting beyond it. I will yet go forward."[27] For Christian, safety is a future promise, but he can never be sure that the promise will be fulfilled--hence the uncertainty that characterizes his view of the road, as opposed to the total knowledge of the dream narrator who described that road to us.

This contrast in perspectives is evident even in isolated details of the narrative. When for instance, Christian approaches the Palace Beautiful, at first he has no idea what this place actually is. He sees lions at the entrance and is frightened and despondent. And so we see the palace through the eyes of the pilgrim. But then at once the dream narrator changes the perspective by remarking: "The Lions were chained, but he saw not the chains."[28] The effect of this change on the reader is that instead of sharing in Christian's fears as if they were his own he can stand outside them again and view them more as an expression of the general human condition. He is no longer exclusively caught up in Christian's experiences, but is given the chance to assess the latter's situation and his reactions to it. The same applies to the temptations offered by Worldly Wiseman. Christian has no idea whose hands he has fallen into--for him the tempter appears to be nothing if not a thorough gentleman--but the narrator has already told the reader all about him. Christian has to learn by experience who this "gentleman" really is.[29] And so again, the reader has been given extra information which puts him in a superior position and enables him to recognize and evaluate the trials and tribulations along the road to salvation.

And so the narrative technique alternates between omniscient narration and dialogue, and the increasing preponderance of dialogue is an indication of the increasing importance of subjectivity within an objective context. But the reader is never allowed to be totally absorbed in the immediacy of the characters' reactions; he is constantly reminded or made aware of the overall situation, so that he can attain a more balanced judgment of human conduct generally, and, ultimately, of his own in particular. This change of perspective is an integral feature of the edification provided by Pilgrim's Progress, and it also brings about a dramatic switch of tensions: although the reader knows right from the start that the pilgrim will arrive safely in the Promised Land, the dialogue is so direct and alive that this knowledge at times fades right out of the reckoning; at others, he is aware of the end result, and so his interest lies not in whether the pilgrim will arrive, but in what the pilgrim has to do in order to get there. This latter form of tension is epic, since the outcome of the adventures is already known. But at those times when the reader loses sight of the end result and shares in the pilgrim's uncertainty as to whether he will arrive or not we have a different form of tension. "And so in the tension of the 'whether at all' there is contained a time element in the form of a conception of the future, in which the accent lies on the obscurity and opaqueness of everything future."[30] The future along the road to salvation is always present in the dialogues as an either/or that can never be resolved through preestablished ideals but only by the course of time. This tension is characteristic of the novel.

We can now see clearly the two poles between which the action takes its course: at the one extreme we have the objective, exemplary road to salvation, described directly by the dream narrator; at the other, we have the increasing, subjective certitude of salvation, developed during the dialogues. Salvation is an a priori precondition for all events in the book; certitude must be gained a posteriori. Man's destiny--the search for salvation--is clear from the beginning; the certainty of finding the fulfillment of this destiny is identical with death. The objective goal can only be reached through subjective "self-experience,"[31] and this process is communicated to the reader by the alternation between dream vision and dialogue and the respective tensions arising from this alternation.

For the most part, Pilgrim's Progress is

SELECTED EXAMPLES OF CRITICAL STUDIES

written in prose, but at various specific points the language changes to verse. It is unlikely that Bunyan's intention was merely to conform to the old form of the 'prosimetrum', for he only makes use of rhetorical means to serve his own particular strategic ends. The verse passages are generally very short, and so they act rather as interruptions to the otherwise prevailing prose. If we are to understand the significance of the verse, it might be advisable to take a closer look at the prose.

As we have seen, it is in the dialogue that certainty is sought after; here the speaker endeavors to ascertain his own situation and to open the eyes of his partner to the signs of increasing knowledge of salvation. Inevitably then the language takes on an argumentative character, for experiences have to be weighed and the significant elements singled out. The argumentation demands a discriminating use of language, not only in order to increase its effectiveness but also to incorporate all the given factors that make up the pilgrim's experiences. It is only by bringing out all the apparent trivia and contingencies of individual situations that the speaker can enhance his partners' awareness of their own positions. As virtually all the characters are passing along the road to salvation, they do not need to inform each other of the necessity of the journey. But in order for them to know where they stand on this allegorical road, they need a constant analysis of what they are and of the empirical situation they are in. Many of the dialogues therefore take the course almost of a trial, and the discussion--typified by a profusion of causal particles--gives rise to knowledge, though this need not always have a positive value, as we can see from the discussion between Christian and Worldly Wiseman. "Only prose can embody with equal power the tribulation and the triumph, the conflict and the coronation, the search and the sanctification; only its unlimited flexibility and its rhythmless linkage can capture with equal force fetters and freedom, the given weight and the fought-for lightness of the world that is now immanently radiant with the discovered sense."[32]

AN OVERVIEW

The prose dialogues of Pilgrim's Progress unfold the characters' fluctuations of mind and efforts to conquer their own uncertainty. They give rise to the whole picture of the pilgrim's empirical situation, and they reflect the Puritan reader's own inner conflicts. And it is precisely because the nuances of the prose unfold the empirical conditions surrounding the pilgrim that the verse passages take on such a special significance, for they offer something of which the Puritan reader could never be sure.

Many of the incidents in Pilgrim's Progress are rounded off with a few verses, which, as it were, sum up the conflict that has just taken place. After Christian has recognized his error in following Worldly Wiseman, the verse starts: "When Christians unto Carnal Men give ear."[33] The verse abstracts from the concrete instance in order to offer all Christians general criteria of conduct arising out of the individual error. This is another edifying element of the book, for here the Puritan reader is shown how to overcome the doubts and temptations which the prose dialogue enabled him to experience virtually as his own. But if the end result given by the verse is to be unambiguous and universal, it must separate itself from the single situation from which it arose, and so frequently the subject of the verses is no longer the individual pilgrim, but pilgrims in general.[34] If the name of the particular character is retained, however, the message takes on an increased degree of exemplariness, as shown for instance with Faithful's conduct in Vanity Fair.[35] The need to explain Faithful's significance once more in verse is an indication of the extent to which his behavior was oriented by ideas which sprang from his character as a human being, rather than from his ideality as a personification. The scaling down of characters to their exemplary values is a predominant feature of most of the verses.[36] But this very fact gives extra significance to those verses that are spoken by the pilgrim himself. Undoubtedly their edifying effect is all the more striking. After Christian has been given a scroll which symbolizes for him the first unmistakable sign of a gradual certitude, he reaches Hill Difficulty.

SELECTED EXAMPLES OF CRITICAL STUDIES

As he comes to climb the hill, the narrative breaks off into verse:

> This Hill, though high, I covet to ascend;
> The difficulty will not me offend;
> For I perceive the way to life lies here:
> Come, pluck up, Heart, let's neither faint nor fear:
> Better, though difficult, the right way to go,[37]
> Than wrong, though easy, where the end is woe.

These lines lay emphasis on Christian's firm resolve to continue his quest. As he has just received the first sign of grace, he is no longer put off by the difficulty of the way, but he talks of the effort required to conquer his own typically human weakness and fear, which might otherwise make him take the wrong way. The fact that Christian speaks these verses himself draws attention to his ability to extract the right conclusions from his own situation. And in this he satisfies a basic requirement of Puritan edification.

The function of the verse, then, is to pinpoint the general significance of particular events. While the prose unfolds the personificatio of the characters, the verse extracts the significatio. So long as events and reactions are the subject of the narrative, the language remains prose, but when the abstract, edifying idea behind these events is to be placed in the forefront, prose gives way to verse.

The distinctions we have observed in the language and the narrative perspectives apply also to the characters themselves. Basically there are two separate groups of characters in Pilgrim's Progress: the one purely functional, the other extending beyond mere function. Such characters as Evangelist, Pliable, and Obstinate only appear on the scene at set moments in the story and then disappear again. Evangelist, for instance, always comes when Christian is in need of heavenly guidance.[38] Once this has been given, he withdraws. Pliable and Obstinate have similarly fixed functions: they allegorize Christian's situation at his departure and embody the conflict that arises within him. Obstinate is Christian, insofar as he seems determined to take the road to salvation at all costs; Pliable is Christian in that he remains completely open to all the suggestions of those that want to divert him from his quest. But once Christian is actually on the way, Obstinate and Pliable diappear-- they have played their part and fade from the scene.[39] They are only functional, representing an abstract idea in a situational context, and so they cannot be developed as characters in their own right. In this respect they correspond to the pattern of the epic and the allegory.

The second group of characters, however, is not purely functional. The principal member of this group is, of course, Christian himself, but he is also accompanied for much of the way by Hopeful and Faithful, who are far more than just embodiments of a single idea. In them the reader has to recognize the reflection of his own doubts as well as his own hopes, and for this purpose it is essential that they should at times fall out of their allegorical character, for if they were to behave as ideal pilgrims, the link with the Puritan reader would be broken and the work would lose much of its edifying effect. The importance of these characters is indicated technically by a sort of narrative close-up, in marked contrast to the paucity of description with which the functional figures are presented. This is particularly true of Christian. Right at the beginning we are offered a thoroughly detailed picture of him. He reads, weeps, trembles, and finally gives vent to a cry of despair. In torment he rushes home from work, and then at first tries to hide his agony in order that his wife and children should not notice his suffering. But he cannot remain silent for long, as his anguish steadily increases. Finally he tells them what is troubling him. They are all amazed and think "that some frenzy distemper had got into his head."[40] As night approaches, they hope his health may improve with sleep, and so they hurry him off to bed. But Christian sighs and weeps right through the night, and next morning everything seems even more hopeless to him than it did the previous day. Now people begin to mock him,

SELECTED EXAMPLES OF CRITICAL STUDIES

then they remonstrate with him, and finally they ignore him, in the belief that this will cure him. But Christian retires to his room, not knowing what has happened to him, and then prays and feels sorry for himself. After this he goes out to the fields again, reads and prays$_{41}$ in the hope that this may calm the inner storm. This description of the initial situation in <u>Pilgrim's Progress</u> offers a series of concrete details. Christian is observed much more closely than the other characters, and the vividness of his portrayal is in obvious contrast to their comparative anonymity: Christian is not shown to us as and exemplary pilgrim, but as a man plunged into the despondency that in fact is the first sign of grace.^{42} This opens up a particular perspective which continues right through to the end of the book. When Christian reaches the River of Death and sees the towers of the Celestial City beyond, in spite of the many signs of salvation he has received, he once more gives way to black despair. Again the human side of the pilgrim takes over in the form of care, fear, and hopelessness. It is because of this emphasis on the human side that Christian is not surrounded at the beginning by allegorical figures that might interpret his conduct; instead he is shown with his wife and children--"Children of my bowels"^{43}--who indicate the human situation in which the quest for grace can only appear as a disturbance. For the family, this preoccupation with an obscure salvation is explicable only as a form of madness.

There is another important side to the opening scene of the book. Although he is in anguish, Christian is by no means resolved to set out on the quest for salvation; on the contrary, he would like to be rid of this oppressive feeling, which takes on the image of a burden he has to bear.^{44} He is far from being the ideal pilgrim joyfully preparing for his journey; instead he is shown as a man whose one concern is to be relieved of his suffering. And this is why on the way he is subjected to so many different temptations, for he has to learn that he can only obtain the relief he longs for when he has left behind those weaknesses that determine his character as a human being. The very theme of the

99

pilgrim's way is that Christian has to become aware of the paradoxical fact that the desire for relief, which arises out of his humanity, is only to be fulfilled by overcoming that same humanity. The pilgrim himself, as a man, is the actual source of the temptations--whether they be to lead him astray, or to make him doubt his incipient certitude, because nothing in this world can ever be truly certain. This is why, at the Palace Beautiful, Christian acknowledges the fact that humanity is an annoyance to the man set on salvation.[45]

The two groups of charcters then reveal the same two perspectives we have already observed in relation to narrative techniques and use of prose and verse. If the characters are purely functional, then it is the abstract idea of salvation that is uppermost; when the characters cease to be mere personifications, emphasis is thrown on human conduct and motivation. The two planes are complementary, in that the <u>certitudo salutis</u> can only be subjective, with the pilgrim extracting the signs from his own individual human experiences.

IV

The alternation of perspectives and the mixture of 'human' and 'functional' characters have certain far-reaching effects on the allegorical mode of presentation in <u>Pilgrim's Progress</u>. As from Prudentius's <u>Psychomachia</u> onward, the allegory, as <u>bellum intestinum</u>, possessed certain specific structural characteristics,[46] and these remained consistent right through to the Renaissance. The vices and virtues struggling for the soul did not personify any psychological qualities, but put the soul in the context of an overriding reality.[47] Consequently the soul was only the object of the allegorical presentation, while the superior truth was the subject. This is why the soul--still regarded by Prudentius as corresponding typologically to the Church--and the allegorical self in medieval court allegories were both presented more or less as abstractions. "An allegorical being, however human may be the form given to it, can never take on the individuality of a Greek god or a saint or any other real subject: because in order for it to correspond to the abstraction of its meaning, it must hollow out all subjectivity so that any fixed individuality disappears completely."[48] This idea is prevalent both in Anticlaudianus and in the Roman de la Rose. The 'homo perfectus' and the 'amant' remain abstract figures, and are only real within the limits of a nonsubjective world. The allegory--as Walter F. Otto put it so succintly--represents "not a personification, but in actual fact a depersonification."[49]

Despite these impersonal elements of the allegory, we must not overlook the vital interaction that takes place between the abstract ideas and the concrete situations they are transposed into. The character in the allegory is not the subject matter, but neither is the theological or moral canon. "As a literary form it [i.e., the allegory] effects a concordia discors. Its achievement lies in combining what discursive thought can only conceive of as separate. It links the significance of the general with the situational present of the concrete."[50] This link results from the basic feature of the allegorical mode of presentation, which is a "noun with a fixed, general, abstract connotation fitted into a particular situation in the text,"[51] thus bringing about the paradoxical idea of "a contextual merging of the mutually exclusive linguistic poles of abstraction and situation."[52] It is no doubt this structure of interaction that explains the fascination which allegory has had down through the ages as a mode of presentation. But this same structure is also an important key to historical insight, for the framework of interaction shown by the "contextual merging of ... abstraction and situation" has been filled with a variety of pictures, depending on the historical function it has had to serve.

Historically, the 'situation' became increasingly important within this structure, and in Bunyan's allegory--against the background of predestination--it is unmistakably in the forefront. This shift in the balance of the structure brings about a far-reaching change in the

AN OVERVIEW

conception of the allegorical figures. In <u>Pilgrim's Progress</u> there are three distinct types of figures, and the interaction between them brings out the originality with which Bunyan manipulated abstract ideas in the context of a situation. There are personified virtues and vices, personified qualities, and the central figure of the pilgrim himself, who steps out of the allegorical framework at various turning-points in his life. The fact that the virtues and vices do not fight with Christian all at the same time arises out of the journey metpahor. Simultaneity here gives way to a succession of stages, in accordance with the Stoic convention. But in fact the virtues--Good-Will, Charity, Piety, Prudence, etc --do <u>not</u> fight with the pilgrim at all; nor do the vices, from Worldly Wiseman to Ignorance. Only once is the pilgrim ever involved in a fight, and that is with Apollyon who, as the Devil, embodies the absolute opposite to the quest for salvation. Like Evangelist, he represents the spiritual level of the Scriptures, in the form of a symbol. Apollyon and Evangelist mark the two spiritual poles of the salvation process and as such transcend the allegorical pattern.

The individual relationships between virtues and vices and Christian himself are established by discussions. The virtues and vices are constantly appealing to him, thereby presupposing that there is a side of Christian's character on which they can work. And so the object of the dialogue is persuasion, which means that the allegorical figure must have an inner self that is open to persuasion. It is through this inner self that the character outstrips the allegory, and the pilgrim takes on a sort of double role.

This is made clear by the second group of figures which--like Faithful and Hopeful--represent personified qualities and are of greater importance than the others by virtue of the fact the they are Christian's closest companions along the road to salvation. The change of emphasis in the allegorical pattern of interaction is clear from the very names--Faithful and Hopeful, not Faith and Hope. Christian is no longer the object but the subject of the action, with his inner qualities—set as they are on salvation—being personified as his companions. When Christian leaves the Palace Beautiful, he learns from the watchman that Faithful is also on the road. Christian remarks: "I know him; he is my Townsman, my near Neighbour, he comes from the place where I was born."⁵³ This quality of faith is already inherent in Christian, but it only takes on a real form after he has gone through the torments of the awareness of sin and has begun to view these as signs of future grace. But before Christian can actually join up with Faithful, he has to fight Apollyon and go through the Valley of the Shadow of Death in order to test the certainty of the faith now developing. Finally, in Vanity Fair, this faith gives testimony of its unshakableness through the death that Faithful is ready to suffer. And so it is only after this vital confirmation that Hopeful comes on the scene as the new companion, whose support Christian needs right up to his death. If the sequence of Faithful/Hopeful is principally an indication of the uncertainty of the Puritans' road to salvation, nevertheless it also shows how a readiness to believe can turn into hopeful perseverance, And so the allegorical schema is less an illustration of the Calvinist doctrine of predestination than an attempt to take the sting out of this doctrine by concentrating on the possibilities of experience open to the believer. The fact that Faithful and Hopeful become the pilgrim's companions gives precedence to the human situation. This must in any case be predominant within the schema of allegorical interaction, if only because the idea of predestination presented as an allegory would inevitably lead from a need for faith to black despair. Here the virtues and vices do not struggle exclusively for the soul, as they did in the medieval allegory; instead, it is the soul itself, filled with its own resolve, that yearns for the Celestial City. As the longing cannot incorporate its own fulfillment, the allegorical sense is conveyed by adjectives. The numinous is allegorized by nouns when it is concerned with the human soul; the self is allegorized by adjectives when the only impulsion is a longing for the transcendental world beyond.

AN OVERVIEW

So long as the allegory personifies abstractions, naturally all individuality is bound to be excluded; the significatio dominates, and its concrete representation is limited to its single function. However, when it is human qualities that are being allegorized, the allegorical figure does not have to be confined to the feature it represents, for it does not personify any theological or moral canon, but relates the inner self to a particular goal. And so personified qualities contain an inherent duality, such as we see in Faithful and Hopeful. Although Faithful represents man's pious resolve, he departs from this 'character' whenever he confesses to features that are not connected with this function—for instance, when he admits to occasionally giving way to the lusts of the flesh[54] (which can scarcely be regarded as essential to the personification of faith). At such moments, the personification takes on individual features which even begin to compete with the abstract function, incorporating human frailties into the allegorical significatio.[55] The same applies to Hopeful, who confesses his past enjoyment of "Rioting, Revelling, Drinking, Swearing, Lying, Uncleanness, Sabbath-breaking, and what not."[56] These characters do not merely personify the pilgrim's readiness to believe and to hope, but they show that this readiness can only come from the conquest of human weakness. And in this way they depart from the traditional schema of the allegory and approach that of the novel, in that they first have to work out the meaning of their own destiny. In the medieval allegory, this meaning was given a priori, but Bunyan's work is for much of the time concerned with overcoming weakness precisely by the character's finding out this meaning for himself. In this respect we find literary fiction trying to accomplish that which the Calvinist dogma had excluded, and it is little wonder that Pilgrim's Progress was read as a book of devotion, for it filled a psychic gap that had been created by the doctrine of predestination.

In the character of the pilgrim himself, the

SELECTED EXAMPLES OF CRITICAL STUDIES

guidelines for edification are given concrete form. If, with Faithful and Hopeful, the allegorical function still outweighs the human aspect, the same cannot be said of Christian. Faithful and Hopeful take on their human characteristics through their occasional departures from their allegorical function, but they never develop this contrast themselves, whereas Christian reflects on everything that happens to him in a number of highly individual monologues.[57] The very form of the monologue presupposes an inner self as addressee, and it transcends the allegorical structure of the work insofar as Christian's inner voices are no longer allegorized. C.S. Lewis has pointed out that with the medieval allegory, the moment a character starts 'thinking' about a certain conflict, the different sides are at once translated into allegorical figures.[58] Christian, however, does his own thinking; he forms a relationship with himself and does not need a superimposed reality to gain a clear vision of his own situation. Instead, he looks for motives and reasons that can eventually enable him to correct himself, and this preoccupation with himself mirrors the radical isolation of man as brought about by the doctrine of predestination. As has already been pointed out, the Calvinist pilgrim could do nothing to ensure his own salvation, but could only search for signs. And so the lack of any certitude meant that the pilgrim's one and only source of information about his ultimate destiny was himself. This was why the monologues in the Pilgrim's Progress were of particular interest to Puritan readers, for Christian's search for reassurance offered them a guideline as to how they should examine themselves.

The pilgrim's monologues are already a departure from the traditional schema of the allegory; through them he becomes what Forster called a "flat character,"[59] but this is only one departure from tradition: another lies in the frequent repetition of particular events. After Christian has been led astray by Wordly Wiseman and made to believe that the road to salvation is the wrong one for him to take, Evangelist comes on the scene. Through a series of questions, Evangelist compels Christian to repeat his meeting with Worldly Wiseman and to see it in a completely different light. Christian is then able to reassess his own conduct, to recognize his mistakes, and to understand the consequences which he has not been aware of when he was directly involved in the events.[60] Similar situations recur during other phases of his pilgrimage. For instance, when he reaches the Wicket-gate and meets the watchman, Good-Will,[61] the latter questions him in an almost Socratic manner, compelling him to relive various experiences he has already been through. As a result, Christian is able to gain insight into these events and to find his own way toward clearing up his own confusion and correcting his own mistakes. He is not punished for having strayed from the path of salvation; instead he is induced by the functional and allegorical figures to think over his situation. When, in the Palace Beautiful--one of the most important stages of his journey--he is again forced to relive past events, his insight is so developed that he recognizes his own human nature as the greatest obstacle along the path to salvation. Prudence asks him: "Do you not yet bear away with you some of the things that then you were conversant withal?" Christian replies: "Yes, but greatly against my will, especially my inward and carnal cogitations; with which all my countrymen, as well as myself, were delighted; but now all those things are my grief; and might I but choose mine own things, I would choose never to think of those things more; but when I would be doing of that which is best, that which is worst is with me."[62]

The pilgrim has obviously come a long way since his despairing cry of "What shall I do?"[63] at the beginning of the book. He realizes now that human weakness stands in the way of the longed-for certitude, but through his own reflections he can gradually overcome this weakness. The actions arising from his self-correction lead to experiences which enhance this insight and take him in a direction that promises a greater degree of certainty and consolation.

The experiences gained during the early part of the book--up to the Palace Beautiful episode--

SELECTED EXAMPLES OF CRITICAL STUDIES

are often invoked again during subsequent episodes. At the beginning Christian was constantly being made more aware of himself by the various allegorical figures, but he now proceeds to use his insight, in accordance with the idea of the Puritan mission, in order to enhance the self-awareness of his fellow pilgrims. When he meets Faithful, he begins to explore the latter's life history, for he wants to spur him on to the same insight that he achieved through his encounter with the vices and virtues. Faithful has naturally already recognized many of his own human errors, and so Christian does not need to induce him to self-correction, in the manner of Evangelist, Good-Will, or Prudence. But Christian's questions still have an important influence on Faithful, who is sometimes rather too ready to believe and, for instance, unexpectedly falls victim to the glib speeches of Talkative, until he is enjoined to be more vigilant by Christian, who has seen through this chatterbox straight away.[64]

Christian's experiences have an even greater effect in his relations with Hopeful. The vital event here is the discussion they have when crossing the Enchanted Ground.[65] The subject of this discussion is the certitudo salutis. Christian asks Hopeful the customary question how the expectation of salvation formed itself within him. This makes Hopeful think about himself, and he learns to distinguish between the true and false signs. The content of this dialogue is virtually a psychological exposé of the salvation process, for it revolves continually around the subject of how the certitudo salutis awakens in man: "Why, what was it that brought your sins to mind again? ... And how did you do then? ... And did you think yourself well then?"[66] Hopeful feels himself compelled to confront his expectations of salvation with his own human disposition, because only such a conscious confrontation can bring about the necessary degree of security for a proper evaluation of the signs. The process that the allegorical figures set in motion during Christian's period of development is now begun by Christian himself for Hopeful. Thus Christian's experiences are confirmed, and we know that in the context of Calvinist orthodoxy such a confirmation marked an important stage in the devotional account of incipient certitude. Through correcting his own mistakes, Christian gradually takes on the role of guide; it is he that is now the 'presbyter.' The extent to which experience qualifies him for this role is apparent from something Hopeful says. When Christian asks him the vital question about the origins of his expectations, Hopeful replies: "Nay, do you answer that question yourself, for you are the older man."[67] Greater experience is the basic criterion in evaluating expectations of grace, although in the light of the doctrine of predestination these must always remain basically subjective and approximate. But experience only takes place when preconceptions are called in question by a process of self-examination. Christian tries to inspire this insight in others, in order to prevent them from blocking the road to salvation through the prevailing uncertainty of their expectations. The vital importance of reflection is stressed by Christian during his encounter with Ignorance; "There is none righteous, there is none that doeth good.... The imagination of man's heart is evil from his youth. Now then, when we think thus of ourselves, having sense thereof, then are our thoughts good ones, because according to the Word of God."[68]

Ignorance--to whom this admonition is addressed--had exalted the feelings of the heart to the position of highest authority, and so had lost the ability to distinguish between certitude and illusion. He embodies pure subjectivity, believing he can do without experience because he regards the voice of the heart, like the law, as an adequate guide for his own conduct. But a blind faith in one's own heart, or in the precepts of the law, means relinquishing the possibility of conscious acquaintance with one's own situation, for such an insight can only come about through experience; it is experience that reconciles the pilgrim's human distress with the idea of salvation, relieving the unbearable tensions of the soul leading eventually to increasing certitude. Christian has learned this lesson, and subsequently corrects in others the naive belief that the promptings of the heart can offer an infallible guide. From the pilgrim's self-inspection there arise a series of experiences as he sallies forth into the world and puts his own body and soul in jeopardy in order to triumph over himself. This series of experiences foreshadows the history of the hero which forms the basic pattern of the eighteenth-century novel.[69]

The significance of experience is clearly brought out during one of the key episodes of the whole story. Christian tells Hopeful the tale of Little-Faith, who on the road to salvation was attacked and robbed by three bandits, Faint-Heart, Mistrust, and Guilt.[70] After a brief description of what happened, there comes a long dialogue between Christian and Hopeful, and in the course of this Christian corrects the false conclusions which Hopeful draws from the conduct of Little-Faith. Hopeful's viewpoint is theologically relevant and understandable, for he remarks that after the robbery Little-Faith clearly lacked the courage to go along the road he knew to be the right one. One would have expected Christian to accept this judgment, for it fits in with the demands any pilgrim had constantly to make of himself in the face of the hardships he was bound to encounter on the way. But Christian's extremely revealing reply is unmistakably a reproach.[71] For him any abstract argument that is not based on concrete experience is a source of irritation, and he proceeds to justify Little-Faith's reaction by referring to just such experience:

> As for a great heart, Little-faith had none; and I perceive by thee, my Brother, hadst thou been the man concerned, thou art but for a brush, and then to yield. And verily since this is the height of thy stomach, now they [i.e. the robbers] are at a distance from us, should they appear to thee as they did to him, they might put thee to second thoughts. But consider again ... I myself have been engaged as this Little-faith was, and I found it a terrible thing ... I was clothed with Armour of proof. Ay, and yet though I was so harnessed, I found it hard work to quit myself

like a man: no man can tell what in that Combat attends us, but he that hath been in the Battle himself.[72]

Only someone who has been in a similar situation is qualified to judge Little-Faith, for only through a similar experience can one feel the degree of anguish that torments the pilgrim on his journey. If this anguish were merely measured by the abstract demands of religious creeds, it would inevitably turn into despair. But the presentation of the exemplary pilgrimage is meant to <u>cure</u> the faithful of their despair. This is why Christian defends Little-Faith's despondent reaction, for this is something that all pilgrims have to face at one time or another. However, once it has been faced, the question is how much one is able to learn and benefit from one's anguish. Christian himself is no longer afraid, but it is only <u>after</u> one has passed through such fears that one can assess their true significance.

Here, then, we are shown the meaning and importance of experience. The <u>certitudo salutis</u> does not arise out of the one-sided guidance of theological commandments, and this is why Christian corrects Hopeful, who can only think in theological terms and therefore overlooks the spontaneity of human reaction in moments of danger. Neither the promptings of the heart nor the precepts of religious dogma are adequate guides for the pilgrim on his journey: the former will make him lose his way in self-justification and the latter in despair. The fact that Christian went through the same despondency as Little-Faith and yet still took his place in the scheme of salvation, because he was able to transform his distress into beneficial knowledge, is what constitutes the instructional basis of <u>Pilgrim's Progress</u>. The members of Calvinist sects discovered themselves in Christian--not only in their weak humanity but also through the promise that by self-examination they could overcome their weakness and so attain an increasing degree of certitude. As far as the composition of <u>Pil-</u>

SELECTED EXAMPLES OF CRITICAL STUDIES

grim's Progress is concerned, the episode of Little-Faith occupies a special position in that it is the only story in the whole book that is told by one of the characters for the purpose of demonstration. It has the nature of an exemplary narrative[73] concerned not with different stages along the road to salvation, or with the theological demands arising out of these, but simply and solely with human motivation. It throws emphasis on typically human behavior which offers a different view of events than that demanded--or even allowed--by the abstract idea of salvation. This is why there is very little of the allegory about this episode, particularly in the vital second part. Hopeful cannot really understand Little-Faith's behavior, because from the standpoint of salvation it seems inconsistent; but for Christian this inconsistency is removed through his own experience in a similar situation.

Experience then is the force that mediates between the human character and its hidden destiny. The withholding of certitude activates the human potential, the manifestations of which orientate the character toward the goal he is striving after. Consequently the focal point of attention is no longer the goal, i.e., salvation, but the means of attainment, i.e., self-examination through experience. This process is fraught with difficulties, because each experience can only call forth subjective and, therefore, unreliable reactions. In order to mitigate the ensuing dangers, the pilgrim must undergo and observe more experiences through which he may accumulate a degree of insight into himself and thereby into his goal. There thus evolves a history of the pilgrim in which the attainment of the objective virtually coincides with the activation of his own human potential through experience. And so in Pilgrim's Progress the theological withholding of certitude stimulates human self-assertion, the development of which foreshadows the pattern of the eighteenth-century novel.

AN OVERVIEW

V

"Wherever there prevails a mood of intense piety, and wherever life beyond is regarded as the true one, and life here as merely transitory, this life is experienced and shaped as a migration."[74] This is the starting-point of Pilgrim's Progress. But the journey is not treated by Bunyan just from one point of view, for there are temporary reconciliations as well as lasting conflicts in Christian's encounters with the world. The pilgrimage in fact begins before the journey, in the sense that there are certain as yet incomprehensible signs of salvation which lead to the progressive isolation of the pilgrim before he even knows that he is going on a journey. In Christian's case, this is when he experiences the familiar world as something repugnant. He leaves his family and his birthplace, because he feels "the Powers and Terrors of what is yet unseen."[75] The decision to seek salvation involves cutting all ties with the familiar world, and this in turn means isolation. As Talon has pointed out, it is only after he has taken this decision that the pilgrim is given the name Christian.[76] Through his inner distress, the pilgrim has freed himself from the anonymity of the City of Destruction, and so he becomes a person in his own right. But these sacrifices gain him nothing positive. When Pliable asks Christian " ... but, my good Companion, do you know the way to this desired place?", Christian can only answer: "I am directed by a man, whose name is Evangelist, to speed me to a little Gate that is before us, where we shall receive instruction about the way."[77] There is a striking contrast between the radical decision to leave the familiar world and the unknown mystery of the road now opening up before Christian. And so at first most of his actions have a negative quality, because there is no concrete promise as yet to fill the gap of the repugnant world he has rejected. His motivation is not the prospect of future bliss, but a desire to escape from the distressing present. All he does know is that his radical devaluation of his past life can lead

SELECTED EXAMPLES OF CRITICAL STUDIES

him closer to the expectation of something as yet concealed from him. Thus his journey becomes a probing search, which occasionally leads him astray, because the goal remains uncertain and because his only guidelines are his objections to the familiar world and to the weaknesses of human nature. Christian's sharp conflict with the world--which marks the beginning of the salvation process--is developed thematically in the course of the various adventures that follow. Time and again he is exposed to the dangers and temptations of this world, and it needs all his physical and mental strength to overcome them. But in contrast there are also episodes in which the conflict fades away. Palace Beautiful,[78] Plain Ease,[79] The River of the Water of Life,[80] The Delectable Mountains,[81] and the Country of Beulah[82]--these are all points along the journey at which the pilgrim feels a fairy tale harmony with his surroundings. At such times there is a sense of paradisal security, and the pilgrim has a foretaste of the bliss which is at most a vague inspiration for him during the conflicts of his other adventures. The surprising aspect of these episodes is that they are direct descendants of medieval secular romances, finding their way into this exemplary conduct-book[83] despite the Puritan abhorrence of literature. Both the name and the various features of the Palace Beautiful are a direct reference back to romances of chivalry, to whose enchantments, as Schirmer has stressed, the Puritans were not altogether unsusceptible in their childhood years.[84] The castle by the wayside, the lovely ladies, the Round Table, and the display of treasures are all component parts of vulgarized court romances.[85] These basic features, however, undergo a definite transformation in Bunyan, for they are set in a different frame of reference. Thus the Palace is changed into the Church,[86] and the ladies into cardinal virtues, while the discussion at the table concerns salvation, and the sight of the treasures provides inner reassurance; romantic wrappings are filled with Christian contents. The same applies to the other places where the pilgrim feels tempted to linger awhile. At such moments we

AN OVERVIEW

find the trappings of the locus amoenus mixed with those of the hortus conclusus, and they convey an unmistakable atmosphere of Paradise. The repertoire of motifs from medieval romances is called upon whenever the fundamental conflict between man and world is to be temporarily relieved. With the disappearance of this opposition, the world seems ideal and idyllic, its transfiguration bringing about a surprising harmony between man and reality. But as the orthodox Puritan believed that man's situation was characterized by the conflict and not by the harmony, this inner bliss could only be illustrated through a repertoire from outside the Puritan tradition. The very fact that Bunyan used such a repertoire shows the extent to which the Calvinists abandoned their radical contempt for the world when it had to serve as the setting for an unmistakable manifestation of grace. Although the pilgrim sets forth in the hope of ensuring salvation through overcoming the contemptible world, this very world miraculously changes into a nascent paradise the moment he feels his expectations might come true. "Just as entrance into the sacral precincts means for the believer participation in the hierophany, so the literary fiction of the enclosure offers the possibility of an illusory integration of the self into the totality of salvation.... The form of the Romance, which reconciles extremities ... , offers a literary matrix in which the inner world of the believer and the transcendent world of salvation --which Calvinism had completely separated--can once more be reconciled to one another."[87] The fictionally presented certainty of fulfillment of the yearnings shared by all Puritans was a vital feature of the process of edification, because it offered the imaginary achievement of what was excluded by the doctrine of predestination. The pattern of the romance, with its sequence of fight--pathos--fulfillment,[88] corresponded to typical expectations insofar as the genuine anguish of faith was shown, as it were, in the mirror of its possible relief. The fact that the inner struggles and conflicts dominate the pilgrim's journey is representative of the situation of all believers. But only through reflections

SELECTED EXAMPLES OF CRITICAL STUDIES

of and on such a situation can the preconditions be brought about whereby the fairy tale glow surrounding all the places of blissful security can take on the form of a real promise. Thus it is the doubts and despair of the pilgrim that make credible the certitude of fulfillment presented in the schema of the romance.

Of course the havens of security are only sketched in very briefly, for they mark endpoints or transitions in the series of past and future ordeals. Indeed this very sparsity indicates on Bunyan's part an acute psychological sense for the effectiveness of the edifying process he had set in motion. A glimpse is far more inspiring than overexposure. It is also worth pointing out that his use of the romance sequence of fight--pathos--fulfillment shows how the same schema can be used for different purposes at different times. This is true not only of medieval court literature as compared with Bunyan's work but also of that same literature compared with the early novel, which during the eighteenth century was to use this same schema in a quite unforeseeable manner.

If the pattern of the romance smacks of triviality through its removal or fulfillment of fears and longings, this affirmative outcome in a Puritan context has a definite historical significance, which considerably outweighs the triviality. For here the affirmation is an indication of how great must have been the distress and despair of the ordinary believer, since his negative situation could only be compensated by fiction. As far as the history of the novel is concerned, this affirmative tendency has undergone a gradual but irrevocable reversal, until now, with the modern novel, we have a high potential of negation in fiction that seeks to break up all the fixed structures of expectation and conduct in the reader.

VI

The epic and allegory of the Middle Ages were firmly based on what Lukács called "God-given security";[89] Bunyan's <u>Pilgrim's Progress</u> arises

115

out of the total withdrawal of such security. This vital loss gives human existence an unexpected significance, because only through self-observation was it possible to attain any degree of assurance. Thus the transcendent nature of salvation increases the value of man himself in a manner that counterbalances the devaluation brought about by the doctrine of predestination. This is why in Pilgrim's Progress so much emphasis is laid on human situations. In this way, individuality increasingly becomes an end in itself, "because it finds in itself that which is essential to it and which makes its life an authentic life--not as the given basis of life, but as something to be searched for."[90] Christian's story is one of an increasing self-awareness, and in this respect it is indisputably a novel, or at least a novel in-the-making. Self-awareness requires experience, and this is what Christian gains in his confrontation with the world. In the novel, experience is the keynote of the action, whereas in the epic and allegory everything was subsidiary to the idea. In Pilgrim's Progress the increasing importance of experience is an indication of the fact that this was the only way to get over the consequences of the doctrine of predestination. In a 'God-forsaken' world, it offers the one chance of human self-understanding. Through it, the self and the world can be reconciled in a new way, but since there can be no paradigmatic, universally applicable reconciliation, literary fiction can only offer situational answers to each of the historical problems that need to be solved. The history of these problems and answers constitutes the history of the novel.

Bunyan was faced with the paradoxical task of adapting the conduct-book--which for all its systematic orientation remained essentially private--in such a way that he could ensure the general applicability of individual certitude necessary for edification. The conduct-books were first and foremost 'statements of account,' which were edifying to the extent that they showed the possibility of attaining certitude of election here and now. But this depended on the absolute truth of the experiences recorded, and the pri-

AN OVERVIEW

vate nature of these was more of a hindrance than a help to the process of edification. And so gradually fabricated stories, which could generalize distress and certitude, provided the most appealing form of edification. One would have assumed that the fictionalization would devalue the trustworthiness of the certitude, but this was clearly not the case, as can be seen from the history of responses to Pilgrim's Progress. Obviously, the fictional humanizing of theological rigorism must have fulfilled an elementary historical need, since the Calvinists' strict distinctions between truth and fiction were allowed to fade into the background. And from this historical observation, we might draw a conclusion that will apply to all forms of fiction, from Pilgrim's Progress right through to the experimental works of today: namely, that literature counterbalances the deficiencies produced by prevailing philosophies.

AN OVERVIEW

NOTES

[1] Herbert Schöffler, *Protestantismus und Literatur* (Leipzig, 1922).

[2] Ernst Troeltsch, *Gesammelte Schriften*, I (Tübingen, 1912).

[3] Max Weber, *Gesammelte Aufsätze zur Religionssoziologie*, I (Tubingen, 1920).

[4] Schöffler, *Protestantismus*, p. 154.

[5] *Ibid.*, p. 156.

[6] *Ibid.*, pp. 165 f. Schöffler is referring to the conference at Salters' Hall in 1719.

[7] This term is used by Frank Kermode, *The Sense of an Ending. Studies in the Theory of Fiction* (New York, 1967), pp. 63 f.

[8] Schöffler, *Protestantismus*, p. 154.

[9] E.M.W. Tillyard, *The English Epic and its Background* (London, 1954).

[10] *Ibid.*, p. 386.

[11] H. Talon, *John Bunyan: L'Homme et l'Oeuvre* (Paris, 1948), p. 252; see also E.A. Baker, *The History of the English Novel*, III (London, 1929), p. 57.

[12] The structure of the epic distance has been systematically described by H.R. Jauss, *Zeit und Erinnerung in Marcel Prousts 'A la Recherche du Temps Perdu'* (Heidelberg, 1955), following B. Groethuysen; see esp. chap. 1.

SELECTED EXAMPLES OF CRITICAL STUDIES

[13] John Bunyan, The Pilgrim's Progress (Everyman's Library) (London, no date), p. 6.

[14] One consequence of the Norman Conquest was the fact that it took a long time for a native English form of the epic to come into being. In contrast to the traditional epic, the English epic of the late Middle Ages and the Renaissance is typified by a lack of any historical restrictions. The English epic, as regards its form, stands on the borderline between the classical epic and the allegory.

[15] Tillyard, The English Epic, p. 393.

[16] See C.S. Lewis, The Allegory of Love (London, 1953), p. 268.

[17] See also Tillyard, The English Epic, p. 393.

[18] See G. Thiel, Bunyans Stellung innerhalb der religiösen Strömungen seiner Zeit (Sprache und Kultur der germanischen und romanischen Völker. A. Anglistische Reihe, VII) (Breslau, 1931), pp. 136 ff. In this otherwise well-informed study, Thiel does, however, overlook the vital fact that the certitudo salutis can only be subjective; see p. 142.

[19] See, Bunyan, Pilgrim's Progress, pp.156 f.

[20] The consequences for the history of economics have been shown in detail by Max Weber and R.H. Tawney, Religion and the Rise of Capitalism (London, 1926). See also H. Bock, "Typen burgerlich-puritanischer Lebenshaltung in England in 17.und 18. Jahrhundert," Anglia 65(1941): 153 ff.

[21] Gerd Birkner, Heilsgewissheit und Literatur. Metapher, Allegorie und Autobiographie im Puritanismus (Theorie und Geschichte der Literatur und der schönen Künste, 18) (Munich, 1972), p. 102.

[22] Georg von Lukács,"Die Theorie des Romans," Zeitschrift für Ästhetik und Allgemeine Kunstwissenschaft 11 (1916): 226 f.

[23] Tillyard, The English Epic, p. 386.

[24] Bunyan, Pilgrim's Progress, pp. 6 f.

[25] R. Sharrock, John Bunyan (London, 1954), pp. 73 f., rightly emphasizes the uniformity of the first part of Pilgrim's Progress: "The First Part of The Pilgrim's Progress is a complete and self-sufficient narrative; it has no need of a sequel to make plain either its religious meaning or its unity of atmosphere."

[26] See Bunyan, Pilgrim's Progress, pp.4 and 6.

[27] Ibid., p. 45.

[28] Ibid., p. 47.

[29] Ibid., pp. 23 f.

[30] C. Lugowski, Die Form der Individualität im Roman (Neue Forschung, 14) (Berlin, 1932), p.42.

[31] This term is taken from E. Harding, Selbsterfahrung (Zürich, 1957) (German translation), but is not used in the psychological context which this book discusses.

[32] Lukács, "Theorie des Romans," p. 247.

[33] Bunyan, Pilgrim's Progress, p.24.

[34] Ibid., pp. 44, 75, 134, passim.

[35] Ibid., pp. 94 and 99.

[36] Ibid., pp. 148, passim.

[37] Ibid., p. 43.

[38] Ibid., pp. 12 f. and 22.

[39] Lugowski, Form der Individualität, p. 99.

[40] Bunyan, Pilgrim's Progress, p. 12.

SELECTED EXAMPLES OF CRITICAL STUDIES

[41] Ibid., pp. 11 f.

[42] See also A. West, The Mountain in the Sunlight (London, 1958), p. 28.

[43] Bunyan, Pilgrim's Progress, p. 11.

[44] Ibid., p. 23.

[45] Ibid., pp. 51 f.

[46] Re the conception of the allegory in the ancient tradition and the renewed discussion of the difference between allegory and symbol, see H.R. Jauss, "Form and Auffassung der Allegorie in der Tradition der Psychomachia," in Medium Aeuvum Vivum (Festschrift für Walther Bulst) (Heidelberg, 1960), pp. 179 ff.

[47] See also H.E. Greene, "The Allegory as employed by Spenser, Bunyan, and Swift," PMLA 4 (1888/89): 145 ff., though his definitions are much too formalistic. The distinction he tries to draw between symbol and allegory is not convincing. On the same problem, see W. Benjamen, Schriften I (Frankfurt, 1955), p. 283. Re the conception of the allegory in the eighteenth century, see B.H. Bronson, "Personification Reconsidered," ELH 14 (1947): 163 ff.

[48] G.W.F. Hegel, Ästhetik, ed. F. Bassenge (Berlin, 1955), p. 393.

[49] Quoted from Germanisch-Romanische Monatsschrift 39 (1958): 314.

[50] Birkner, Heilsgewissheit und Literatur, p. 115; for this aspect of the allegory I am indebted to Birkner's work.

[51] H. Engels, "Piers Plowman--Eine Untersuchung der Textstruktur mit einer Einleitung zur mittelalterlichen Allegorie," Dissertation, Cologne, 1968, p. 38.

[52] Ibid., p. 44.

121

[53] Bunyan, *Pilgrim's Progress*, p. 57.

[54] *Ibid.*, p. 70.

[55] See, amongst others, Talon, *John Bunyan*, pp. 232f.

[56] Bunyan, *Pilgrim's Progress*, p. 137.

[57] *Ibid.*, pp. 45 f., passim.

[58] See Lewis, *Allegory of Love*, p. 30.

[59] See E.M. Forster, *Aspects of the Novel* (Pocket Edition) (London, 1958), pp. 43 ff.

[60] See Bunyan, *Pilgrim's Progress*, pp. 23 ff.

[61] R. Sharrock, "Spiritual Autobiography in *The Pilgrim's Progress*," *RES* 24 (1948): 114, interprets the "Wicket-gate" as the entrance to the community of the faithful.

[62] Bunyan, *Pilgrim's Progress*, p. 51.

[63] *Ibid.*, p. 11.

[64] *Ibid.*, pp. 79 f.

[65] *Ibid.*, pp. 136 ff.

[66] *Ibid.*, p. 138.

[67] *Ibid.*, p. 149.

[68] *Ibid.*, p. 145.

[69] See also, W.F. Schirmer, *Antike, Renaissance and Puritanismus* (Munich, 1924), pp. 209 f., and W. Kayser, "Die Anfänge des modernen Romans im 18.Jahrhundert und seine heutige Krise," *Deutsche Vierteljahrsschrift für Literaturwissenschaft und Geistesgeschichte* 28 (1954): 434.

[70] Bunyan, *Pilgrim's Progress*, p. 125.

[71] *Ibid.*, p. 128.

SELECTED EXAMPLES OF CRITICAL STUDIES

[72] Ibid., pp. 129 f.

[73] Re the form of the exemplary narrative, see Lugowski, Form der Individualität, pp. 139 ff.

[74] E. Dabcovich, "Syntaktische Eigentümlichkeiten der Fioretti," in Syntactica und Stilistica (Festschrift für Ernst Gamillscheg) (Tübingen, 1957), p. 100.

[75] Bunyan, Pilgrim's Progress, p. 15.

[76] See Talon, John Bunyan, pp. 165 f.

[77] Bunyan, Pilgrim's Progress, p. 15.

[78] Ibid., pp. 47 ff.

[79] Ibid., p. 107.

[80] Ibid., p. 111.

[81] Ibid., pp. 119 ff.

[82] Ibid., pp. 153 f.

[83] See Schirmer, Antike, Renaissance und Puritanismus, p.209.f. and Sharrock,"Spiritual Autobiography," pp. 102ff., who looks at Pilgrim's Progress entirely from the standpoint of the conduct-book.

[84] Schirmer, Antike, Renaissance und Puritanismus, p. 200.

[85] See H. Golder, "Bunyan and Spenser," PMLA 45 (1930): 216, who also discusses the difficult problem of sources.

[86] See Talon, John Bunyan, p. 173.

[87] Birkner, Heilsgewissheit und Literatur, pp. 109 and 150.

[88] Ibid., p. 152,

[89] Lukács, "Theorie des Romans," p. 394.

[90] Ibid., pp. 260 f.

The Implied Reader: Patterns of Communication in Prose Fiction from Bunyan to Beckett (Baltimore: John Hopkins Univ. Press, 1974), pp. 1-28.

SELECTED EXAMPLES

OF CRITICAL STUDIES

BUNYAN AND THE HOLY COMMUNITY

JOHN R. KNOTT, JR.

The second part of The Pilgrim's Progress has always been over-shadowed by the more engaging story of Christian's uneven spiritual progress toward the New Jerusalem. Bunyan's sequel lacks the dramatic force of the first part and will never be as widely read, yet it presents dimensions of spiritual life that he was unable to explore in his account of Christian's solitary pilgrimage. Recent critics have characterized Part II as, among other things, a study of the corporate rather than the individual aspects of Christian life, a "novel of manners" rather than a "novel of character or action," and a picture of the "cheerful" life of a separatist church rather than of the agony of Christian.[1] The dominant emphasis of this criticism has been upon the differences between the two parts and the ways in which they are complementary. More recently, N.H. Keeble has argued for the unity of the work as a whole.[2] We have come far enough from the earlier tendency to deprecate Part II as a work for women and children to be able to recognize the value of diverse critical approaches, emphasizing its continuity with Part I as well as its distinctive differences. My own approach will emphasize the contrasts between the two parts and, especially, Bunyan's concern with the nature and importance of the Christian community in Part II, a concern that becomes increasingly prominent in his late writings. One needs to step back from the work to consider Bunyan's sense of the holy community more broadly to appreciate the ways in which it functions in Part II.

In the later stages of his career John

AN OVERVIEW

Bunyan presents a strikingly different figure from the one that emerges in his spiritual autobiography, Grace Abounding to the Chief of Sinners (1666). In that relatively early work one sees the young Bunyan blown from terror to joy and back until he emerges from his spiritual storms with confidence in his saving faith. In the period of his ministry that he summarizes in Grace Abounding, Bunyan remains vulnerable to fears and temptations. He recounts how as a preacher he was driven to seek out "in the darkest places in the Countrey" those still in the condition from which he had just escaped, laboring "to find out such a Word as might, if God would bless it, lay hold of and awaken the Conscience" (84). Bunyan's evangelical emphasis on "awakening and converting Work," though never wholly lost, yielded in the last decade of his life to a concern with the nature and spiritual health of the Christian community. Many who had felt the awakening power of the Word looked to him for assurance that would quiet their doubts and provide guidance that would help them to live godly lives.

In the eighties Bunyan was known as the author of the widely read first part of The Pilgrim's Progress (1678) and as a popular preacher to Independent and Baptist congregations as well as to his own Bedford meeting. When he preached in London, he drew large crowds, including at times John Owen and other leading Independents. His congregations were made up largely of the converted seeking to confirm and strengthen their faith. Bunyan had by this time become a formidable preacher of assurance.[3] His Come and Welcome to Jesus Christ (1681), on John 6:37 ("All that the father giveth me shall come to me; and him that cometh to me I will in no wise cast out"), argues the power of Christ to "execute his word" and the mercy of God toward lost sheep. It concludes with a series of "encouragements" to believe in the reality of grace, including a memorable image of the soul experiencing "a sweet and still gale of the Spirit of God": "Thou ridest at those times as upon the wings of the wind, being carried out beyond thyself, beyond the most of thy prayers, and also above all thy fears and temptations."[4] Other works from this period describe the organization and life of the church and speak to the condition of its members.[5] Bunyan's growing concern with the Christian community takes various forms in the major imaginative works of the eighties: The Life and Death of Mr. Badman (1680), The Holy War (1682) and the second part of The Pilgrim's Progress (1684).

Modern readers of Bunyan are likeliest to know the two works that best dramatize the fears and trials of the individual Christian seeking salvation, Grace Abounding and the first part of The Pilgrim's Progress. The mixture of uncertainty and emotional intensity that these works present in their different ways produces a kind of dramatic tension that Bunyan never matched in his other imaginative writing. The individual struggles would make no sense, however, without a defining context, and Bunyan established this by creating powerful images of the ideal community which the individual Christian seeks to join. The ultimate form of this is of course the New Jerusalem with its fellowship of saints in the presence of God, for which Christian flees the City of Destruction. More immediately, it is the holy community of the faithful in this world, and this is what increasingly attracted Bunyan's attention.

In Grace Abounding Bunyan describes the critical influence of his chance sight of several poor women of Bedford "sitting at a door in the sun, and talking about the things of God." The scene prints on his mind a haunting image of the satisfactions of the godly life: "And me thought they spake as if joy did make them speak: they spake with such pleasantness of Scripture language, and with such appearance of grace in all they said, that they were to me as if they had found a new world, as if there were people that dwelt alone, and were not to be reckoned among their Neighbours, Num. 23.9."[6] The moment is transformed in his vision of the women "on the Sunny side of some high Mountain" (19) while he shrinks below in the cold, then struggles through a gap in the wall to join them in the sun. This episode dramatizes Bunyan's sense of the inadequacy of his earliest religious experience and provides an allegorical statement, repeated in the image of the wicket gate of The Pilgrim's Progress, of the way to salvation through Christ. Bunyan describes the mountain as "the church of the living God" and the sun as "the comfortable shining of his merciful face."

The key elements of this early image of the church are the separateness of the elect from the rest of the world and their experience of joyful fellowship under the influence of divine favor. It is complemented by the image of the heavenly church in Hebrews (12:22-24) that confirms Bunyan's assurance of salvation and forms the climax to the first part of his narrative: "Ye are come to mount Zion, to the City of the living God, to the heavenly Jerusalem, and to an innumerable company of Angels, to the general assembly and Church of the firstborn, which are written in heaven, and to God the Judge of all, and to the spirits of just men made perfect" (82). Bunyan develops the scene sketched here at the conclusion of the first part of The Pilgrim's Progress, drawing upon Isaiah and Revelation as well as Hebrews to represent the fellowship of the saints that Christian joins upon the completion of his pilgrimage. The narrative insists upon the reality of this transcendent community of the blessed who enjoy actual communion with God and express their joy in melodious praise. Christian's experience in the New Jerusalem simply overwhelms his memories of Vanity Fair, Bunyan's version of the self-centered and violent city of man.

Bunyan's vision of the poor people of Bedford on their mountaintop offers a figurative representation of the independent church of Bedford, first led by John Gifford and eventually, after 1672, by Bunyan himself. An entry in the Church Book describes the gathering in 1650 of godly people of the town "zealous according to their light, not only to edify themselves, but also to propagate the Gospell, and help it forward."[7] They were responding to the biblical imperative that underlay a separatist tradition in England reaching back to the gathered churches of Robert Browne and Henry Barrow in the late sixteenth century: "Wherefore come out from among

SELECTED EXAMPLES OF CRITICAL STUDIES

them, and be ye separate, saith the Lord" (2 Cor. 6:17).[8] The Christians of Bedford who had joined together to worship as they chose welcomed others who could satisfy the congregation "of the truth of the work of grace in their heartes."[9] As required by other Independent or Baptist churches, newcomers had to give sufficient evidence of their faith and holiness to be accepted as "visible saints." Lapses from holiness could lead to disciplinary action including, for extreme cases, expulsion from the congregation.

Bunyan became a vigorous defender of the principle of separation and the purity of the fellowship of the elect. He appealed primarily to the example of the New Testament churches to justify his insistence upon a congregation of the godly: "I dare not have [church] communion with them that profess not faith and holiness; or that are not visible saints by calling."[10] His severe ideal of purity, fostered by Old Testament as well as New Testament texts, led him to condemn communion with the "open profane" as polluting God's ordinances, violating His law, profaning His holiness, and defiling His people.[11] Following Paul, he saw "the word of faith and holiness" as the spiritual rule that distinguished the "children of Abraham," superseding the ritual of circumcision: "This is the gospel concision knife, sharper than any two-edged sword ... by which New Testament saints are circumcised in heart, ears, and lips."[12] Bunyan supported the ordinances of baptism and the Lord's supper, at least "in their first and primitive institution," but he argued against the Particular Baptist claim that baptism should be a condition for admission to the church.[13] He found baptism in the Holy Spirit sufficient. In fact, Bunyan deplored doctrinal disputes among Presbyterians, Independents, and Baptists; he urged unity in the church. Maintaining the separation of the godly from the ungodly was his real concern.

Bunyan's sense of the elect as a separate community whose purity must be guarded helps to explain the treatment in his imaginative works of the ungodly and those of insufficient faith. In *The Holy War* Emmanuel refuses any compromise that would permit the Diabolonians to remain in contact with Mansoul, much less live there. Inhabitants convicted of being followers of Diabolus are put to death. In The Pilgrim's Progress Bunyan defines the godly community in part by his exclusions. One could compile a long list of those who cannot meet the tests of faith and holiness and thus will never become true pilgrims, including the faint-hearted (Timorous), the openly skeptical (Atheist), and those who profess religion (Talkative, By-Ends) but show themselves unwilling to act upon it in the radical way that Bunyan's faith demanded. Christian's abrupt departure from the City of Destruction dramatizes the need to come out of the world, and his experience in Vanity Fair reveals the continuing need to set oneself against it.

In the second part Madam Bubble represents the sensuous allure of "this vain World," with its promise of wealth and luxurious life, which Stand-fast must reject absolutely if he is to continue in the way of faith. Bunyan's defense of his conception of faith and holiness can seem harsh to modern readers, many of whom have been troubled by the exclusion of Ignorance at the gate of Heaven. Occasionally one is startled by a sudden shift of tone, as when Mercy says of Simple, Sloth, and Presumption, hung up in irons for hindering pilgrims in their way: "let them hang and their Names Rot, and their Crimes live for ever against them."[14] Here as often in Bunyan the harshness can be traced to the Bible.[15] Bunyan found ample biblical warrant for rigor in the defense of holiness.

In The Life and Death of Mr. Badman, written as a sequel to the first part of The Pilgrim's Progress, Bunyan anatomized the ways of the ungodly and by contrast illuminated the life of the godly. Badman's manifold sins can be traced to his early rejection of godly influences and his continuing association with bad companions. Bunyan says of his youth that he "wanted not good Books, nor good Instruction, nor good Sermons, nor good Examples."[16] Fundamentally, Badman rejects the "rule of the Word," which Bunyan pictures as providing comprehensive directions for holy living, even including standards for the honest management of business. Badman errs in

SELECTED EXAMPLES OF CRITICAL STUDIES

shutting himself off from "wholsom words" of Christian counsel and the influence of the Word as expounded by ministers. One of the most flagrant sins is forbidding the pious wife he tricked into marrying him to go to sermons. As Bunyan puts it, he "robbed her of the Word of God" (77). In his proud scorn for Scripture as well as for good advice, Badman can be rescued from sin only if "God shall smite him in his conscience by the Word" (126). His unrepentant death, body and soul worn out by a life of sin, forms the inevitable conclusion to Bunyan's moral tale. The reader is left with this lurid example and the author's injunction to "gravely enquire concerning thy self by the Word, whether thou art one of his [Badman's] linage or no" (4).

The outlines of the godly society from which Badman falls away and against the background of which his sins stand out so boldly emerge more clearly in Bunyan's works of practical divinity. This society is made up of those to whom the Gospel has come not "in word only" but in power; they attempt to walk "in and after the Spirit." In his Christian Behaviour (1674) Bunyan assumes that its members will keep to their rank and station, like flowers "that stand and grow where the gardener hath planted them."[17] With others in the Puritan tradition, he saw the Bible as governing the behavior of members of the household toward each other, and he derived a series of "duties" from it. His expectations for the head of the family are very like those for a minister. He should be sound in doctrine, "exemplary in faith and holiness," and able to pray and preach so that servants and children will be brought "under subjection to the word of God."[18] Among the examples he cites are Abraham in the Old Testament and Gaius in the New.

In Christian Behaviour and subsequently in The Holy Life Bunyan emphasized the importance of holy living, insisting that "good works do flow from faith."[19] One is not saved by works, but they give evidence of the nature of one's faith. Identifying the signs of true faith was one of the preoccupations of Puritan ministers and their congregations. Bunyan questions whether "that can be called a justifying faith that has not as

131

its fruit good works."[20] If one plants in the sinner "good doctrine" and lets it be "watered by the word of grace," one can expect the "fruits of holiness."[21] Bunyan's rules for godly living and his descriptions of the working of grace assume the interdependence of members of the community, acting toward each other in charity and fostering each other's spiritual growth. Near the end of Christian Behaviour he offers a persuasive metaphoric statement of the ideal: "The doctrine of the gospel is like the dew and the small rain that distilleth upon the tender grass, wherewith it doth flourish, and is kept green. Deut. 32.2. Christians are like the several flowers in a garden, that have upon each of them the dew of heaven, which being shaken with the wind, they let fall their dew at each other's roots, whereby they are jointly nourished, and become nourishers of one another."[22]

Bunyan's most effective representations of the life of the holy community, and the spiritual sustenance and joy this affords, are the idealized versions of this life found in the imaginative works, particularly in the second part of The Pilgrim's Progress. Before looking more closely at these, however, it is important to recognize a corollary of Bunyan's insistence upon separation, his conviction that following the dictates of the Word can be expected to lead to suffering: "persecution always attends the word, that of the tongue or that of the sword."[23] Bunyan could speak from experience, of course, having spent twelve years in Bedford gaol for refusing to stop the preaching that he believed the Bible commanded, even when this was forbidden by law. He had seen the consequences for nonconformists of a series of laws that imposed heavy penalties upon those who engaged in any kind of worship other than that according to the Book of Common Prayer.[24] In the letter to the reader with which he prefaced Mr. Badman Bunyan casts himself in a role like that of the apostles bringing truth to the ungodly: "Christ sends his Lambs in the midst of Wolves, not to do like them but to suffer by them for bearing plain testimony against their deeds."[25]

Like other nonconformist ministers, Bunyan

felt the need to justify the suffering of his people at a time when many of them were imprisoned or stripped of their possessions by severe laws, applied unevenly. In Seasonable Counsel: Or Advice to Sufferers (1684) he demonstrates that "the people of God are a suffering people" and shows why and how suffering should be endured. He could argue that suffering should be borne patiently because he believed that it was invariably sent by God for a reason and that it could not touch the soul. Bunyan reminded his readers that their persecutors were subject to the power of God: "God's bridle is upon them. God's hook is in their nose ... God hath determined the bounds of their rage."[26] He saw those who suffered for truth in his own day sustained by God as their predecessors had been. Foxe's stories of the Marian martyrs "who could shout for joy, and clap their hands in the very flames for joy"[27] furnished a precedent to which he appealed repeatedly. In fact, Bunyan looked back with some nostalgia to the Marian period and the early days of Puritanism that followed as a heroic time in which one could see "another life than is now among men, another kind of conversation than now is among professors."[28] The ultimate precedents were biblical, heroes such as Daniel in the Old Testament and, most important, martyrs of the apostolic church such as Peter, Paul, and Stephen. The tradition was a living one for Bunyan, made vivid by his own experience of persecution in what he came to see as the dangerous "last days." In justifying his refusal to stop preaching to "private meetings" he cited to his examiners the case of Paul, "often in prison."[29]

Bunyan's most important efforts to render the life of the holy community can be found in the second part of The Pilgrim's Progress, which both complements the first part and extends its range. While the experience of Christiana and her companions depends critically upon Christian's and inevitably falls short of the intensity of that experience, Christiana exemplifies a kind of spirituality in some ways richer than Christian's. In Part I Bunyan emphasized the terrors and uncertainties of the way. In Part II he offered a message of assurance to the whole

Christian community. The greater confidence of the pilgrims in Part II, reinforced by the presence of Great-heart and nurtured by the welcome that they receive along the way, makes possible a kind of uninterrupted growth in holiness that one could not really expect of Christian. In Part II examples of fellowship and communal life stand out rather than solitary confrontations with spiritual enemies. We remember the support members of the company of pilgrims give each other in crossing the Valley of the Shadow of Death, the way they draw strength from their communal experience at the house of Gaius, the dignity and mutual concern with which they meet death. To grasp the character of Part II one needs to understand both the experience of the individual in this version of the fundamental Christian pilgrimage and the ways in which this depends upon the life of the community. The two most important stories in Part II are the interrelated ones of Christiana and Mercy, the key figures around whom the community of pilgrims develops.

Monsignor Knox's famous comment,"Christian goes on a pilgrimage, Christiana on a walking tour,"[30] has enough truth to it to bear repeating. Christiana's journey is leisurely, with prolonged stays in the various places where she finds shelter, and she enjoys a kind of guidance and protection that make it seem unlikely that she will succumb to attackers or wander out of the way. Yet one should not ignore the trials that she and her companions face. She must learn that "'The bitter is before the sweet'" (180), and she is reminded more than once of the need to be wary, by her own experience and that of others, such as Heedless, whose cases serve as object lessons for pilgrims. Great-heart wards off real dangers, sometimes with difficulty, as in his prolonged battle with the Giant Maul. Valiant-for-Truth's bloody story of fighting off thieves, armed with the sword of the Spirit, makes him an even better exemplar of Christian warfare than Christian himself: "I fought till my Sword did cleave to my Hand, and when they were joyned together, as if a Sword grew out of my Arm, and when the Blood run thorow my Fingers, than I fought with most Courage" (291).

SELECTED EXAMPLES OF CRITICAL STUDIES

One key difference between Christian and those who follow him is the greater certainty of the latter. Valiant-for-Truth shows none of the doubt that makes Christian vulnerable. Christiana, though capable of fear, remains confident that she can follow the way marked by her husband, particularly because she knows that help is available from Great-heart and other defenders. Old Honest bluntly characterizes the way in response to a question about how the country is affected toward the pilgrims: "It happens to us, as it happeneth to Way-fairing men; sometimes our way is clean, sometimes foul; sometimes up-hill, sometimes down-hill; We are seldom at a Certainty" (275). If they were wholly certain of what to expect, the pilgrims would have no need to exercise faith. Yet the uncertainty of Part II has more to do with the nature of the "Rubs" they will encounter, to use Honest's word for the difficulties of the way, than with where they must go and whether they will get there. The song that these pilgrims sing after leaving the shepherds of the Delectable Mountains reflects their cheerful assumption that God will make possible an orderly progress toward the end they seek:

> Behold, how **fitly** are the Stages set!
> For their Relief, that Pilgrims are become:
> And how they us receive without one let,
> That make the **other** Life our **Mark** and Home.
> (289)

In the second part the Bible functions more characteristically as a guide than as a weapon. When the pilgrims come to the Enchanted Ground, "a place at which a man is apt to lose his Way" (297), Great-heart consults his "Map" and saves them from the pit just ahead. A little farther on he gets them through the darkness by lighting his lantern, another symbol for the Word of God.

Readers have been quick to note the greater ease with which Christiana and her party traverse places where Christian faced great danger. In the Valley of Humiliation, to take the most obvious example, she finds a delightful pastoral scene instead of Apollyon blocking the path. To her it appears "fat Ground,"with meadows "beautified with Lillies" (237) and grazed by sheep. Viewed from the perspective of Christian's adventure, the episode appears anticlimactic. The trials of the proud will always make better drama than the satisfactions of the humble. Yet Bunyan attempted something quite different in Part II, exploring the implications of a spiritual state beyond the reach of Christian through a kind of folk pastoral. The fertility of the valley serves as a metaphorical statement of the effects of the grace enjoyed by the humble, suggesting that they will be fruitful in the good works that Bunyan saw as flowing from a vital faith. Biblical landscape shades into something reminiscent of Elizabethan pastoral with the song of his shepherd boy:[31]

> He that is down, needs fear no fall,
> He that is low, no Pride:
> He that is humble, ever shall
> Have God to be his Guide.
> I am content with what I have,
> Little be it, or much.
>
> (238)

Great-heart observes that he "lives a merrier Life," and "wears more of that Herb called Hearts-ease in his Bosom, then he that is clad in Silk and Velvet." Bunyan here blends traditional pastoral contentment, arising from the "otium" of literary Arcadias, with the Pauline "peace of God."

Great-heart notes that these meadows where Christ loved to walk foster the contemplative life: "Here a man shall be free from the Noise, and from the hurryings of this Life; all States are full of Noise and Confusion, only the Valley of Humiliation is that empty and Solitary Place. Here a man shall not be so let and hindred in his Contemplation, as in other places he is apt to be" (238). The implication is that pilgrims should be capable of meditation as well as struggle, and that they can create mental space for this through the practice of humility. Bunyan's Valley functions as a natural part of the way of the pilgrim rather than as a pastoral refuge from

SELECTED EXAMPLES OF CRITICAL STUDIES

heroic striving of the sort that Calidore finds in the sixth book of The Faerie Queene. He suggests that pilgrims can retreat from the noise and hurry of the world to contemplate God, growing in holiness in the process, without threatening the quest for the New Jerusalem. In his view of Christian life, pastoral and heroic modes of experience are perfectly compatible.

The greater ease of the journey in Part II reflects a general shift of emphasis away from the doubt and despair that may afflict the individual pilgrim to the benefits of a more secure faith and the ways in which such a faith is nurtured, chiefly through spiritual guidance and the support provided by other Christians. Christiana and Mercy find the steps across the Slough of Despond without difficulty, escaping the despair that engulfed Christian early in his journey. They are so far from despair in the later stages of their pilgrimage that Doubting Castle poses no threat and can in fact be destroyed by Greatheart. The contrast between Christiana's departure and Christian's establishes a critical difference in tone early in Part II. Although she is stricken as he was with a sense of sin and of the hopelessness of her present state, compounded in her case by guilt at having ignored her husband's plea to follow him, she is summoned by Secret with his message of pardon from God, and an invitation: "He also would have thee know that he inviteth thee to come into his presence, to his Table, and that he will feed thee with the Fat of his House, and with the Heritage of Jacob thy Father" (179). This striking introduction of the divine presence, quite different from anything in Part I, makes for the beginnings of an assurance impossible for Christian at a comparable point. Christiana receives a letter from God with a promise of the joy of the heavenly city, Christian a parchment from Evangelist with a command to "'Fly from the wrath to come'" (10). Christiana's dream of Christian bliss, reinforced by Secret, powerfully supports her resolve to break with the old life. The example of his success overcomes potential doubts and ensures an eager welcome for her and her party at those places that harbor pilgrims.

AN OVERVIEW

Given the various ways in which Christiana is encouraged, one does not expect her to undergo the crises that Christian does or to show a comparably dramatic spiritual development; yet she does mature in faith and holiness as she moves through the stages of her pilgrimage.[32] At a relatively early point she proves her courage by defying Giant Grim and his lions, in the company of Great-heart to be sure. The words with which she declares her resolve to stay in the "kings High-way" come from the Song of Deborah (Judges 5:7): "Now I am Risen as Mother in Israel" (219). With this act of self-assertion, she establishes her identity as a true pilgrim and one of the children of Abraham. Such heroism is not typical, however. Mainly, we observe Christiana learning to be watchful and to seek help when she needs it. We also see her growing in knowledge and extending the range of her affections. After Great-heart's explanation of Christ's sacrifice, she professes her heart "ten times more lightsome and joyous" and demonstrates a new capacity for devotion: "Oh! thou loving one, Oh! thou Blessed one" (212).

One of Christiana's most important functions is to serve as an example for Bunyan's female readers. In leading her children through to Beulah she justifies Gaius's praise of women as "sharers with us in the Grace of Life" (261) and fulfils the role that those who greet her along the way expect her to play: "Come in thou Wife of that Good Man, come in thou Blessed Woman" (221). The spiritual odyssey of her young friend Mercy holds more real interest, however, and better illustrates the skill at representing the experience of the more timid pilgrims that Bunyan shows in Part II. Mercy receives no special call and must depend initially upon Christiana's encouragement. She is so apprehensive about her reception at the wicket gate that she faints. Her progress from fearfulness to joy, and from illustrating the comprehensiveness of divine mercy to exemplifying mercy herself, is the most engaging in the second part.[33]

Two encounters figure importantly in Mercy's spiritual development, the first with the Keeper of the Gate and the second with the Interpreter.

SELECTED EXAMPLES OF CRITICAL STUDIES

In both instances her fear that she will prove unworthy temporarily disables her, and in both the gentleness of her host overcomes this fear. The most striking thing about the first scene is that this host is revealed to be Christ rather than Good Will, who welcomed Christian. As in The Holy War, where Emmanuel receives the trembling emissaries of Mansoul and forgives them, Bunyan boldly brings Christ into the action to dramatize the extent of divine mercy. The individual encounter in the second part of The Pilgrim's Progress is more intimate, with Christ gently reviving Mercy and questioning her about her coming: "Then he took her again by the Hand, and led her gently in, and said: I pray for all them that believe on me, by what means soever they come unto me" (190). The situation and the attitudes expressed are reminiscent of Herbert's "Love III." Mercy is transformed from someone who stood before the gate with her spirit struggling "betwixt life and death" to an assured pilgrim who can fall before her Lord and worship with fluent praise. The scene works largely because of Bunyan's remarkable talent for blending the numinous and the ordinary. He shows Mercy and Christiana discussing the happenings at the gate, in the absence of their host, as they might talk over any experience. Mercy subsequently finds a way to satisfy the curiosity of the group about the dog that harassed them at the gate. The pilgrims remain entirely credible because of such natural human reactions.

Mercy's transformation continues, though less dramatically, in her encounter with the Interpreter. Again she falters, unable to respond to his questions about why she came until he tactfully draws her out. The Interpreter's praise of Mercy at the end of his interrogation confirms her identity as a pilgrim by associating her with the Israelites: "Thou are a Ruth, who did ... go with a people she knew not heretofore" (207). Afterwards, Bunyan tells us, she "could not sleep for joy" but lay praising God, so great was her confidence that she would succeed in her pilgrimage. Mercy's dream in the House Beautiful, in which she fears the hardening of her heart and then sees herself comforted by an angel, suggests a lingering concern. The clear direction of her evolution, however, is toward greater assurance and the fruitfulness of charitable deeds, manifested in her making of clothes for the poor. She grows into the embodiment of mercy, and of other spiritual virtues as well. It is Mercy who expresses the potential for devotion of the Valley of Humiliation: "Here one may think, and break at Heart, and melt in ones Spirit" (239).

Christiana and Mercy cannot be understood in isolation from the group of which they are a part and the sustaining communities that they encounter along the way. Their immediate group begins as a family and evolves, as more pilgrims join their company, into something that Bunyan describes as a church by the end of the work. Christiana defines her role in relation to her children and to Mercy, and in response to the example of Christian. She imagines herself as a "Mother in Israel." Mercy depends upon Christiana, whom she follows like a Ruth. Both of course depend upon their appointed "Conductor," Great-heart, to help them understand the way and ward off its evils. Great-heart, is an idealized version of a minister of a separatist church and perhaps of Bunyan himself in his pastoral role.[34] His solicitude for the pilgrims recalls the preface to Grace Abounding, in which Bunyan, addressing his flock, tells them of "fatherly care and desire after your spiritual and everlasting welfare" and "longing to see your safe arrival into the desired haven." Great-heart's role differs from that of Evangelist in Part I in his responsibility for the continuing welfare and spiritual growth of those he tends. He combines the roles of minister and Christian father, very similar as we have seen, and wins the trust of the pilgrims by his knowledge of the way and his great confidence that spiritual danger can be overcome.

Great-heart performs in some measure the duty that Bunyan, in the preface to Grace Abounding, complained that his imprisonment prevented him from pursuing, the "further edifying and building up in Faith and Holiness" of those for whom he is responsible. Yet Great-heart shares this duty with others, many of whom we have already met in Part I. These tend to play a larger or at least a different role in Part II, given its greater emphasis on edification. The Interpreter presents emblematic scenes to Mercy and Christiana as he had to Christian, but he takes them into new rooms where these are simpler and more suited to their needs and comprehension than the dramatic scenes illustrating the dangers of despair and the demands of Christian warfare that speak to Christian's condition. Some resemble emblems in Bunyan's A Book for Boys and Girls (1686).[35] One in particular, designed to illustrate the various ways God calls His people by showing a hen calling her chicks, suggests that the Interpreter's House offers a homely kind of assurance of divine concern.

In House Beautiful Christian is interrogated at length about his experiences and his intentions and shown "Rarities" that illustrate the heroism in the service of God that he will soon have to demonstrate. Once Christiana gives her name to the Porter she and her company are welcomed with rejoicing, without further questioning. Their month-long stay is marked by Prudence's catechising of the children and their questioning of her, Mercy's courtship by Mr. Brisk, and Matthew's illness and purging. We see what amounts to a stage in the pilgrims' lives, dominated by the Christian education of the children, rather than preparation for specific challenges of the way as with Christian.[36] Piety's act of sending Chrisitiana away with a "Scheme" of what she has seen is characteristic of the emphasis upon the edification in this episode of Part II. The rarities they are shown upon leaving (Eve's apple, Jacob's ladder, the golden anchor that Christiana is given to take with her, Abraham's offering up of Issac) mingle warning, hope, and an exhortation to sacrifice. Their preparation seems designed to strengthen them for Christian living and, by exposing them to a comfortable and loving environment as well as to instruction, to increase their assurance that they are among the elect.

Gaius, a figure drawn from the life of the New Testament church and a major new character in Part II, contributes to the edification of the pilgrims with his riddles and stories.[37] As Christian's host, he provides not only comfort and nourishment but godly discourse on such topics as charity toward the poor and the workings of grace. He also offers the good counsel that leads to the marriage of Matthew and Mercy. The shepherds of the Delectable Mountains play a somewhat different role in Part II, especially welcoming the "Feeble and Weak" to their palace (they only had tents in Part I) and instructing the pilgrims in charity and innocence rather than cautioning them about the perils of the way. They adorn the pilgrims with jewels, as if confirming their holiness, and give Mercy the treasure she craves, the looking glass that represents the Word in its seemingly marvellous capacity to reveal the features and the life of the "Prince of Pilgrims."

Bunyan's pilgrims receive stronger support from such nurturing figures in Part II, and they do more to support each other. Christiana and Mercy, and even Christiana's precociously pious children, contribute to the edifying discourse that accompanies their journey. As the godly family grows to something more like the congregation of the faithful, the circle of the conversation expands to include others such as old Honest, who acts the part of the a wise Elder with his blessings and shrewd observations. The company functions most like a congregation in accepting new pilgrims, not only the strong (Standfast, Valiant-for-Truth) but also those who falter in the way (Feeble-mind, Fearing, Ready-to-halt). Fearing presents the acute case of the spiritual state that Mercy demonstrated earlier, and the fact that Bunyan gives several pages to his story reflects the importance of the problem and its appropriateness to the concerns of Part II. His example gives the other pilgrims, Christiana and Matthew as well as Mercy, the opportunity to recognize their own past fears and Greatheart the chance to comment on the right use of fear, like many a Puritan preacher: "<u>the fear of God is the beginning of Wisdom</u>" (255).

Bunyan's attention in Part II to the problems of the weak, and their need for reassurance and support, has often been noted. By the end of

SELECTED EXAMPLES OF CRITICAL STUDIES

the work he has illustrated both the diversity of the Christian community as he understood it and the solicitude of its members for each other's welfare. In Part II Beulah appears as a wonderfully harmonious "Town" where all pilgrims live out their lives waiting for the summons to cross the river. It remains a lush pastoral setting reflecting the spiritual satisfactions of its inhabitants, as in Part I, but Bunyan's attention has shifted to the communal aspects of life there, including the celebration of new arrivals ("<u>More Pilgrims are come to Town</u>" [303]). Christiana and her company will become part of the "History" of pilgrims' deeds that helps shape the consciousness of the universal church.

The experience of the pilgrims on the road and at the houses in which they are entertained offers numerous glimpses of the life of the separatist church. We see this life in the singing, in the communal meals with their overtones of the Lord's Supper, in the various kinds of godly discourse that contribute to the edification of the pilgrims, in the relationship between the pilgrims and their "Conductor," and in Bunyan's emphasis upon the sustaining fellowship of the godly, united in their opposition to the world's evil and their commitment to growth in holiness. Yet for all Bunyan's apparent realism the composite picture of the church that he presents is a highly idealized one. Some episodes, such as Prudence's catechising of Matthew, seem close to the life of the church Bunyan knew. Others, such as the "Bath sanctification" enjoyed by the pilgrims in the Interpreter's House, belong to the distinctive world of <u>The Pilgrim's Progress</u>. This "Bath" obviously suggests baptism, but it is neither a simple allegory nor a representation of actual practice. The episode owes its power to Bunyan's ability to fuse physical and spiritual experience. Dusty travellers clearly welcome such a bath: "They then went in and washed, yea they and the Boys and all, and they came out of that <u>Bath</u> not only sweet, and clean; but also much enlivened and strengthened in their Joynts" (207). Bunyan makes one believe in the supernatural, here the power of grace to cleanse and strengthen spiritually, by making it seem a natural part of life. By focusing on the pilgrim's experience, their joyful sense of refreshment and renewal, he suggests the spiritual force of baptism without needing to use the word.

The Interpreter's House, House Beautiful, and the Inn of Gaius can all be thought of as representing the church in some sense, but one must look at the experience of the pilgrims in each place to understand its particular character as well as Bunyan's expectations for the life of the church. While their experience in these places has common elements--communal meals, music, instruction, a sense of Christian community--different aspects of the life of the church predominate in each place. The Interpreter's House suggests its mystery, at least as much mystery as Bunyan would allow. The Interpreter himself, with his candle of "Illumination," plays the role of the Holy Spirit.[38] He explains the ways of Christ and plays his traditional role of comforter, providing relief in the form of rest, assurance of election, and a meal that suggests, with its accompanying song, the nurturing presence of God:

> The Lord is only my support,
> And he that doth me feed:
> How can I then want anything
> Whereof I stand in need?
>
> (204)

The greatest mystery surrounds the rituals of purification that conclude the pilgrims' stay in the House of the Interpreter. Following their sanctifying bath, they are marked with a seal that identifies them as "Children of Israel" and then clothed with "<u>fine Linnen, white and clean</u>" (208). The ceremony recalls a similar one in <u>The Holy War</u> in which Emmanuel clothes the inhabitants of Mansoul in the same white linen, described in Revelation (19.8) as "the righteousness of saints."[39] In both instances the garments serve as confirmation of holiness and admonition to practice holy living. Emmanuel makes the admonition explicit in <u>The Holy War</u>: "<u>Keep them always white, for if they be soiled 'tis dishonour to me.</u>" In <u>The Pilgrim's Progress</u>

SELECTED EXAMPLES OF CRITICAL STUDIES

Bunyan concentrates on the response of the pilgrims, struck with wonder and humility by the sudden transformation of their companions. The sum of their experience in the House of the Interpreter, culminating in this symbolic robing, constitutes an initiation into the church.

House Beautiful offers perhaps the fullest view of the ongoing life of the church of all the various "Stages" that mark the pilgrims' journey, certainly of the church in its concern with edification. As we have seen, Prudence, Piety, and Charity confirm and strengthen the pilgrims' understanding of what it means to be a Christian. The sacrament of the Lord's Supper plays a more prominent role in the House Beautiful of Part II. Its communal aspects are suggested by the initial meal of lamb and it efficacy in combating sin by the purging of Matthew with pills made, we are told, from the body and blood of Christ.[40] Music is also more prominent, as Mercy's exclamation makes us aware: "Wonderful! Musick in the House, Musick in the Heart, and Musick also in Heaven, for joy that we are here" (222).

The frequency of song in The Pilgrim's Progress reflects Bunyan's fondness for congregational singing. With Benjamin Keach, who produced the first hymnal, he helped move nonconformist worship beyond the singing of metrical psalms.[41] Mercy's comment gets at the underlying reasons for music's importance to Bunyan, its capacity to express both the joy of holiness and the harmony of heaven and earth. This joy is intensified in Beulah, where bells and trumpets "continually sound so Melodiously" that the pilgrims cannot sleep and yet are refreshed as if they had. It is perfected when they join the saints praising God in heaven. Bunyan's preoccupation with hearing helps to explain the significance of music in The Pilgrim's Progress. Characters in his imaginative works are beset by the hideous noises associated with evil and saved by the thundering of preachers or by the text that sounds the voice of God in the inner ear. Those who have truly heard the word naturally express their praise and celebrate their victories in song, demonstrating their holiness by this capacity for making a joyful noise.[42]

AN OVERVIEW

In the Inn of Gaius, and also in the house of Mr. Mnason in Vanity Fair,[43] the pilgrims experience their strongest sense of the Christian fellowship that Bunyan associated with the church. These two figures from the apostolic period bring into focus the ideal that stands behind Bunyan's various representations of the holy community in The Pilgrim's Progress: the primitive church. The "passionate desire to recover the inner life of New Testament Christianity" that Geoffrey Nuttall finds in the Independents characterizes Bunyan as well.[44] In the responses of the pilgrims and those who shelter them to each other one sees the emphasis on charity of the primitive church. Honest salutes the pilgrims with the "holy Kiss of charity" urged by Paul.[45] Bunyan shows the pilgrims greeted with a kiss at House Beautiful and adds a marginal note: "Christians love is kindled at the sight of one another" (221). Gaius and Mnason exemplify charity with their hospitality; at Gaius's "Inn" pilgrims are not allowed to pay. Bunyan's references to peace, as in the words of the angel who appears in Mercy's dream, "Peace be to thee" (222), also recall the early church.[46]

The world of Bunyan's pilgrims, with its communities of faithful planted in a hostile environment, strongly suggest that of the early Christians. Their progress from one to another of these holy communities recalls the journeys of Paul described in Acts. Although they do not share Paul's evangelical mission, they do stimulate the faith of those who shelter them, particularly the Christians of Vanity Fair. The pilgrims linger with Mnason and his friends, becoming a part of the life of the community, and are finally sent on their journey, as Paul was by the inhabitants of Melita, "laded ... with such things as was necessary" (Acts 28:10). Bunyan's pilgrims must also be prepared to suffer for their special calling, as Paul and the apostles did. In the prefatory verses to Part II he emphasizes this implication of the life of faith and shows a robust confidence in the outcome of the pilgrims' struggles:

Tell them that they have left their House and Home

SELECTED EXAMPLES OF CRITICAL STUDIES

> Are turned Pilgrims, seek a World to come:
> That they have met with hardships in the way,
> That they do meet with troubles night and Day;
> That they have trod on Serpents, fought with Devils,
> Have also overcome a many evils.
> (167)

Gaius links Christian and his progenitors to the original stock ("their Ancestors dwelt first at Antioch" [260]) and the early martyrs, beginning with Stephen and including Ignatius and Polycarp, that Foxe had celebrated. The story of Faithful's martyrdom, indebted to Foxe as well as to contemporary criminal trials,[47] belongs to this tradition. In Part II the threat of persecution has subsided, reflecting an easing of the actual restrictions on nonconformists, but the sense of belonging to an embattled elect is crucial to the experience of fellowship that the pilgrims find with Gaius and Mnason. The faithful in Vanity Fair are still "few," Mnason tells them, and the godly friends who gather at his house stress the need for watchfulness and courage. Their militant spirit is exemplified by their readiness to join with Great-heart in battling the local monster, who suggests the growing menace of Catholicism.

The supper that the pilgrims share with Gaius is the most prominent example of the communal meals that they enjoy throughout their journey and that anticipate "the Feast that our Lord will make for us when we come to his House" (262), as Gaius puts it. This supper suggests the communal meals recounted in Acts and New Testament "feasts of charity" as well as the observation of the Lord's Supper described by Paul.[48] Although the pilgrims drink "the Juice of the true Vine," the meal becomes much more than a simple allegory of the Lord's Supper. It begins with portions of sacrificial offerings traditionally due the priest of Israel, which Bunyan associates with David and hence with the tradition of praising God. Most of the foods the pilgrims enjoy suggest some form of divine nurture.[49] Nuts and the dish of milk given the children point to the nurturing properties of the Word. The simple foods that Isaiah saw as the dish of the Lord, butter and honey, become a means to the knowledge of good and evil. Gaius offers apples with verses adapted from the Song of Solomon which play on the traditional reading of that work as an allegory of the marriage of Christ and the church.

<u>Drink of his Flagons then, thou, Church, his Dove,</u>[50]
<u>And eat his Apples, who are sick of Love.</u>
(262)

These apples, which affirm the goodness of nature despite the fall, suggest not only divine nurture but an intimacy with God that looks forward to the pilgrims' enjoyment of the divine presence in heaven.

Bunyan's pilgrims are drawn progressively into the life of the church as they are sanctified, instructed, nurtured, and supported by those they encounter in the "godly mansions" that mark the stages of their journey. By the time they arrive in Beulah they themselves offer a powerful example of the life of the holy community. When they reach the Delectable Mountains, they have already grown in number to the point where the shepherds, "seeing so great a train following Mr. <u>Great-heart</u>," comment on the "goodly Company" (284). As the final trial of the Enchanted Ground illustrates, they have learned to care for each other and to trust to their guide, who himself trusts to the Word to show the way through darkness and rough ground. The last song ("What Danger is the Pilgrim in ..." [303]) celebrates their collective victory as well as that of Stand-fast over Madam Bubble, and also reflects the watchfulness that no Puritan could afford to lose, even in the state of holiness suggested by their presence in Beulah.

The way the pilgrims meet death offers the best illustration of the kind of community they have become. At the conclusion of Part I Bunyan focuses on the fears of Christian as he enters the river and, more insistently, on the glories of the city on the other side. In Part II he emphasizes a succession of brave deaths, stressing the way each person to be summoned takes his or her leave of the community. One is struck by the dignity of these leavetakings and by the mingling of natural grief and rejoicing in the reactions of those who remain behind. The manner of those who are summoned is disarmingly natural, particularly that of Christiana: "however the Weather is in my Journey, I shall have time enough when I come there to sit down and rest me, and dry me" (305). Yet the episode itself is highly stylized.[51] Those who cross the river receive a divine summons validated by a token (usually a verse from Ecclesiastes), make bequests, and speak last words to the attending community of friends. Our sense of the orderliness of the episode and the fitness of such deaths owes a great deal to these repetitions.

Bunyan's use of passages from Ecclesiastes is especially effective. The images themselves offer powerful symbols of mortality: "<u>I have broken thy golden Bowl, and loosed thy silver Cord,</u>" "<u>Thy Wheel is broken at the Cistern,</u>" "<u>All thy Daughters of Musick shall be brought low.</u>" Yet Bunyan created an atmosphere radically different from that of Ecclesiastes, with its gloomy emphasis upon the vanity of human activity and the unpredictability of death: "so are the sons of men [like birds] snared in an evil time, when it falleth suddenly upon them."[52] Man "knoweth not his time" in The Pilgrim's Progress as in Ecclesiastes, but Bunyan makes the time of death seem right when it comes. The summons is both comprehensible and acceptable to the pilgrims. There is no surprise, or despair, because they are ready and with Christian hope anticipate the joys of the heavenly city on the other side. The strength of their faith enables them to meet death courageously and to find apt words with which to take their leave.

Sir Charles Firth once observed that the farewell speeches of Bunyan's pilgrims were probably suggested by those of Foxe's Marian martyrs.[53] The influence of Foxe in the final scenes of Part II is in fact larger than Firth's astute observation suggests and deserves more comment. Foxe's accounts of the Protestant martyrs established a widely familiar pattern for courageous and holy dying. Bunyan imitated aspects of the pattern (the examination, the cruelty of the executioners) in presenting the martyrdom of Faithful. In Part II he adapted it to give the ordinary deaths of the pilgrims some of the heroic qualities of the extraordinary deaths that Foxe reports.

Foxe's martyrs usually receive a summons, give away possessions, offer parting advice in the form of letters that Foxe scrupulously reproduces, and speak a few last words at the stake. Foxe shows most of them ready for their summons, some even eager for it. They typically conquer the terrors of death, in Foxe's retelling, by such actions as kissing the stake and continuing to pray aloud amid the flames. The calmness of Bunyan's pilgrims reflects this tradition. Standfast in particular suggests the martyrs' habit of reassuring the faithful as he speaks from the river of death: "This River has been a Terror to many.... But now methinks I stand easie" (310). Christiana's parting advice recalls the farewell letters of the martyrs. For example, Foxe's George Marsh writes "a certain godly Friend": "Only tarry ye the Lord's leisure; be strong; let your heart be of good comfort; and wait ye still for the Lord."[54] At the stake the martyrs were usually prevented from addressing their supporters, but they did this indirectly through prayer and the witness of their faith. Their last words, usually in the form of a cry to God, offered a pattern that Bunyan may well have imitated, especially in the cases of Christiana and of Stand-fast, whose final words are "Take me, for I come unto thee" (311).[55]

Bunyan would have known accounts of holy dying other than those Foxe provided and may have been influenced by them.[56] Yet Foxe's stories of the Marian martyrs offered the most compelling evidence outside the Bible of individual acts of faith and courage and of the strength of a holy community in a period of fierce persecution. Their spiritual triumph would have recalled for him as for Foxe that of the primitive church, the ultimate model for holy living as well as holy dying. Together with New Testament accounts of the early church Foxe's book established a tradition in which Bunyan could place the holy communities that he and his readers knew firsthand. In

SELECTED EXAMPLES OF CRITICAL STUDIES

the second part of The Pilgrim's Progress he attempted much more than a reworking of Christian's pilgrimage for the benefit of women and children. By shifting his focus from the experience of the individual Christian to that of the community Bunyan could draw upon a side of his own experience, as preacher to separatist churches concerned with the spiritual growth of all their members, and a tradition that could not come into play fully in Part I.

The opportunity of writing another version of his basic story allowed Bunyan to elaborate on the original episodes and add new ones in such a way as to show the importance of the holy community to the individual pilgrim and to distill the essence of the life of this community. The preoccupations that characterize Part II--with the separateness of God's people, the faith and holiness that testify to their distinctiveness, the suffering that their different way entails, the joy arising from their fellowship, their sense of being nurtured by God--testify to Bunyan's pastoral concern with instructing his readers in the ways of holy living and assuring them that they can belong to a living community of the elect. All the pilgrims that we see or hear of in Part II are members of the larger community that constituted the universal church for Bunyan. Those who remain behind in Beulah ("I heard one say, that they were yet alive, and so would be for the Increase of the Church in that Place where they were for a time" [311]) will perpetuate the earthly church. Bunyan's focus on the life of the holy community in this world throughout Part II gives his sequel a special kind of immediacy and human appeal. The second part of The Pilgrim's Progress remains his best testimony to the vitality of the separatist church.

AN OVERVIEW

NOTES

[1] Roland M. Frye, God, Man, and Satan (Princeton, 1960), p. 148; Henri Talon, John Bunyan (London, 1951), p. 219; Roger Sharrock, John Bunyan (London and New York, 1968), p. 138.

[2] "Christiana's Key: The Unity of The Pilgrim's Progress," in The Pilgrim's Progress: Critical and Historical Views, ed. Vincent Newey (Liverpool, 1980), pp. 1-20. Keeble offers a useful review of modern criticism of Part II. See also S.J. Newman, "Bunyan's Solidness," Newey, pp. 225-50, for a discussion of contrasts between Parts I and II, especially with regard to language.

[3] Roger Sharrock comments briefly on the relationship between the emphasis upon mercy and hope in Part II and Bunyan's activities as a preacher. See "Life and Story in The Pilgrim's Progress." The Pilgrim's Progress: Critical and Historical Views, ed. Newey, p. 64.

[4] The Works of John Bunyan, ed. George Offor (Glasgow, 1859), 1. 299. Hereafter cited as Works.

[5] A discourse of the Building, Nature, Excellency, and Government of the House of God (1688); A Holy Life the Beauty of Christianity (1684), Seasonable Counsel: Or Advice to Sufferers (1684).

[6] Grace Abounding to the Chief of Sinners, ed. Roger Sharrock (Oxford, 1962), p. 15.

[7] The Church Book of Bunyan Meeting, 1650-1821, facs. ed. and intro. G.B. Harrison (London, 1928), p. v.

[8] See Edmund Sears Morgan, Visible Saints: The History of a Puritan Idea (New York, 1963), pp. 14ff., and Geoffrey F. Nuttal, Visible

SELECTED EXAMPLES OF CRITICAL STUDIES

Saints: The Congregational Way, 1640-1660 (London, 1957), chap. 1.

[9] Church Book, p. ix.

[10] A Confession of My Faith, And A Reason of my Practice in Worship (1672). Works, II, 602.

[11] Ibid., p. 604.

[12] Ibid., p. 608.

[13] For a careful analysis of Bunyan's thinking on the church, as reflected in his doctrinal writings, see Richard Greaves, John Bunyan (Abingdon, Berkshire, 1969), chap. 5. See also Gordon Campbell, "The Theology of The Pilgrim's Progress," Newey, pp. 25-62, for a discussion of Bunyan and the separatist church.

[14] The Pilgrim's Progress, ed. J.B. Wharey, 2nd ed., rev. Roger Sharrock (Oxford, 1960), p. 204. Quotations from The Pilgrim's Progress are taken from this edition.

[15] Mercy echoes Proverbs 10:7.

[16] The Life and Death of Mr. Badman and The Holy War, ed. John Brown (Cambridge, 1905), p. 43. Quotations from Mr. Badman are taken from this edition.

[17] Works, III, 550.

[18] Works, III, 556-7.

[19] Ibid.

[20] A Holy Life. Works, III, 507.

[21] Christian Behaviour. Works, III, 571.

[22] Works, III, 570.

[23] A Holy Life. Works, III, 523.

[24] Among them the Act of Uniformity, the Con-

venticle Acts of 1664 and 1670, and the Five Mile Act. See Gerald R. Cragg, Puritanism in the Period of the Great Persecution, 1660-1688 (Cambridge, 1957), chap. 1.

[25] See Matt. 10:6 "Behold, I send you forth as sheep in the midst of wolves."

[26] Seasonable Counsel. Works, III, 725.

[27] Works, III, 700. A visitor to Bunyan in Bedford gaol reported that the only book in his library besides the Bible was Foxe's Acts and Monuments. See John Brown, John Bunyan: His Life, Times and Works (London, 1885), p. 54.

[28] A Holy Life. Works, III, 545.

[29] A Relation of my Imprisonment. Grace Abounding, p. 124.

[30] Ronald Knox, Essays in Satire (London, 1928), p. 206.

[31] Sir Charles Firth commented upon the relationship of Bunyan's scene to Elizabethan pastoral in an 1898 introduction to The Pilgrim's Progress. See his Essays Historical and Literary (Oxford, 1938), pp. 159-60.

[32] I would challenge Talon's assertion that "Christiana does not develop at all in her pilgrimage." John Bunyan, p. 162.

[33] See U. Milo Kaufmann's discussion of Mercy's experience as evidence of divine mercy. The Pilgrim's Progress and Traditions in Puritan Meditation (New Haven, 1966), pp. 95-7.

[34] Critics have noted the similarity to Bunyan. See, for example, Talon, John Bunyan, p. 191, and Sharrock, John Bunyan, p. 144.

[35] See Wharey and Sharrock, eds., The Pilgrim's Progress, p. 342n., and Lynn Veach Sadler, John Bunyan (Boston, 1979), chap. 7 passim. Kaufmann, The Pilgrim's Progress and Traditions

SELECTED EXAMPLES OF CRITICAL STUDIES

in Puritan Meditation, pp. 190-5, discusses the scenes in Part II in relation to the tradition of occasional meditation.

[36] Sharrock finds House Beautiful in Part II a "symbol of the communal life of the church" rather than "a preparation for the individual's spiritual warfare." John Bunyan, p. 145.

[37] See Romans 16:23 ("Gaius mine host, and of the whole church, saluteth you") and 3 John, addressed to Gaius, who is praised for walking in the truth and for his charity "before the church" (2, 6).

[38] See James's response to Prudence's question about how the Holy Ghost saves one: "By his Illumination, by his Renovation, and by his Preservation" (224). Critics have commonly identified the Interpreter with the Holy Spirit. R.M. Frye comments that the Interpreter "suggests, rather than represents, the Holy Spirit" and goes on to discuss his function. See God, Man, and Satan, pp. 145 ff. In The Holy War Bunyan describes the "Lord chief Secretary," who represents the Holy Spirit in that work, as "well skill'd in all mysteries" and the chief teacher in "all high and supernatural things." The Holy War, eds. James F. Forrest and Roger Sharrock (Oxford, 1980), p. 139. Conscience, described as "a Minister and a Preacher to the Town of Mansoul," is confined to teaching "all things humane and domestick" (142). Their relationship is akin to that of the Interpreter and Great-heart, represented as serving at the Interpreter's behest.

[39] Forrest and Sharrock, eds., The Holy War, pp. 146-7.

[40] See R.M. Frye's helpful discussion of the sacraments in The Pilgrim's Progress, God, Man, and Satan, pp. 152-8, and also Greaves's exploration of Bunyan's understanding of the sacraments, John Bunyan, pp. 135-45.

[41] See Sharrock, John Bunyan, p. 150, and Horton Davies, Worship and Theology in England:

AN OVERVIEW

From Andrewes to Baxter and Fox, 1603-1690 (Princeton, 1975), pp. 281-5, on Keach and the rise of hymnody.

⁴²The Puritan emphasis on hearing the Word, reflected in the importance attached to preaching, had biblical basis in Romans 10:17: "Faith cometh by hearing." See Kaufmann, The Pilgrim's Progress and Traditions of Puritan Meditation, chap. 10, for a discussion of aural aspects of The Pilgrim's Progress.

⁴³Acts 21:16 refers to "one Mnason of Cyprus, an old disciple, with whom we should lodge."

⁴⁴Visible Saints, p. 3.

⁴⁵See Romans 16:16.

⁴⁶See Paul's customary salutation, "Grace be unto you, and peace" (1 Cor. 1:3), and Christ's "Peace be unto thee" (Luke 24:36). Paul linked charity and peace in his epistle to the Colossians (3:14-15): "And above all these things put on charity, which is the bond of perfectness. And let the peace of God rule in your hearts." The pilgrims are described at the beginning of Part II as going to be with Christian "and his Companions in Peace" (181).

⁴⁷See Wharey and Sharrock, eds., The Pilgrim's Progress, p. 328n.

⁴⁸Acts 2:42, Jude 12, 1 Cor. 10:16. The most relevant passage in Acts comes from the beginning of a description of the life of the primitive church: "And they continued stedfastly in the apostles' doctrine and fellowship, and in the breaking of bread, and in prayers." R.M. Frye, God, Man, and Satan, pp. 157-8, sees the communal meals as indicating "communal support and sharing" and, when they suggest the Lord's Supper, "the Church in communion with God."

⁴⁹The sense of divine nurture runs through Part II and is strikingly apparent in Bunyan's

description of the shepherd by the River of Life, to whom Christiana urges her "Daughters" to commit their children: "that by these Waters they might be housed, harbored, suckered, and nourished, and that none of them might be lacking in the time to come" (280). Marginal references to Jeremiah and Ezekiel invoke God's promises to be a shepherd to the people of Israel.

[50] See Song of Solomon 2:5: "Stay me with flagons, comfort me with apples: for I am sick of love."

[51] John Bunyan, pp. 152-3. Sharrock has called attention to the formulaic character of the final scenes.

[52] Eccles. 9:12.

[53] Essays Historical and Literary, p. 138.

[54] John Foxe, The Acts and Monuments of John Foxe, ed. Rev. Josiah Pratt (London, 1877), 7, 67.

[55] See. for example, Ridley's "Lord, Lord, receive my spirit" Ibid., p. 550. Stephen had said "Lord Jesus, receive my spirit" (Acts 7:59).

[56] Sharrock notes that quoting the twelfth chapter of Ecclesiastes may have become a convention of Puritan death-bed scenes and cites Edward Bagshaw's The Life and Death of Mr. Bolton. John Bunyan, pp. 153, 154n.

VIEWPOINTS ON GRACE ABOUNDING

Robert Bell

... <u>Grace Abounding</u> depicts Bunyan's "castings down and raisings up" (p.2) in the plural, because his process of redemption is a continuous, on-going struggle. Unlike Augustine, with his stunning conversion in the garden, Bunyan never turns a sharply demarcated corner; the encounter between humanity and divinity persists, yielding both the mystery and the ambivalence of the story.... Throughout the narrative, Bunyan appears to inhabit a land mid-way between the city of God and the city of man. He seems to suspect that he remains the vehicle of a metaphor: a man <u>like</u> a saint. Thus he systematically and self-consciously compares himself to the saints and the prophets, as much to test as to affirm his salvation.

In this regard, Bunyan's conception of metaphor is extremely telling, because it expresses a distinctly Puritan attitude toward experience. He seems incessantly and acutely aware as in <u>The Pilgrim's Progress</u>, that "I have used similitudes...."

A comparison between <u>Grace Abounding</u> and <u>The Confessions</u> inevitably invites more general speculation about the subsequent direction of autobiography as a genre. Bunyan wrote at a particularly complicated historical moment, when fervid spiritual ardour jostled with doubts about its efficacy. Between the birth of Bunyan in 1628 and his death in 1688, the values and assumptions men lived by began to shift.... In <u>Grace Abounding</u> we can discern a dim but significant approach to a new state in which both nature and grace are characteristically defined in terms of this world. It is a paradox that this burdensome condition in itself helps account for the rise of secular autobiography in the eighteenth century.

What we recognize as the "modernity" of most autobiographies after Bunyan is, typically, their secular premises and empirical inclinations. The

Augustinian shaping form and spirit which inspired Bunyan deteriorated, leaving prominent vestiges and nostalgic aspirations, but too little force to structure coherent life stories.

From: Bell, Robert. "Metamorphoses of Spiritual Autobiography," ELH (1977): 107-126.

AN OVERVIEW

Anne Hawkins

It is my intent to look at Grace Abounding as a narrative which derives its thematic properties and structural unity from Bunyan's personal experience of conversion--an experience which is itself derivative of existing models in the theology and cultural milieu of seventeenth-century England. In the Varieties of Religious Experience, William James introduces his discussion of conversion by defining it as "the process, gradual or sudden, by which a self hitherto divided, and consciously wrong, inferior and unhappy, becomes unified and consciously right, superior and happy, in consequence of its firmer hold upon religious realities." The distinction which James introduces so casually between the gradual and the sudden has come to be repeated in the literature on the psychology of conversion, with only slight modifications, in book after book. One might be tempted to see this as evidence of the psychologist's tendency (and we are all psychologists) to deal with the unsettling ambiguities of heart and mind by labels, classifications, and categories. But in the case of conversion, these two categories of the gradual and the sudden are not classifications imposed from without, but represent alternative possibilities of response which are inherent in the experience itself. In other words, it is my assumption that these two types of conversion can be treated as morphological categories, each having its own specific form and function. Thus whether the personal experience of conversion conforms to the gradual or the sudden paradigm (or whether it involves both models) becomes crucial in understanding the autobiographical narrative which records that experience.

But perhaps James's most suggestive contribution to the psychology of the two forms of conversion is the analogy he draws between spiritual and physical healing: "The older medicine used to speak of two ways, lysis and crisis, one gradual, the other abrupt, in which one might recover from a bodily disease. In the spiritual realm there are also two ways, one gradual, the other sudden, in which inner unification may occur." The medical matrix from which James draws his terminology of lysis and crisis is important, for conversion is here implicitly defined as spiritual healing, then we might well expect these two models of conversion to function as alternative religious therapies for different spiritual maladies.

. . .

That Bunyan's conversion is an example of the lysis model (James's gradual, educative type of spiritual regeneration) is supported by the Calvinism of the times, where conversion is conceived not as an event but as a process, and a lifelong one at that. Yet Bunyan's religious experience, as he presents it to us in Grace Abounding, cannot be summed up as simply a gradual and voluntary process of unification. As he himself writes in the Preface, it is a record of "my castings down and raisings up." And few were cast down so low, or raised up so high, as was Bunyan in the course of his conversion. Also, there is the fact of the attempts of Bunyan scholars, though they all recognize that the Calvinist conversion is not an event but a process, to try to find in Grace Abounding the turning point, or definitive moment, or crisis episode of conversion to which they can affix a sense of structure.

. . .

This great need for there to be a single, dramatic episode in a conversion is indeed striking--especially when accompanied by the stated recognition that there is no such definitive turning point. Also striking is the fact that there is such confusion as to precisely when this turning point occurs. There is both a traditional and structural explanation of the fact that the crisis conversion model exerts such a formidable suggestive power over our expectations of an individual conversion. The explanation by tradition is to point to the Augustinian and Pauline examples, which have been imitated both in life and in literature to such an extent that they have unconsciously shaped our very definition of conversion.

...

... we may define the <u>lysis</u> conversion as a gradual process of spiritual maturation which generally conforms to a dyadic structure. In <u>Grace Abounding</u>, this means that Bunyan's conversion is represented as a process which unfolds gradually over a long period of time, but also that there are two specific transitional modes in this gradual proess; in other words, that there are two conversion events.

...

The dyadic nature of conversion is also quite clearly articulated by William Ames, whose work precedes Bunyan's by some forty years, and whose English transposition of the original "Calvinese" may be said to be typical of the theology of the times. Ames observes that conversion "is twofold, relative and absolute (or real)."

...

These two stages in conversion, the "relative" and the "absolute," correspond to Bunyan's own idea of repentance as having two aspects.

...

The iterative theology of repentance--nature to grace/grace to glory--is structurally represented in <u>Grace Abounding</u> as the two conversions.

From: Hawkins, Anne. <u>Philological Quarterly</u> 61 (Summer 1982): <u>259-76</u>.

VIEWPOINTS ON GRACE ABOUNDING

Felicity H. Nussbaum

Bunyan alters the traditional pattern of spiritual autobiography so that the two ways of conceptualizing the self both compete with and complement each other in the text. We may be better able to understand the altered form Bunyan uses if we examine the complexity of his relationship to the divine patriarchal authority, as he substitutes his own personal authority for God's. Bunyan struggles with the tension between the providential and the existential explanation of his life in Grace Abounding before the novel of the eighteenth century makes it familiar.

. . .

The autobiography recounts the development from a self who longed to be other than himself (someone whom God might have called) to a self converted, an adult who merits the birthright and the blessing, and can, as a new father, pass it on to his children. The child becomes the father who can provide others their birthright through the medium of the text, the guidebook for the soul, Grace Abounding.

Bunyan uses the early conversion to create a temporal and spatial arena for the exploration of a series of possible selves which test the patriarchal authority of God. At the same time that Bunyan explores the possibilities of rebellion against God, of Bunyan the father rather than God the father, the autobiographical text begins to compete for authority with the Scriptural texts. After finding God in the early conversion, he then tests the limits of his own newfound authority. The period of temptation allows for both a mask and a purge; it provides a crisis of authority, but also a safe and secure position from which to struggle, for the narrator, the protagonist, and the reader know the outcome from the beginning of the text. We are certain that the conclusion will find the transgressor safe in the abounding grace of the authority of God. The autobiographer will achieve his goal of becoming God's child and becoming the father of the reader. Bunyan stresses that he seeks a home, a place, and he also attempts to make himself a paternal spiritual guide for his flock of children. Bunyan disobeys God within the autobiography, but he disobeys within the limits of authority.

The autobiography, the text, becomes a validation for Bunyan that the temptations will not have to occur again, and the text, like Scripture, is a text of authority for the reader. At the same time, a subversive element creeps into Grace Abounding as the personal text replaces the scriptural one. Narrator, protagonist, and reader assume the authenticity of the autobiographical account of Bunyan's conversion, but while Bunyan uses the words of Scripture as a corollary text to Grace Abounding, it is finally the private, individual account of conversion which competes with the Bible as a substitute text. There is nothing in Bunyan's account which resembles the Scriptural exegesis concluding Augustine's confessions. Instead, Bunyan presents his individual experience, his own conversion, as possessing the possiblity of equal authority. One might even say that while Bunyan seems to proclaim the authority of God's word, the force of the autobiographical text suggests that Bunyan is creating a substitute personal text to replace the Scriptures as a devotional guide. And simultaneously, as the father of his flock and the spiritual guide for his devoted followers, he creates himself in a role as an earthly father who substitutes for the heavenly father to make the work more ambiguous and more modern than many earlier spiritual autobiographies.

From: Nussbaum, Felicity. "'By These Words I was Sustained': Bunyan's Grace Abounding." ELH 49 (1982): 18-34.

VIEWPOINTS ON THE PILGRIM'S PROGRESS

(PART ONE)

Dayton Haskin

Bunyan wrote a work for simple puritans who could afford a book printed on cheap paper, and he offered them the charms of familiar types, in native English settings, with realistic dialogue and characters. But for those who were concerned to know whether they were saved or damned and were disposed to think that "the Bible only" would answer them, Bunyan's book offered also a benign interpretation of the book that threatened to lay upon them burdens that might drive the conscientious to despair. There was a special attractiveness in the figure of the lonely, burdened Christian, learning to interpret for himself, making his way through the wilderness of the world. The Reformation rhetoric that had glorified the individual Christian had also imposed on him weighty duties. The Pilgrim's Progress helped to render the burden light and easy by allowing, confidently and playfully, great interpretive and imaginative freedom in the face of the forbidding text. Bunyan showed several generations of readers, who not only knew their Bibles well but believed that they were under a moral imperative to know them, that the book can be reread--even rewritten--with considerable freedom and pleasure.

From: Dayton Haskin, "The Burden of Interpretation in The Pilgrim's Progress," SP 79 (1982): 256-78.

AN OVERVIEW

John R. Knott, Jr.

To appreciate the nature of Bunyan's commitment to the metaphor of the way one must recognize that he used this metaphor in two basic senses, both of which are important. His genius for exploiting the dramatic potential of biblical metaphor is perhaps most apparent from his success at holding in suspension these two senses of his central figure. The way is the path of all Christians through the wilderness of the world, the way "From This World To That Which Is To Come," and simultaneously the inner way of faith of the indivivual believer. Without a strong conviction about <u>where</u> the way leads, the pilgrim would never set <u>out</u> at all, yet he cannot arrive at the promised end unless he understands how to walk.

Bunyan talks about the second sense of his metaphor, what it means to walk in the way of faith, in <u>The Holy City</u>, his commentary on Revelation.

. . .

This sense of the way as determined by the faith of the individual pilgrim coexists with the other sense of the way as a common journey of all the faithful from the City of Destruction to the New Jerusalem.... Bunyan saw that he did not speak any less truly for speaking "metaphorically." The metaphor, which he saw as embodying God's promise that his saints would succeed in making their way through the wilderness of the "Land of Promise," is the key to his conception of <u>The Pilgrim's Progress</u> and to the appeal of the work for his Puritan readers. His "dream" could succeed because the habit of thinking of the world metaphorically, as a wilderness to be journeyed through, was ingrained in his readers
. . . .

. . .

VIEWPOINTS ON THE PILGRIM'S PROGRESS (PART ONE)

The encounter of Christian and Hopeful with the shepherds of the Delectable Mountains provides a revealing illustration of Bunyan's ability to combine the two basic senses of the metaphor of the way. The episode offers one of the best examples in The Pilgrim's Progress of the subjectivity of the individual way of faith.... The deliberate ambiguity forces one to recognize that the nature of the way--its length and the specific dangers to be encountered--depends upon the faith of the individual pilgrim. The shepherds can assess the spiritual health of the wayfarers at the moment ("You are just in your way"), but this spiritual condition is dynamic and precarious. To give definite answers to the pilgrim's questions would be to ignore the uncertainty with which faith must live.

...

Yet Bunyan's shepherds are also talking about the one true way that leads to the New Jerusalem (and not just "somewhere") and the Delectable Mountains mark a station along the way, as the Interpreter's House and House Beautiful mark earlier stations. Christian'a actions describe a progression through stages of spiritual life. This progression is clearer in some places than in others--notably near the beginning and the end of the journey--but its outlines would have been familiar to readers acquainted with Puritan spiritual autobiography.

From: Knott, John R. Jr. "Bunyan's Gospel Day: A Reading of The Pilgrim's Progress." English Literary Renaissance, 3 (1973): 443-61.

VIEWPOINTS ON THE PILGRIM'S PROGRESS
(PARTS ONE & TWO)

N.H. Keeble

Much of the immediacy of <u>The Pilgrim's Progress</u> derives from the fact that, as in drama, we hear the characters directly in dialogue. And, again as in drama, this make for ironic misunderstandings and misapprehensions as the limited points of view of these characters lead them to misjudge both themselves and others. <u>The Pilgrim's Progress</u> is built up of a series of such ironic encounters. Beneath their superficial exchanges, new acquaintances are engaged in weighing each other up, trying to determine whether or not they will make suitable travelling companions. Christian is constantly taxed to tell his friends from his foes, and it is a measure to what he (and the reader with him) learns by experience that, while at the outset he falls an easy prey to Mr. Worldly Wiseman, he is later able to see through Talkative and to lay bare the fallacies of Mr. Money-love, until he achieves the independence of judgment evidenced in the wisdom and generosity of his comments on Little-faith. To attain and maintain this discerning perception demands a constant mental alertness.

...

Bunyan has an uncommonly sharp eye for the appearances, mannerisms and behaviour of ordinary people, and vivifies his characters, as Henri Talon has put it, by the 'slightest flick of the brush', such as Ignorance's 'briskness' (p. 101), Atheist's 'very great laughter' (p. 110), or Madam Bubble's "Swarthy Complexion' (p. 252). Such details, however, do not merely vivify and particularize: they suggest moral states.... That they do suggest, rather than embody, is important. U. Milo Kaufmann has well cautioned us against speaking of Bunyan's characters as 'types'. Certainly, they do have a symbolic function within the allegory, but they fulfill it as examples: they 'do not incarnate but exemplify a particular quality'.... Even such a minor character as Pliable illustrates the consequence. He is pliable, in his readiness first to join and then to abandon Christian when the going gets tough. Our later glimpses of him 'sneaking among' his neighbors and 'leering away' from acquaintances (pp. 14, 56) are, however, of a man whose behaviour declares guilt and embarrassment at what he has done. Guilt and embarrassment are no part of the abstract quality of pliability: they are the experiences of a pliable man. Bunyan, that is to say, recognizes that moral qualities have their reality in people's lives, but he appreciates further that, though people may be virtuous or vicious to a degree, no human personality is ever wholly consumed into a particular virtue or vice. His moral realism is the source of his artisitic realism.

So it is that, despite his Calvinism, that most discriminatory of theologies, Bunyan never rigidly categorizes. On the one hand, his villians are never impressive in their villiany, never wholly evil. Evil in The Pilgrim's Progress is a pervasive meanness, pettiness and selfishness, which yet allows a kind of friendliness: it is not a defiant amorality, nor a deliberate policy, nor a demonic power (though that is its source). We shall find nothing to compare with Marlowe's Dr. Faustus and Mephostophilis, Shakespeare's Iago, Tourneur's Vendice, Webster's Vittoria Corombona or Milton's Satan. What we do find is more familiar: the narrow-mindedness of Obstinate which has no patience with 'Craz'd-headed Coxcombs' (p. 10): the smugness of Formalist and Hypocrisy who look at each other and laugh at Christian's strict adherence to the way (p. 34): the snobbery of Shame who, anxious to be in the social swim, objects to religion as a 'pitiful, low, sneaking business' unbecoming 'the brave spirits of the times' (p. 59). On the other hand, our saints are not rare exemplars: Evangelist discerns 'many weaknesses' in Christian and Faithful (p. 71). Anyone who doubts that Bunyan was keenly aware that faith coexists with failings need only read over the stories of Little-faith and Mr. Fearing, true pilgrims both. Indeed, in Part II Bunyan deliberately associates with the women, Christiana and Mercy the young, the old, the infirm, the despondent, the tiresomely scrupulous, the fearful and the anxious. These seem improbable saints and unlikely literary heroes. Yet, that they hardly look any different from ordinary people is both the theological point and the source of the fictional verisimilitude.

...

... "Realistic allegory' may appear an oxymoron, if not a contradiction, but there is in Bunyan's execution no indecorousness and little tension because he was habituated to treating the sublunary world as an allegory of translunary truth. And, however engaging the realism, the allegory, as its marginalia remind us, requires of its reader the same interpretative effort as Bunyan believed the natural order demanded: Both were 'Metaphors' to be 'Turned up' (p. 134). And he clearly expected his reader to share his own delight in the challenge this presented. He openly entices the would-be reader of <u>The Pilgrim's Progress</u> with the promise of 'pleasant' and teasing 'Riddles' ('Wouldst thou divert thy self from Melancholly?') and speaks of his work in terms which recall the 'metaphysicals' and their penchant for cunning and obscurity: it is 'something rare' whose 'Riddles' that 'lie couch't within' its 'misterious lines' 'nimble Fancies' are invited to solve. To accept the invitation is not, however, to engage in the merely enjoyable: it is a 'profitable' exercise; to 'loose thy self' in his allegory is 'to find thy self'(pp. 6,7,141). Small wonder, then, that the aftersupper entertainment at Gaius' house is riddling or that the progress of the pilgrim's to the full self-knowledge of sanctity is measured in part by their skill in solving riddles.... When Mercy and the boys blush for failing to solve the 'Riddle' of the spider, it is not merely the application which affects them: it is also their want of percipience, of wit. Christiana, by contrast, is a 'Woman quick of appre-

VIEWPOINTS ON PILGRIM'S PROGRESS (PARTS I & II)

hension' (p. 165). Her companions have been caught out, and that ill becomes a saint....

...

... Bunyan read the Bible, not, like Archbishop Tilloston, as an eminently reasonable and lucid handbook of ethics, but as 'some curious riddles of secrets.'

From: "Introduction," The Pilgrim's Progress. The World's Classics. Edited by N.H. Keeble. Oxford paperbacks. Oxford University Press, 1984. The references to Bunyan's works in Keeble's Introduction are from his edition of The Pilgrim's Progress.

VIEWPOINTS ON THE PILGRIM'S PROGRESS

(Part Two)

James F. Forrest

The years of success following the publication of The Pilgrim's Progress in 1678 gave him [Bunyan] reason enough to ponder afresh the meaning of his art. That he thought about it sufficiently to become convinced of its crucial importance as a means of picturing God's ways to man is evidenced by this fact alone, that he judged it worthwhile to produce a sequel; and the pages of the Second Part of 1684 everywhere attest the strength of the belief. There is about the second narrative an artistic selfconsciousness that is far more pronounced than in the earlier piece. No doubt much of this is the natural reaction to the comments of his critics, whom he answers in the apologetic verses again attached to his work, but mainly the awareness of what he is about springs from creative zest and newly-won admiration for the instrument of art. At least, this is one inference to be drawn from the more plainly metaphorical method of the Second Part, in which catechisms and riddles are frequently employed to pluck the heart out of the mystery of the Christian life, and in which emblem jostles emblem in the Interpreter's House and House Beautiful ...

But nothing betrays the self-awareness of the creative artist more than an exaggerated concern with the form of his work; and it is this that most plainly announces Bunyan's reappraisal of the practical worth of dream or vision. Most noticeable at the beginning of the Second Part is his apparently inept handling of the dream-form.

...

Now the interesting thing about this form, dream-within-dream, is the steroscopic effect it gives to the vision as a whole. At the outset the two dreams come together and interact to produce a solidity and depth in the vision of the pilgrimage that follows. Hence the import of Christiana's dream is that it has a meaning quite beyond itself, for not only does it show how God may sometimes use the dream to move the human mind and start the soul on its long journey home, but it also sets up an awareness of the impressive effect of dream or vision that must surely qualify the reader's response and thus be crucial to his appreciation of the entire work. Indeed, The Pilgrim's Progress, Second Part, opens with an allegorical comment on the usefulness of its own allegory; and it is difficult not to feel that Bunyan is here prefacing his dream with a grand and proud apologia, based on his experience of the first part ...

Perhaps it is not surprising that this artistic effect of Bunyan's dream-within-dream has been largely overlooked by critics, for the form initially gives an ambiguous indirectness that seems alien to the allegory as a whole. More remarkable, however, is the readiness with which otherwise sensitive critics have sold Bunyan's art short by refusing to acknowledge an artistic function behind his choice of form ....

...

Bunyan's preoccupation with vision in the Second Part of The Pilgrim's Progress is in the end the measure of the pleasure he delights in to see the soul so well. His earlier happy dream had taught him the heights to which the human soul could rise, had humbled him in the knowledge that we are often greater than we know ... Not surprisingly, therefore, the visionary gleam became for him one of the clearest intimations of immortality; and since such insight he believed to be the gift of divine grace, it was only natural that he should come to regard his art more than ever as a peculiar manifestation of the Holy Spirit and cherish it as such. A deepened awareness of the ultimate significance of art and the art-form is thus what most clearly separates the Second Part of The Pilgrim's Progress from the first.

AN OVERVIEW

From: "Vision, Form, and the Imagination in the Second Part of The Pilgrm's Progress (1684)." The Journal of Narrative Technique 13 (Spring 1983): 109-116.

ANNOTATED BIBLIOGRAPHY OF CRITICAL STUDIES ON

GRACE ABOUNDING

AND

THE PILGRIM'S PROGRESS (PART ONE AND PART TWO)

Adeney, Elizabeth. "Bunyan: A Unified Vision?" Critical Review, 17 (1974): 97-109.

   Contends that during the journey of The Pilgrim's Progress a split occurs between the narrator and Christian. Indicates that Bunyan's feeling for life is stronger than his religious beliefs.

Adrian, Daryl B. Introduction to The Pilgrim's Progress. New York: Airmont Publishing Co., Airmont Classics, 1969, pp. 1-9.

   Suggests that Christian's story is a symbolic depiction of the Calvinist view of salvation with focus on the daily walk of disciples. Christian's story stresses personal witness and brotherly concern for those weak in the faith.

Alpaugh, David J. "Emblem and Interpretation in The Pilgrim's Progress." ELH: A Journal of English Literary History 33, no. 3 (September 1966): 299-314.

   His thesis is that "The art of emblem interpretation that Christian learns ... is in a larger sense the art that all aspiring pilgrims must learn before they enter the Celestial City." Classifies the emblems which Christian encounters into two general types: emblems of brightness and emblems of darkness.

Alter, Robert. "Mirrors for Immortality." Saturday Review 55, no. 46 (December 1972): 72-74, 76.

AN OVERVIEW

Considers *The Pilgrim's Progress* as one of the literary models for Nabokov's *Transparent Things*. Bunyan shows death transcended through Christianity, but Nabokov confronts death with art, offering "incandescence without transcendence...."

Bacon, Ernest W. *John Bunyan, Pilgrim and Dreamer*. Grand Rapids: Baker Book House, 1983, pp. 132-42.

Glances at *Grace Abounding* in various sections throughout the book. Chapter IX (pp. 132-42) is entitled *The Pilgrim's Progress*. Makes observations on symbolical sights and pictures and on several characters depicted in Part One and Part Two. Obviously designed for the general reader with emphasis on biographical information rather than on critical analyses.

Baird, Charles W. *John Bunyan. A Study in Narrative Technique*. Port Washington, New York and London: Kennikat Press, 1977.

Sections pertinent to *The Pilgrim's Progress* and *Grace Abounding* are scattered throughout the book.
Shows a "coherent pattern" in the development of Bunyan's writings from *Grace Abounding* to the second part of *The Pilgrim's Progress*. Thoroughly shows Bunyan's growth and development as an artist.

Bartell, Shirley Miller. "Uncertainty in Bunyan Versus Assurance in Fox." *Quaker History* 58, no. 2 (Autumn 1969): 93-103.

Bunyan's imprecise use of language and biblical quotation, his struggling over the meaning of scripture and the nature of God as manifested in *Grace Abounding* show that his theological beliefs left him in doubt. Fox, on the other hand, demonstrates linguistic accuracy, resolute view of God, and a serenity of spirit.

ANNOTATED BIBLIOGRAPHY

Batson, E. Beatrice. "John Bunyan: Conscious Artist." Christianity Today 13 no. 6 (December 1968): 10-12.

    Argues that Bunyan works as a conscious artist as evidenced in his use of dialogue, the levels of meaning, and the handling of character.

------. "Teaching The Pilgrim's Progress." Improving College and University Teaching 21 (1973): 105, 107, 109.

    Urges teachers to show the significance of the journey through life with its adventurous action balanced with interludes of resting places, its varied characters, its dramatic dialogue, and the allegory's appeal to all readers.

------. "Bunyan as Creative Artist." Crux (Winter 1983): 4-10.

    Argues that Bunyan had obviously given thought to qualities inherent in imaginative literature. Shows that his rhymed preface to The Pilgrim's Progress practically contains a theory of poetics.

------. John Bunyan: Allegory and Imagination. London: Croom-Helm, New York: Barnes and Noble, 1984.

    Comprehensive study of the literary art of Bunyan's writings, which are most often considered only for their theological, economic, social, and political outlook. The literary art, moreover, is analyzed from the standpoint of Bunyan's philosophy of imaginative literature, consistent with St. Augustine's view (and with the view of other medieval and Renaissance theorists and authors including Dante and Chaucer) that literature by its metaphors, similitudes, and other devices embodies spiritual understanding.

AN OVERVIEW

------. *John Bunyan: The Pilgrim's Progress*. Literary Study in Master Guides Series. London: Macmillan (forthcoming, Feb. 1988).

    Summary and critical commentary on *The Pilgrim's Progress*. Discusses special themes, characterization, style and language. Carefully examines a specimen passage to show literary qualities. Comments on reception of allegory from seventeenth century to the present.

Beal, Rebecca S. "*Grace Abounding to the Chief of Sinners*: John Bunyan's Pauline Epistle." *Studies in English Literature* 21 no. 1 (Winter 1981): 147-60.

    Claims *Grace Abounding* is a Pauline Epistle rather than autobiography.

------. "Bunyan in Prison, Ministry in Suffering." *Christian History* 5 no. 3 (1986): 14-15, 34.

    Shows the way in which Bunyan thought of suffering as a part of his ministry as recorded in *Grace Abounding*. Some reference to Bunyan's intimate understanding of fears Christians face in their suffering as depicted allegorically in *The Pilgrim's Progress*.

Beatty, Bernard. "Rival Fables: *The Pilgrim's Progress* and Dryden's *The Hind and the Panther*." In *The Pilgrim's Progress: Critical and Historical Views*. pp. 263-81. Edited by Vincent Newey. Liverpool: Liverpool University Press, 1980.

    Both Bunyan and Dryden describe a changed life which is based on faith. Dryden's faith is a "submission to the understanding of the will," which enables one to affirm inexplicable doctrine such as that of the Trinity. Bunyan's faith is the assurance of salvation. Whereas Bunyan em-

ANNOTATED BIBLIOGRAPHY

phasizes the individual art of interpretation, Dryden points to the Church as interpreter of scripture.

Bell, Robert. "Metamorphoses of Spiritual Autobiography." ELH: A Journal of English Literary History 44 no. 1 (Spring 1977): 108-126.

    Contends that Bunyan's spiritual autobiography conforms to the pattern of Augustine's Confessions. Since Bunyan defines nature and grace in terms of worldly experience, he paradoxically assists in promoting the rise of secular autobiography.

Bellamy, Joan. "John Bunyan and the Democratic Tradition." Zeitschrift Fur Anglistik und Amerikanistik 27 no. 3 (1979): 218-24.

    Suggests that The Pilgrim's Progress embodies in literary art the historical movement toward a more democratic church and state. Puritans intensified the individualism of democracy by regarding life as an extended spiritual trial and by taking upon themselves the burden of persecution. The Pilgrim's Progress, as well as Grace Abounding, shows this individual struggle. John Bunyan and Martin Bostwick, an Elizabethan pamphleteer, cultivated a style of dramatic immediacy--a democratic mode of expression particularly suited to the common man.

Bennett, Rachel. "Punch Versus Christian in The Old Curiosity Shop." Review of English Studies 22 no. 88 (November 1971): 423-34.

    Contends that opposing tendencies in Dickens' novel are embodied in two opposing motifs, The Pilgrim's Progress and Punch.

Bizzell, Patricia Lynn. "Willful Simplicity: The Charm of John Bunyan's Poetry." Ph.D. dissertation. Rutgers University, 1975.

    This study is part two of a three-part

dissertaion. Asserts that Bunyan cleverly uses verse in The Pilgrim's Progress in order "to emphasize significant episodes and to vary the pace of the prose." Thinks the shepherd boy's song and "Who would true valour see" to be "fully independent lyrics," and considers Bunyan an important minor lyricist of the seventeenth century.

Bloom, Morton W. "Allegory as Interpretation." New Literary History 3 (1972): 301-317.

Reviews various concepts of allegory from the development of the allegorical method in Alexandria to the various views of allegory in modern times. Holds that the crux of the problem of allegory as interpretation is "the surface of the work." Argues that the greatness of any work of art lies "in the literal sense: that which gives it shape and being."

Bridges, Margaret. "The Sense of an Ending: The Case of the Dream Vision." Dutch Quarterly Review of Anglo-American Letters 14 no. 2 (1984): 81-96.

Asserts that given the movement toward closure of the dream-vision form, so many works of its kind are open-ended (fail to close) or exhibit "surprising" or "disappointing" closure. Argues that Chaucer's House of Fame, a dream-vision, classified as unfinished, exemplifies feature of closure, that Piers Plowman undermines closure, and The Pilgrim's Progress, composed of its two distinct parts, polarizes closure and open-endedness. Unlike medieval dreamers who participated in their fictions, Bunyan seems to reduce his role to that of an eyewitness.

Brink, Andrew. "Bunyan's Pilgrim's Progress and the Secular Reader: A Psychological Approach." English Studies in Canada I no. 4 (Winter 1975): 386-405.

ANNOTATED BIBLIOGRPAHY

Offers a psycho-analytical reading of the allegory, while seeing it as the climax of an earlier attempt in Grace Abounding "to settle ego disturbance." Attempts to show the "intra-psychic" conflict lying behind Grace Abounding and asserts that "loss of alienation of parental affection" can explain the intensity of Bunyan's struggle.

Brittain, Vera. "Literary Testaments." In Essays by Divers Hands, Being the Transactions of the Royal Society of Literature pp. 19-35. Edited by L.P. Hartley. London: Oxford University Press, 1966.

Briefly examines Grace Abounding as the most important religious testament to appear between Augustine and Cardinal Newman.

Broes, Arthur T. "Journey into Moral Darkness: 'My Kinsman, Major Molineux' as Allegory." Nineteenth-Century Fiction 19 (September 1964): 171-84.

Shows influence of episodes from Bunyan's The Pilgrim's Progress on Hawthorne.

Bruss, Elizabeth W. Autobiographical Acts. The Changing Situation of a Literary Genre. Baltimore and London: Johns Hopkins University Press, 1976, pp. 33-60. (Chapter One, pp. 19-32, is also helpful.)

Considers Grace Abounding as "an act rather than a form," or more accurately, it is "in many ways an act groping for a form." It has the conventional divisions of a Saint's Life, yet Bunyan does not seem "to borrow for his own endeavor the respectability surrounding hagiography." It resembles a Pauline Epistle, for "like Paul's letters, Grace Abounding is conceived as an address from a distant missionary to the 'children' and converts...." Grace Abounding does not desert the pattern of "sectarian autobiographers," and the autobiography also bears resemblance to didactic and controversial pamphlets which circulated during the seventeenth century. It is also "an argument rather than merely an attractive rhetorical display." Bunyan plays the part of a patriarch whose struggles are interpreted typologically.

Bzowski, Frances. "A Continuation of the Tradition of the Irony of Death." Dickinson Studies: Emily Dickinson (1830-86). (1984): 33-42.

    Suggests that Bunyan's Pilgrim's Progress is a fitting place to begin the analysis of Dickinson's poem, "Because I could not stop for Death." Holds that the dreamlike entrance into eternity of the character in Dickinson's poem is similar to that of Christian's entrance into the Celestial City at the end of Part One of The Pilgrim's Progress.

Campbell, Gordon. "The Theology of The Pilgrim's Progress." In The Pilgrim's Progress: Critical and Historical Views, pp. 251-62. Edited by Vincent Newey. Liverpool: Liverpool University Press, 1980.

    Argues that the allegory is a religious rather than a theological work and states that the "overtly theological passages in the book tend to be incidental to Christian's journey...."

Cantarow, Ellen. "A Wilderness of Opinions Confounded: Allegory and Ideology," with comments by Nancy Hoffman. College English 34 no. 2 (November 1972): 215-55.

    Through an examination of Langland, Spenser, and Bunyan, argues that allegory arises out of a particular class and social order. The Pilgrim's Progress supposedly emerges from the bourgeoisie and the artisan class.

Carlton, Peter J. "Bunyan: Language, Convention,

ANNOTATED BIBLIOGRPAHY

Authority." <u>ELH: A Journal of English Literary History</u> 51 no. 1 (Spring 1984): 17-32.

    Offers a "demythologizing" of <u>Grace Abounding</u> as well as of various critics of the work.

Clifford, Gay. <u>The Transformation of Allegory</u>. London and Boston: Routledge and Kegan Paul, 1974.

    Concentrates on special characteristics of the allegorical mode. Suggests the "ideal and non-mimetic features" of the mode but also shows concern with its "inner flexibility" and with "the power of allegorical forms to undergo a complex evolution and multiple transformations." Offers a description of the reading experience sensitive to the reality of narrative allegory. Argues that "to write allegorically is not merely to create a particular kind of literature, but also to make assumptions about its functions and about a particular way of reading." The study focuses on several works, including <u>The Pilgrim's Progress</u>; references are primarily illustrative examples of stated views on allegory. Chapter One, "The Concept" is probably most pertinent to Bunyan's allegory.

Cobau, William Weinschenk. "Historical Modes in <u>The Pilgrim's Progress</u>: John Bunyan's Quest for Literary Art." Ph.D. dissertation. The Pennsylvania State University, 1964.

    Declares that Bunyan twice told the Puritan story of religious conversion. Contends that he describes conversion in the utilitarian confession of <u>Grace Abounding</u> and later tells the same story in the controlled art of <u>The Pilgrim's Progress</u>. Claims that Bunyan desires to transcend the "utilitarian, associative procedures" of <u>Grace Abounding</u> and to give conversion the order of art. In order to accomplish his desired purpose, Bunyan draws upon specific rhetorical and literary sources, such as allegory, the exemplum, the bestiary, the catechism, martyrology, and the saints' legend.

Cowan, Michael. City of the West: Emerson, America, and Urban Metaphor. New York and London: Yale University Press, 1967, pp. 76-77, 80, 82, 107-109.

    Demonstrates the relation of Bunyan's journey metaphor and images of the city, including "City of Destruction" and "Celestial City" to Emerson's (and other American Renaissance writers') use of the urban metaphor.

Curley, Thomas M. "The Spiritual Journey Moralized in Rasselas." Anglia 91 (1973): 33-35.

    Contends that The Pilgrim's Progress provides a structural pattern for Rasselas.

Damrosch, Leopold, Jr. God's Plot and Man's Stories. Chicago and London: The University of Chicago Press, 1985, pp. 121-86.

    Views Bunyan's Grace Abounding as an autobiographical narrative founded on "psychic dividedness and ontological dualism." Argues that Grace Abounding shows that Bunyan needs a faith that will not only "promise him election, but will accommodate that promise to the fact of continued sin and guilt."
    The Pilgrim's Progress, Part One and Part Two, both embody "novelistic" details in that the characters are allowed to be characters. In Part One, particularly, events and images change as the experiencing self changes. Part Two, in tending toward the novel, sacrifices much of what makes the first part immortal, primarily the psychological intensity.

Daniells, Roy. Milton, Mannerism and Baroque. Toronto: University of Toronto Press, 1963, pp. 119, 141, 145-69.

Extended comparison of Milton and
Bunyan (particularly through comments on
Part One and Two of The Pilgrim's Progress)
by showing methods of the two authors to
achieve unity of effect. Claims that Bunyan
is motivated by his milieu to create a new
art form from romance, allegory, and Puritanism as is Milton to write a Christian
epic.

Davie, Donald. A Gathered Church. The Literature
of the English Dissenting Interest, 1700-
1930. London and Henley: Routledge and
Kegan Paul, 1978, pp. 7-10, 12-16, 34, 77.

Claims that it is no longer possible to
study The Pilgrim's Progress in university
without also understanding Calvinist theology. Later dissenting literature fails to
meet Bunyan's standards of "the heroic."

Davis, Nick. "The Problem of Misfortune in The
Pilgrim's Progress." In The Pilgrim's Progress: Critical and Historical Views, pp.
182-204. Edited by Vincent Newey. Liverpool: Liverpool University Press, 1980.

Studies Bunyan's allegory in the context of the tradition of medieval romances.

Delaney, Paul. British Autobiography in the
Seventeenth Century. London: Routledge and
Kegan Paul, 1969, pp. 28-30, 78, 88-93, 95-
97, 174.

Investigates the influence of St. Paul
on Grace Abounding and contends that the
success of the autobiography is primarily
due to Bunyan's ability to show readers that
the results of the spiritual struggle are
always questionable.

------. "Bleak House and Doubting Castle."
Dickens Studies Newsletter 3 no. 4 (December
1972): 100-106.

Shows through internal and external evidence that there is a relationship between Krook's house and Doubting Castle, especially seen in the fact that visitors to both places fall into a state of despair.

Donaldson, Ian. "<u>Bartholomew Fair</u> and <u>The Pilgrim's Progress</u>." <u>Notes and Queries</u> 29 (April 1982): 142-43.

Cites parallels between comments and attitudes of Busy in Jonson's Smithfield Fair with those of Christian and Faithful in Vanity Fair. Inquires what scholars should make of parallels, which seem "to go beyond the bounds of mere coincidence."

Dutton, A. Richard. "'Interesting, but tough': Reading <u>The Pilgrim's Progress</u>." <u>Studies in English Literature 1500-1900</u> 18(1979): 439-56.

Believes that Huck Finn's difficulty with <u>The Pilgrim's Progress</u> is understandable, particularly since the work merely offers Calvinism in fictional form and presents the problems that arise in following Calvinistic beliefs.

Ebner, Dean. <u>Autobiography in Seventeenth Century England. Theology and Self</u>. The Hague: Mouton, 1971, pp. 22-71.

Investigates the manner in which theological ways of knowing the self and God influenced the style, structure and content of various seventeenth century autobiographers. Chooses <u>Grace Abounding</u> to illustrate Baptist autobiography.

Edwards, Philip. "The Journey in <u>The Pilgrim's Progress</u>." In <u>The Pilgrim's Progress: Critical and Historical Views</u>, pp. 111-17. Edited by Vincent Newey. Liverpool: Liverpool University Press, 1980.

Thinks of the journey at first as an escape, not a pilgrimage until later. Also argues that Bunyan's "progress" is not improvement but traveling.

El-Gabalawry, Saad. "The Pilgrimage: George Herbert's Favorite Allegorical Technique." College Language Association Journal 13 no. 4 (June 1970): 408-419.

    Concentrates on George Herbert but suggests that Herbert's allegorical method is similar to that of Bunyan (and Dante) in that the method of the three writers depicts struggle in the pursuit of a spiritual goal.

Finch, Geoffrey. "The Puritan Imagination of John Bunyan." Orita (Ibadan) 7 (1974): 45-47.

    Claims that Bunyan is at the end of a long medieval tradition which saw no separation between the natural and the supernatural. Shows through various episodes in Grace Abounding and The Pilgrim's Progress how doctrine is transformed into pictorial representations that are perceived imaginatively as truth.

Fish, Stanley Eugene. Surprised by Sin: The Reader in "Paradise Lost." London, Toronto: Macmillan; New York: St. Martin's Press, 1967, pp. 19n, 48n, 142-43, 198-200.

    Offers Bunyan analogues to show Milton's method of involving the reader. Illustrations include the episode of Flatterer, Christian's leaving his family, and Christian's battle with Apollyon.

------. "Progress in The Pilgrim's Progress." English Literary Renaissance 1 no.3 (Autumn 1971): 261-93.

    Holds that "progress" in the allegory is actually illusory and that the narrative subverts the implications of its title, and consequently, undermines the self-confidence of the reader. Shows a relation between the "wayfaring" and the process of reading about it, stating that as Christian must view his struggles in a manner that involves a reliance on a power outside himself so also must the reader interpret the action in a similar way. This means for the pilgrim and the reader the abandonment of "temporal and spatial contexts" in favor of an urgency to "look upward rather than forward." Argues for the work of memory which is capable of bringing to bear "the correcting perspective of what is distant on what is near," and since his prose is both temporal and spatial, Bunyan's allegory continually invalidates itself "as a vehicle of the insight it pretends to convey."

------. Self-Consuming Artifacts. The Experience of Seventeenth-Century Literature. Berkeley, Los Angeles, London: University of California Press, 1972: 224-64.

 Emphasis throughout book is similar to preceding article in that the proper object of analysis is the reader, not the literary work. Chapter 4 is basically a reprint of the preceding article.

Fitch, Robert Elliot. Odyssey of the Self-Centered Self, or Rake's Progress in Religion. New York: Harcourt, Brace & World, 1960, pp. 11-12, 135-36.

 Brief comparison of Bunyan's Vanity Fair to Thackeray's, to Voltaire's Paris, and to Aldous Huxley's City of Dreadful Joy. Contrasts Bunyan's depiction of Slough of Despond with that of the imaginative attitudes of the Existentialist and Analytic Philosopher.

Fletcher, Angus. Allegory: The Theory of Symbolic Mode. Ithaca, New York: Cornell University Press, 1964.

 Claims a one-to-one meaning for allegorical characters, thus limiting complex-

ANNOTATED BIBLIOGRAPHY

ity of characterization for the allegorist. Contends that allegory tends toward one of two patterns, "battle" or "progress." Helpful on various aspects of Bunyan as allegorist.

Forrest, James F. "How Grace Abounded." Scottish Baptist Magazine (March 1960): 8-9.

    Outlines the essential stages of spiritual development which Bunyan names in Grace Abounding.

------. "Ignorance as White Devil: a Bunyan debt to Thomas Adams?" Canadian Journal of Theology 8 no. 1 (1962): 49-50.

    A sermon by Thomas Adams may have influenced Bunyan in his presentation of Ignorance, but there is no basis for believing Bunyan deliberately borrowed aspects of the sermon.

------. "Ready-to-halt's Dance and the Promises: A Bunyan Pun." Canadian Journal of Theology 8 no. 2 (April 1962): 147.

    Clarifies Bunyan's allegorical intent in the second part of The Pilgrim's Progress by identifying a pun in the description of the dance celebrating the slaying of Giant Despair.

------. "Bunyan's Ignorance and the Flatterer: A Study in the Literary Act of Damnation." Studies in Philology 60 no. 1 (January 1963): 12-22.

    Studies sequence of prior events, especially an episode involving the Flatterer to show Bunyan's ultimate rejection of Ignorance as a carefully wrought artistic act.

------. "Mercy with her Mirror." Philological Quarterly 42 no. 1 (January 1963): 121-26.

    Bunyan brings together several traditions in associating Mercy with the looking-glass episode of the Delectable Mountains.

------. "Some Spiritual Symbols in Puritan Literature." <u>Canadian Journal of Theology</u> 9 no. 3 (1963): 185-95.

    Studies the use by Bunyan (and other Puritan writers) of spiritual images, including the journey, warfare, fire, oil, water, tree, and others.

------. "Bunyan's Threatening Hill." <u>Expository Times</u> 86 (October 1974): 23.

    Considers Luther's <u>Commentary on Galatians</u> to be an influence on Bunyan's imagination in creating the hill that threatens Christian during his trek to Mr. Legality's house.

------. "Patristic Tradition and Psychological Image in Bunyan's Three Shining Ones at the Cross." <u>Harvard Theological Review</u> 68 no. 1 (1975): 61-65.

    Recognizes that Bunyan readers would probably associate the Three Shining Ones at the Cross with the Patristic traditional reading of Abraham's three angels of Genesis 18:2 as symbols of the three members of the Trinity, but Bunyan probably also thinks of the emblem of Holy Rood and Augustine's trinity of memory, understanding, and will to show the glorious harmony of the pilgrimage at the Cross.

------. "Vision, Form, and the Imagination in the Second Part of <u>The Pilgrim's Progress</u> (1684)." <u>Journal of Narrative Technique</u> 13 (Spring 1983): 109-16.

    Contends that the second part of <u>The Pilgrim's Progress</u> demonstrates the growing appreciation Bunyan had for art. Holds that Bunyan has an "exaggerated concern with the forms of his work"; and this concern "an-

ANNOTATED BIBLIOGRAPHY

nounced Bunyan's reappraisal of the practical worth of dream or vision."

------. "The Pilgrim's Progress, A Dream that Endures." Christian History 5 no. 3 (1986): 24-27.

Clearly shows the overwhelming popularity of The Pilgrim's Progress in the seventeenth century by the reading public. Learned critics, like Samuel Johnson and Jonathan Swift, of the eighteenth century happily received the allegory. The Age of Reason, however, found it lacking in finesse, but adulations poured upon it in the nineteenth century, and reached a peak in the evangelical fervor of the Victorian era. Influence of the allegory on American Literature is pervasive. As a world classic, the allegory is on the wane in the present era, but there is "a compensating attachment of the work at the academic level."
Explores reasons why the allegory has lasted and identifies features that insure its future.

Frye, Northrop. The Secular Scripture. A Study of the Structure of Romance. Cambridge, Massachussetts: Harvard University Press, 1976, pp. 21-22, 27, 134.

Provocative study of the mythic implications of the Giant Despair episode.

Frye, Roland Mushat. God, Man, and Satan. Patterns of Christian Thought and Life in "Paradise Lost," "Pilgrim's Progress" and the Great Theologians. Princeton: Princeton University Press, 1960; Reprint ed., Port Washington, New York: Kennikat Press, 1972.

Interrelates aspects of Christian theology with two examples of "accommodated" truth: Paradise Lost as portrayal of Milton's view of the Christian faith and The Pilgrim's Progress as Bunyan's vision of the Christian life. With regard to Bunyan, stresses the author's purpose, motives of the pilgrims, nature of good and evil portrayed, and the place of Christ, Scripture, the Holy Spirit and the Church. Concludes that Bunyan with Milton embraces the complete range of Christian belief and behavior.

Furlong, Monica. Puritan's Progress. New York: Coward, McCann & Geoghegan, Inc., 1975.

    Attempts to present Bunyan and his work as reflecting "something true and universal about the human condition." This is completely possible for Bunyan, for he writes within the context of Calvinism, which is an "essentially dramatic conception of human life" and therefore "lends itself to fictional interpretation." Puritanism is "the begetter of his art," and of the author's spiritual tumult in his struggle toward a reconciliation with himself that progresses beyond Puritanism. An intense personal note pervades Grace Abounding, providing a necessary catharsis for Bunyan, but the personal gives way to "Christian as Everyman" in The Pilgrim's Progress. Contends that when he realizes that man is incapable of perfection, Bunyan finds an inner peace and "a new level of creativity," especially evident in the second part of The Pilgrim's Progress.

Gilbert, Sandra M. "Plain Jane's Progress." Signs 2 no. 4 (1977): 779-804.

    Redefines the pilgrimage of Christian's journey in order to show Jane Eyre's life journey. Jane makes something of a mythical progress from one named place to another. The essay focuses primarily on Jane Eyre but shows the influence of Part One of The Pilgrim's Progress on Charlotte Bronte's novel. Slight reference to Part Two of the allegory.

Gillie, Christopher. Character in English Literature. London: Chatto and Windus, 1965, pp.

ANNOTATED BIBLIOGRAPHY

23-24, 101-108.

Examines <u>The Pilgrim's Progress</u> as an allegory somewhere between pure allegory (or fairy tale) and the novel. Characters primarily function to make Christian more intelligible.

Greaves, Richard L. "John Bunyan and Covenant Thought in the Seventeenth Century." <u>Church History</u> 36 (June 1967): 151-69.

Offers splendid insights on Bunyan's theological stance and his place in the stream of covenant theology. Explains the difference between the influence of Luther and Calvin on Bunyan's doctrinal position.

------. <u>John Bunyan</u>. Courtenay Series in Reformation Theology, no. 2. Grand Rapids, Michigan: Eerdmans, 1969.

Studies the stages of Bunyan's life with lucid statements on Bunyan's understanding of God and salvation. Substantiates views from Bunyan's fiction as well as his prose. Helpful in understanding Bunyan's covenant theology and the place of the church and sacraments in that theology. Discusses also the influence of Luther and Calvin, and further contends that there are some ideas taken from the Antinomians and the Separatists.

------. "Bunyan Through the Centuries: Some Reflections." <u>English Studies</u> 64 no. 2 (April 1983): 113-21.

Concise examination of the variety of responses to Bunyan's writing throughout history. Underscores the modern debate concerning Bunyan the isolated genius versus the archetypal Puritan. Also studies his unique artistry and shows his indebtedness to his background.

Greene, Donald. "On <u>The Pilgrim's Progress</u>."

AN OVERVIEW

<u>Christianity and Literature</u> 28 no. 1 (1978): 11-13.

    Demonstrates the excellent features of the allegory, including the archetypal journey narrative, memorable characters, colloquial style, and enigmatic situations.

Guibbory, Achsah. <u>The Map of Time</u>. Urbana: University of Illinois Press, 1986, 270-71.

    Comments helpful in seeing Bunyan's view of time in contrast to and comparison with other seventeenth-century literary figures. Holds that Bunyan, like Bacon and Milton, "insists on the necessity of making a break with the corrupt past." <u>Pilgrim's Progress</u> stresses the necessity "of advancing and the evil temptation of stopping, turning aside or going back."

Guilzo, Allen C. "John Bunyan's Christian at Three Hundred." <u>Christianity Today</u> 22 no. 10 (1978): 13-15.

    A tribute which praises <u>The Pilgrim's Progress</u> for its strong core of Puritan conversion-psychology. Also praises the specifically Christian qualities of the allegory.

Haferkamp, Berta. <u>Bunyan als Kunstler. Stilkritische Studien zu seinem Hauptwerk 'The Pilgrim's Progress.'</u> Tübingen: Max Niemeyer Verlag, 1963.

    Shows that art is no enemy of a moral concept of life. Claims that the one central belief which informs <u>The Pilgrim's Progress</u> is the necessity for strength of the will.

Halewood, William H. <u>The Poetry of Grace. Reformation Themes and Structures in English Seventeenth-Century Poetry</u>. New Haven and London: Yale University Press, 1970, pp. 65-70.

ANNOTATED BIBLIOGRAPHY

Declares *Grace Abounding* to be "an epitome of Augustinian doctrine," particularly with its emphasis on the work of grace in conversion. Explores Worldly-Wiseman episode in *The Pilgrim's Progress* to show how the village of Morality suggests a determined resistance to the superiority of the Celestial City over the earthly city.

Hammond, Brean S. "The Pilgrim's Progress: Satire and Social Comment." In *The Pilgrim's Progress: Critical and Historical Views*, pp. 118-31. Edited by Vincent Newey. Liverpool: Liverpool University Press, 1980.

Examines satirical passages in the allegory and observes that most of the work is satirical. The most brilliant satirical passage is the episode of Vanity Fair. Notes that satiric character portraits are eminently convincing, especially where the sins are less doctrinal and more self-indulgent. Some characters, however, present a thrust which "would be dangerous to trivialize or to expose to laughter." Of such are Apollyon and Giant Despair; for these Bunyan reserves a less sophisticated satire.

Hardin, Richard F. "Bunyan, Mr. Ignorance, and the Quakers." *Studies in Philology* 69 no. 4 (October 1971): 496-508.

Portrays Ignorance as representative of the Quakers who were ignorant of their own natures and of the meaning of the Bible.

Harding, M. Esther. *The "I" and the "Not-I". A Study in the Development of Consciousness.* Bollingen Series 79, pp. 92, 175, 185-86. New York: Pantheon Books, 1965.

Similar to her psychoanalytic study of *The Pilgrim's Progress* published in 1956. Shows Bunyan's concrete depiction of heaven and how his vision differs from that of Dante.

Hardison, O.B., Jr. "Criticism and the Search for Pattern." *Thought* 36 (1961): 215-30.

    Gives attention to allegory and suggests that *The Pilgrim's Progress* is an example of the importance of plot in narrative and asserts that plot follows not the laws of theology, but its own laws.

Harrison, G.B. *John Bunyan: A Study in Personality*. 1928, Reprint ed., Hamden, Connecticut: Anchor Books, 1967; Reprint ed., Folcroft, Pennsylvania: Folcroft Library Editions, 1973.

    Traces the growth of Bunyan's personality and ideas, particularly as embodied in *Grace Abounding*. Suggests that *The Pilgrim's Progress* is another version of his autobiography but holds that the allegory is the story of the Puritan soul, not of the Puritan faith.

Haskin, Dayton William. "The Light Within: Studies in Baxter, Bunyan and Milton." Ph.D. dissertation. Yale University, 1978.

    Contends that at the heart of literary creativity for Baxter, Bunyan, and Milton is the experience of feeling specially enlightened "within" and thus achieving a "unique authority with which to speak." Chapters III and IV examine *Grace Abounding* and *The Pilgrim's Progress* with a view to charting Bunyan's progress as a writer. Holds that Bunyan moves from "feeling that he has arrived 'too late' to a confident conviction that he can rewrite the Book of the Acts of the Apostles ... in a way that will draw latter-day readers into earlier biblical narrative." Believes that Bunyan moves toward accepting a version of the "doctrine of inner light," while resisting a total acceptance.

------. "Bunyan, Luther, and the Struggle with

ANNOTATED BIBLIOGRAPHY

Belatedness in <u>Grace Abounding</u>." <u>University of Toronto Quarterly</u> 50 no. 3 (Spring 1981): 300-313.

    Suggests that Bunyan borrowed a paradigm of Christian experience from Luther, who in turn borrowed it from Paul. Refutes the charge, however, that Bunyan was merely derivative.

------. "The Burden of Interpretation in <u>The Pilgrim's Progress</u>." <u>Studies in Philology</u> 79 (Summer 1982): 256-78.

    Claims that two aspects of Puritan teaching were particularly influential on Bunyan: the "rise of Protestant Scholasticism" in which each individual is given the heavy burden of searching Scripture and interpeting it in order "to work out his own salvation," and the "experimental Predestinarian tradition" of Bayly and Dent, in which the burden is for each one to find the assurance of salvation in Scripture, thus "perfecting his faith." What Haskin sees as the two back-breaking burdens in Puritanism are: 1) idolatry of the Scriptures, and 2) predestination. Haskin sees Bunyan's burden to be a knowledgeable interpreter through his numerous struggles in <u>Grace Abounding</u>. The burden of "right" interpretation lessens in <u>The Pilgrim's Progress</u>. Christian goes through much of what Bunyan shows of himself in his autobiography, but Christian loses his burden rather early, and his new reading material, the parchment roll, comforts rather than torments him.

Hawkins, Anne Olivia. "Archetypes in the Spiritual Autobiographies of Augustine, John Bunyan, and Thomas Merton." Ph.D. dissertation. University of Rochester, 1978.

    Contends that the protagonist of spiritual autobiography fuses "the perceived or recollected self with the mythic or archetypal hero." Bunyan, for example, is at the same time Everyman or the human soul. The hero's development takes the form of a quest or a psychomachia; in Bunyan, the latter predominates. The archetype of psychomachia "dramatizes the conflict of ambivalent and opposing tendencies in the psyche as the battle between good and evil."

Holds that the conversion determines religious meaning and formed structure. The structure of Grace Abounding is based on "a Calvinist lysis conversion pattern, consisting of a repeated bi-polar unit of conversion and relapse, and based on the paternal archetype of an angry, punitive God."

------. "The Double Conversion in Grace Abounding." Philological Quarterly 61 (1982): 259-76.

Study of conversion and asserts its "dyadic" nature--consisting of the gradual lysis conversion, and the abrupt crisis event--and also contends that Bunyan in Grace Abounding demonstrates the lysis type; therefore, the structure of Grace Abounding is "the literary counterpart to the theological anxiety which underlies lysis conversion."

Henson, Gail Clark Ritchie. "A Holy Desperation: The Literary Quest for Grace in the Reformed English Tradition from John Bale to John Bunyan." Ph.D. dissertation. University of Louisville, 1981.

Holds that the doctrine of grace in Reformed English Theology has within it the implicit metaphor of the pilgrimage of life. The doctrine includes the view that God initiates the process of salvation to the Elect through effectual calling. Contends that the theology creates anxieties in individuals who search the Bible and their own hearts for the assurance that they are among the elect. Believes that Grace Abounding and The Pilgrim's Progress (and one of Bunyan's theological treatises) most vividly express the "utter tensions and distresses"

ANNOTATED BIBLIOGRAPHY

precipitated in hearts by the Reformed theology.

Hinds, Carol Louise. "The Implication of Puritan Principles in Restoration and Eighteenth-Century British Literature." Ph.D. dissertation. University of Virginia, 1983.

>Shows the imaginative use to which Bunyan put positive images of Puritans, unlike writers of the Restoration and the Eighteenth-Century English Literature. Also, holds that Puritans--even though the term is ambiguous--served as scapegoats for and justification of some of the licentiousness of Restoration drama.

Honig, Edwin. Dark Conceit: The Making of Allegory. A Boar's Head Book. Cambridge: Walker-DeBarry, Inc., 1960, pp. 40, 47, 52, 71, 75-77, 79, 87, 98-100.

>Examines "the making" of Bunyan's allegory. Contends that Christian's quest combines elements from the "stock medieval tale of the soul's pilgrimage with elements from chivalric romance." Thinks of Christian as a type of everyman and believes that allegorically, The Pilgrim's Progress depicts an "everyman hero following the Christian pattern of suffering and rebirth as an initiation into heavenly life...."

Hough, Graham. An Essay on Criticism. London: Gerald Duckworth & Co., 1966, p. 53.

>Claims that the moral theology of Puritanism is now handled as the imaginative structure of The Pilgrim's Progress.

Howell, Elmo. "Bunyan's Two Valleys: A Note on the Economic Element in Pilgrim's Progress." Tennessee Studies in Literature 19 (1974): 1-7.

>Sees the Valley of Humiliation and the Valley of the Shadow of Death as spiritual

AN OVERVIEW

trials of Bunyan and in keeping with the spiritual variations portrayed by St. John of the Cross in The Dark Night of the Soul.

Hunter, J. Paul. The Reluctant Pilgrim. Baltimore: The Johns Hopkins Press, 1966, pp. 93-124.

    The chapter entitled "The Pilgrim 'Allegory'," gives helpful insights on the way in which the seventeenth-century Puritans, committed to a metaphorical way of thinking, expressed themselves metaphorically. Puritans leaned most heavily on three metaphors: spiritual warfare, the journey, and the wilderness.

Inglis, Fred. An Essential Discipline. An Introduction to Literary Criticism. London: Methuen Educational, 1968, pp. 50-51, 126, 186.

    Slight references to The Pilgrim's Progress which indicate that Bunyan's allegory transcends a "bigoted creed," and his vision is not bound within the confines of dogma.

Iser, Wolfgang. "Bunyan's Pilgrim's Progress: The Doctrine of Predestination and the Shaping of the Novel." The Implied Reader. Baltimore and London: Johns Hopkins Press, 1974, pp. 1-28.

    Strongly exemplifies a facet of reader-response criticism. The Puritan must hunt for signs of his hoped-for salvation since he is already saved or damned. Regardless of the numbers of signs discovered, the certainty for salvation still remains subjective, which means--as in the case of Christian in The Pilgrim's Progress--that doubt persists to the end of life. Christian, and the reader, must discover a new reality through a fiction which is different from the world to which he is accustomed. Experiences cause Christian and the reader to discover imperfections in prevailing stan-

dards and in their own behavior.
A striking element in The Pilgrim's Progress is the varied narrative technique, which alternates between omniscient narrator and dialogue. As dialogue increases, the usual result is an increasing importance of subjectivity. Yet, it is in the dialogue that certainty is sought after, for here the speaker seeks to ascertain signs of his own predicament.
Explores also distinctives in characters: the one purely fictional, and the other extending beyond mere fiction. Concludes that the story of the main character in The Pilgrim's Progress is one of an increasing self-awareness, "and in this respect it is indisputably a novel, or at least a novel-in-the-making."

James, Canon Eric. "The Significance of John Bunyan Today." The John Bunyan Lectures 1978. To Mark the 350th Anniversary of the Birth of John Bunyan and the Tercentenary of the Publication 'The Pilgrim's Progress.' Bedfordshire Education Service, 1978, pp. 53-69.

   Considers Bunyan's images of the journey and the pilgrim to be archetypal. Although there exists a distaste among many modern readers for Calvinism, Bunyan still has wide appeal because of this rigorous introspective analysis.

Johnson, Barbara Ann. "From Piers Plowman to Pilgrim's Progress: The Generic and Exegetical Contexts of Bunyan's 'Similtude of a Dream.'" Ph.D. dissertation. Brown University, 1983.

   Calls for a reevaluation of The Pilgrim's Progress as a literary structure by placing it in "historical and aesthetic contexts that shed new light on Bunyan's purpose and methods." Recalls that in the "Apology" to the allegory, Bunyan claims that his use of allegory and dream vision are justified by the Bible's "mode of discourse" and by the "cryptically described predecessors who pleased God better than modern writers." Contends that <u>Piers Plowman</u> is the only example that "meets the requirements of Bunyan's cryptically-described model, and major parallels of structure, characterization and allegorical mode exist between the two works." Explains that major differences between the works reflect the way in which "the seventeenth century saw the Bible as a literary model and the Reformation emphasis on the role of the individual before the biblical text."

Johnston, Eleanor Isabel. "Puritan Poetics: The Development of Literal Metaphor from John Bunyan to Nathaniel Hawthorne." Ph.D. dissertation. The University of Manitoba, 1985.

Contends that recent critics have begun to argue for a "reformed" aesthetics in order to account for a "Protestant belief in the Real Presence of God in Scripture." The study examines writings which insist upon "a literal identification of the Word with the named 'thing.'" States that the cornerstone of Reformation theology which shaped Puritan writings is "the active power of <u>Logos</u>, God's creative expression in things of this world." Further asserts that the crucial factor which distinguishes Puritan from medieval aethetics is "a kind of 'univocation' which requires metaphor to say 'one thing.'" Holds that in Bunyan's use of Christ's metaphor, "I am the Way," the pilgrim learns to read God's 'Word' in his own heart and "to become the continuing incarnation of God's Word in the world." Believes that <u>The Pilgrim's Progress</u>, Part Two "exchanges metaphor for allegory inasmuch as it falls back upon an absence of the thing referred to; the Real Presence is missing from the mimetic word."

Kaufmann, U. Milo. <u>"The Pilgrim's Progress" and Traditions in Puritan Meditation</u>. New Haven and London: Yale University Press, 1966.

    Investigates Bunyan's complex art by showing the tension between mythos and logos. Examines impact of Puritan meditation on various episodes.

Keeble, N.H. "Christiana's Key: The Unity of The Pilgrim's Progress." In The Pilgrim's Progress: Critical and Historical Views, pp. 1-20. Edited by Vincent Newey. Liverpool: Liverpool University Press, 1980.

    Encourages the reader to treat Part I and Part II of The Pilgrim's Progress as a single unity instead of merely accentuating the differences.

------. "The Pilgrim's Progress: A Puritan Fiction." Baptist Quarterly 28 (July 1980): 321-36.

    Argues that in the sermonic passages, frequently criticized, a reader finds a sense of genuine progress. Clearly shows that as it is only "the human mind (in Bunyan constantly alert and waiting on the guidance of the Spirit) which can, by collecting, comparing and assessing experiences, give purpose and order to a life, so it is in the responses of the hero's mind that the true story lies." This is the explanation for Christian's discussing what he sees on the journey: "there is a progress only because it is a pilgrim who goes on a journey."

------. Richard Baxter, Puritan Man of Letters. Oxford: The Clarendon Press, 1982, pp. 92, 93.

    States that Baxter's The Poor Man's Family Book (1674) contains slight use of detail and characterization which means that fiction "will usurp the didactic purpose of the book: a danger that appeared in the second part of The Pilgrim's Progress."

Considers the ambivalence of Puritanism and its literature: "it appreciates diversity and unity, man and God, this world and the next: and then confounds the reading public by writing realistic allegory as in The Pilgrim's Progress."

------. "Introduction," The Pilgrim's Progress. The Worlds' Classics Paperback. Edited by N.H. Keeble. Oxford: Oxford University Press, 1984, pp. IX-XXIV.

The Pilgrim's Progress captures the stages of Christian experience traced in Grace Abounding and represents these in allegory. Much of the immediacy comes directly through the characters in dialogue, not through the narrator. Although the characters have "a symbolic function within the allegory, they fulfill it as examples." All characters are involved in a powerful drama set against a "realistic background of town and country." The allegory depicts the speech, behavior, emotions and spiritual life of ordinary people and does so in a language of unusual beauty and simplicity.

------. "The Way and Ways of Puritan Story: Biblical Patterns in Bunyan and his Contemporaries." English XXXIII, 147 (1984): 209-232.

Declares that underlying the Puritan story are the two traditions of Israel's origins in "the Abraham legend and the Exodus saga," and the pattern in these traditions is "to leave, journey under divine guidance," to suffer "testing in the wilderness and covenant." That pattern underlies the Puritan story. To comprehend both personal and national English history they must be understood in terms of Israel's history. The latter provides for the Puritan writer a "spiritual geography, a symbolic vocabulary, and a structure by means of which not only to apprehend but to recount" the work of God in the individual soul and 'the signs and

wonders' of God.
Argues that the Puritan story invites analysis in Aristotelian terms: there is a beginning, a middle and an end; in brief, there is progress toward a definite goal. There are numerous allusions throughout the article to The Pilgrim's Progress and a few references to Grace Abounding.

------. The Literary Culture of Nonconformity in Later Seventeeth-Century England. Leicester University Press, Leicester England and University of Georgia Press: Athens, 1987.

Discusses several features of Grace Abounding and The Pilgrim's Progress. Thinks of the ignorance of Bunyan's Ignorance as a "misconception about his spiritual state." Unlike other false pilgrims, he is not confined to a single episode, and the "tenacity of his misconception carries him through even to the gates of the Celestial City." Bunyan is so acutely aware of the threat posed by Ignorance that he gives the last word of his allegory not "to the glorification of Christian and Hopeful but to the damnation of Ignorance."
Other brief discussions of characters or events are helpful. See especially pp. 147, 156, 184, 207-208, 224, 285.

Kelly, Balmer H. "Pilgrim's Existence. A Consideration of the Bible in The Pilgrim's Progress." Interpretation 26 (January 1972): 62-71.

Asserts that The Pilgrim's Progress conveys the meaning of revelation with a "transhistorical significance." Shows the influence of the Bible in citations of Scripture and in the biblical language and imagery. Concludes that the pilgrim's journey is a series of struggles and of decisions to continue on it. Thinks of Bunyan as one in a direct line from the Apostle Paul through Augustine and Luther to Kierkegaard.

AN OVERVIEW

Kelman, John. *The Road. A Study of John Bunyan's "Pilgrim's Progress."* 1911; Reprint ed., 2 vol. Port Washington, New York: Kennikat Press, 1970.

    Considers *The Pilgrim's Progress* as an allegory of the spiritual life and as a romance. Careful study of various experiences which pilgrims encounter as depicted in numerous episodes. Holds that Bunyan recognizes the diversity of Christian experiences, especially seen in Christian, Faithful, and Hopeful.

Knott, John R., Jr. "Bunyan's Gospel Day: A Reading of *The Pilgrim's Progress*." *English Literary Renaissance* 3 no. 3 (Autumn 1973): 443-61.

    Argues against stance taken by Stanley Fish and holds that Bunyan does not subvert his image of the journey but rather shows that the individual Christian's way of faith coexists with the other sense of the way as a common journey of all believers. Clearly shows how Christian, having entered the "Gospel-day," uses the Word "as a means of spiritual survival" and also how the Word "sustains him by offering consolation." Contends that the stages in Christian's spiritual growth are characterized by changes in the nature of his temptations.

------. "John Bunyan and the Experience of the Word," *The Sword of the Spirit*, Chicago, 1980, pp. 131-63.

    The chapter focuses on the imaginative nature of selected writings by John Bunyan, including *Grace Abounding* and *The Pilgrim's Progress*. Shows ways in which Bunyan's Puritan imagination embodies responses to Scripture. Holds that we "still read *Grace Abounding* because Bunyan was able to convey a strongly individual experience in language that compels by its concreteness and its colloquial immediacy" (p. 132). Bunyan is especially sensitive to the terrors of the law and depicts the ways in which such terrors may lead to an enormous struggle which, in turn, brings conviction of sin. Yet, he also shows "the fruition of the soul" under the "quickening power" of the sword of the spirit.

The Pilgrim's Progress imaginatively shows Bunyan's commitment to the metaphor of the way: the way of all Christians from this world to the Celestial City and the way of faith of the individual pilgrim. Knott contends that the "design of The Pilgrim's Progress and much of its force, depends upon the figurative reading of the experience of the Israelites that Bunyan and countless other Puritans learned from Hebrews" (p. 140).

Bunyan defends in the Apology to The Pilgrim's Progress and in the verse Conclusion his figurative and imaginative method. One of his most significant appeals is to the metaphoric nature of biblical truth.

------. "Bunyan and the Holy Community." Studies in Philology LXXX no. 2 (1983): 200-26.

Studies features of the holy community in Part II of The Pilgrim's Progress.

Knox, R. Buick. "John Bunyan and His Pilgrim's Progress." Expository Times 90 no. 2 (November 1978): 40-43.

Contends that the journey metaphor, which involves an escape from the world, lacks special relevance to an era conscious of social engagement and reform. Predicts, however, that the allegory's confrontation of life, suffering, and death will guarantee its survival.

Kornblum, Peter Edward. "The Neighborhood of Reason: A Study in Narration and Relationship." Ph.D. dissertation. University of

California, Berkeley, 1981.

    Asserts that in the debate about the nature of the novel, the form has been related to the "determinations of modern, bourgeois society." This study grants the importance of these determinations, but believes that the argument still seeks to be responsive to traits of characters and nuances of theme. Holds that the structure of "narrative 'neighborliness' combines traditional piety and modern particularism." Believes that in Grace Abounding the narrator's spiritual development is also social and that in both parts of The Pilgrim's Progress, Bunyan dramatizes "the progress of the soul as a movement toward interpretive fellowship, an eternal neighborhood of the elect."

Kuder, Stephen R. "The Literature of Conversion: Religious Background and Literary Achievement in Dante Alighieri, John Bunyan, and James Joyce." Ph.D. dissertation. Graduate Theological Union, 1975.

    Asserts that inherent in the word "conversion" is the metaphor of "turning to God." The metaphor of turning toward God--or away from God--with all of its accompanying imagery, so permeates Grace Abounding (and other "conversion" literature) that insight into its theological and literary distinctiveness produces a new reading of the work.

Lacassagne, Claude. "De Bernard a Bunyan, du Berger Fidele a Evangelistse: Portraits de Ministre au XVII Siecle." Recherches Anglaises et Americaines 5 (1972): 173-93.

    Topical study of the pastor in The Pilgrim's Progress and Bernard's The Faithful Shepherd. Contends that Evangelist is a guide who affirms rather than instructs in doctrinal subjects. Evangelist had an inferior social and intellectual standing in

ANNOTATED BIBLIOGRAPHY

contrast to Bernard's pastor in The Faithful Shepherd.

Leavis, F.R. Afterword to The Pilgrim's Progress, pp. 284-300. Edited by Catherine Stempson. A Signet Classic. New York: The American Library of World Literature, Inc., 1964.

Insists that Bunyan was a highly gifted, imaginative writer and that The Pilgrim's Progress has the vitality and significance of major art. Strongly disagrees with critics who think "puritan" must be taken to "suggest a stern or morose austerity" without any concern for the grace and "good things" of this world. Recognizes William York Tindall's book, John Bunyan: Mechanick Preacher as scholarly work but counters its tone and thesis.

Levin, Harry. "Paradises, Heavenly and Earthly." Huntington Library Quarterly 29 no. 4 (August 1966): 305-324.

Claims that Bunyan is more effective when writing of the dangers of the journey rather than of the glory of the Celestial City.

Lewalski, Barbara Kiefer. "Typological Symbolism and the "Progress of the Soul' in Seventeenth-Century Literature." In Literary Uses of Typology from the Late Middle Ages to the Present, pp. 79-114. Edited by Earl Miner. Princeton, New Jersey: Princeton University Press, 1977.

Contends that Bunyan's pilgrims sometimes meet types and typological situations. Also holds that Christian's progress becomes a type for Christiana's journey.

Lewis, C.S. "The Vision of John Bunyan." Listener 68 no. 1759 (13 December 1962): 1006-1008.

Warned against the bad habit of reading The Pilgrim's Progress as though Bunyan were engaged in cryptography. He insists that it be read as allegory but properly as allegory. According to Lewis, "We ought not to be thinking 'This green valley, where the shepherd boy is singing, represents humility;' we ought to be discovering as we read, that humility is like that green valley." He further observes that readers should practice the habit of moving from the concept to the image, because the image informs and "enriches the concept."

Lindsay, Jack. <u>John Bunyan, Maker of Myths</u>. 1937; Reprint ed., Port Washington, New York: Kennikat Press, 1969.

    Attempts to explain the place of Bunyan's allegories in the area of myth. Focuses on <u>Grace Abounding</u>, <u>The Pilgrim's Progress</u> and other well-known works by Bunyan. Apparently contends that <u>Grace Abounding</u> has its roots in a social problem arising from a conflict between capitalism and the Levellers.

Lyons, John O. <u>The Invention of Self</u>. Carbondale: Southern Illinois University Press, 1978, pp. 71, 73, 82.

    (See Chapter Five entitled "Autobiography") Many journals of public events were written during the seventeenth century. Another form is the confession, "which in Evangelical hands, as in the case of John Bunyan in <u>Grace Abounding</u> follows the tradition of the stunning miracle established by St. Paul rather than the slow intellectual growth of Augustine." The movement of the work is allegorical.

MacCaffrey, Isabel G. <u>Spenser'a Allegory. The Anatomy of Imagination</u>. Princeton, New Jersey: Princeton University Press, 1976, pp. 61, 65, 82, 148.

    All allegory assumes an "anti-nominalist ontology" and old Honest's identifying himself is an illustration from <u>The Pilgrim's Progress</u>. The concluding vision of the allegory shows truth attained after a "metaphorical progress."

MacDonald, Ruth K. "The Case for <u>The Pilgrim's Progress</u>." <u>Children's Literature Association Quarterly</u> 10 no. 1 (Spring 1985): 29-30.

    Not a critical study but offers suggested hints found within the text that serve as means to an understanding of the allegory. Argues also for the inclusion of <u>The Pilgrim's Progress</u> in the historical canon of children's literature.

MacNeice, Louis. <u>Varieties of Parable</u>. Cambridge, Cambridge University Press, 1965, pp. 17, 23-24, 29, 42-45.

    Gives attention to dialogue, story element, dream device, and characters in <u>The Pilgrim's Progress</u>. Slight concern with a comparison of construction of <u>The Pilgrim's Progress</u> with that of Spenser's <u>Faerie Queene</u>.

Mandel, Barret John. "The Autobiographer's Art: A Study of Bunyan, Gibbon, and Cowper." Ph.D. dissertation. University of Connecticut, 1967.

    Asks the questions: "In what sense is autobiography a literary art?" "How is it different from other literary arts?" "By what criteria can it be judged?" Proceeds from the Aristotelian premise that "the art of a literary work may be judged by how well or poorly it carries out its rhetorical or aesthetic purpose." Discusses the value of evaluating the autobiographer's art in "the language of formal or structural literary criticism." Considers the importance of relating author's "self-representation" to his "overall self-conception and governing purpose" as they are embodied in the work.
    Contends that there is a problem in

evaluating Grace Abounding because of its being "unoriginal and typical of a body of Puritan autobiographies." Attempts to show that evaluation of Grace Abounding must take into consideration that is was written "to satisfy a social as well as an artistic end."

------. "Bunyan and the Autobiographer's Artistic Purpose." Criticism 10 no. 3 (Summer 1968): 225-43.

Contends that Bunyan's treatment of time is the one aspect of Grace Abounding which separates it to any obvious degree from other spiritual autobiographies. Bunyan also has a governing principle which defines the artistic end toward which Grace Abounding moved; the governing principle by which he selects episodes is a didactic purpose.

Manlove, C.N. "The Image of the Journey in Pilgrim's Progress: Narrative Versus Allegory." Journal of Narrative Technique 10 no. 1 (Winter 1980): 16-38.

Claims that the distinguishing feature of The Pilgrim's Progress is the focus on one path, the constant sense of the pilgrim moving toward his goal.

Marohl, Joseph William, Jr. Argument and Narrative Technique in John Bunyan's Autobiography. Ph.D. dissertation. University of Miami, 1983.

Contends that Bunyan's literary style was the outgrowth of "the designs and method employed to evangelical ends in the early treatises and thus, by implication, an outgrowth of his pulpit oratory." Argues that the narrative crisis is a crisis of temptation, similar in design to the temptation in the wilderness in Matthew 4:1-11.

Mills, David. "The Dreams of Bunyan and Langland." In <u>The Pilgrim's Progress: Critical and Historical Views</u>, pp. 154-81. Edited by Vincent Newey. Liverpool: Liverpool University Press, 1980.

    Asserts that <u>The Pilgrim's Progress</u> has two different forms: the traditional allegory, which presents a simple world in which our range of responses is limited, and the dream form, which has in it an ambiguity and uncertainty. These two forms are in constant tension in both <u>The Pilgrim's Progress</u> and <u>The Vision of Piers Plowman</u>. Claims also that because of the shifting tones and themes in <u>Piers Plowman</u>, Langland has a more "naturalistic" dream-form than Bunyan. However, Bunyan has a greater simplicity.

Monk, Samuel Holt. Introductions to selections from <u>Grace Abounding</u> and <u>The Pilgrim's Progress</u>. In <u>The Norton Antholgy of English Literature</u>, pp. 1808-1810. Edited by M.H. Abrams <u>et al</u>. New York and London: W.W. Norton & Co., 1979.

    Claims that Bunyan's "psychological insight and vivid narrative make <u>Grace Abounding</u> one of the most enthralling autobiographies in the language." Considers <u>The Pilgrim's Progress</u> to be the most successful allegory in English literature. Its basic metaphor is simple and familiar; the objects that Christian meets are commonplace; the style is modeled on the prose of the English Bible, and the details are "vividly rendered."

Morris, John N. "John Bunyan and the Head of Goliath." <u>South Atlantic Quarterly</u> 64 no.1 (1965): 15-26.

    Commends the account of Bunyan's spiritual experience as recorded in <u>Grace Abounding</u> and considers the author's courage in suffering to be intellectually heroic.

------. "The Example of John Bunyan." <u>Versions</u>

of the Self, Studies in English Autobiography from John Bunyan to John Stuart Mill, pp. 89-104. New York: Basic Books, 1966.

    Maintains that the analytic tone of Grace Abounding gives Bunyan's autobiography a mark superior to many other introspective autobiographies. Grace Abounding is not simply a chronicling of experience but is also a judgment in retrospect of experiences. Claims that despite Bunyan's silence about external details of his life, "the prose of Grace Abounding is rich with physical facts." Further claims that "Bunyan is ingenious at finding in the world objects and actions equivalents for his subjective states."

Nakano, Nancy Yoshiko. "The Authority of Narrative: Technique and Argument in Milton, Bunyan, Dryden, and John Reynolds." Ph.D. dissertation. University of California, Los Angeles, 1973.

    Defines narrative as "all imaginative literature having both a tale and a teller; narrative mediates between drama (which has only a tale) and lyric (which had only a teller)." The configuration of narrative elements (especially plot, character, and point of view) determines the direction of inquiry into a given work. Contends that in The Pilgrim's Progress, the plot follows no causal or dramatic logic but rather the "events of the plot are determined by the order of appearance of the characters that Christian encounters on his journey." Asserts that a "structural sequence based on the relative motion and direction of these characters runs concurrently with a didactic sequence."

Nellist, Brian. "The Pilgrim's Progress and Allegory." In The Pilgrim's Progress: Critical and Historical Views, pp. 132-53. Edited by Vincent Newey. Liverpool: Liverpool University Press, 1980.

ANNOTATED BIBLIOGRAPHY

Claims that The Pilgrim's Progress seems in many respects closer to post-allegorical works than to a traditional allegory because there stands at its center "not a coherent body of thought or a process of developing reflection, as in traditional allegory, but consciousness."

Nevo, Ruth. The Dial of Virtue. A Study of Poems on Affairs of State in the Seventeenth Century, pp. 235-36. Princeton, New Jersey: Princeton University Press, 1963.

Succinct statement on style of The Pilgrim's Progress and its influence in showing the heroic vision of the allegory.

Newey, Vincent. "Bunyan and the Confines of the Mind." In The Pilgrim's Progress: Critical and Historical Views, pp. 21-48. Edited by Vincent Newey. Liverpool: Liverpool University Press, 1980.

Focuses on the "psychological and experiential truth embodied in the work," and to some extent with "reading its psycho-historical message (that is, its meaning in relation to the larger history of the mind)." What Newey offers the reader in this essay is primarily a specimen of a psychological approach to the work. The study aims at getting behind temporal and cultural suppositions in an attempt to extract what is timeless in the history of the mind. Therefore, Christian at Doubting Castle is a "psychodrama: in which an individual [must] live by his own devices."

------., ed. The Pilgrim's Progress: Critical and Historical Views. Liverpool: Liverpool University Press, 1980.

A collection of assorted essays (all are included in this bibliography) which considers its purpose to be "to provide a fresh detailed, and varied consideration of

AN OVERVIEW

The Pilgrim's Progress.

------. "Dorothea's Awakening: The Recall of Bunyan in Middlemarch." Notes & Queries 31 (December 1984): 497-99.

    Shows concern for a subtle, reference to Bunyan's The Pilgrim's Progress in Middlemarch rather than the epigraph in the penultimate chapter which obviously contrasts Bulstrode's pitiable self-contempt with Faithful's "proud knowledge that he is martyred 'for professing the Right.'" Sees a connection between Dorothea's awakening cry to do some positive good towards those in whose crisis she is involved and that of Christian's famous cry at the beginning of The Pilgrim's Progress. Considers various connections (and contrasts) between Christian and Dorothea.

Newman, S.J. "Bunyan's Solidness." In The Pilgrim's Progress: Critical and Historical Views, pp. 225-50. Edited by Vincent Newey. Liverpool: Liverpool University Press, 1980.

    Argues that if religious literature has survived in the twentieth century, it is that critics have transformed the literal language of the text into a literary language, giving expression to the unfulfilled longings of the human heart. "Bunyan's solidness resists this conversion," according to Newman. His "home-made artifact," resists such "contemporary critical rhetoric." The Pilgrim's Progress is important, however, because it is the "last significant product of English religious folk vision."
    To be a pilgrim is to be the humble and despised in society; to write a story about a common wayfaring man means to shun the demands of the rich. Bunyan correspondingly uses a language which is not overtly poetic or rhetorical. By using this common folk-speech, he achieves a solidness, but as the pilgrim draws nearer to the Celestial City,

the exalted language of "the Authorized Version takes over." Furthermore, he contends that in "Part I Bunyan was so concerned to solidify his metaphors that the numinousness of language was excluded. In Part II Bunyan's confidence in his community is reflected in a different attitude to language ... language is once again miraculous, poetic...."

Nussbaum, Felicity A. "'By These Words I Was Sustained': Bunyan's Grace Abounding." Journal of English Literary History 49 (1982): 18-34.

Sees conflict between the "universal allegorical ideal" and the particularized individual in Bunyan's autobiographgical self-representation.

Nuttall, A.D. Two Concepts of Allegory. New York: Barnes & Noble, Inc., 1967.

Only slight attention to Bunyan, but helpful in discussing critical errors inherent in the belief that because "the degree and elaboration of personification is so obviously fictional, the personification itself must be fictional also." Reminds the reader that one need not think that Bunyan believed, for example, that Apollyon existed "exactly as he described him," but he did believe that "something bearing a recognizable resemblance to Apollyon did exist ...." Bunyan would agree "that it is not possible to demythologize all his language, but he would not agree that this admission reduced all his assertions to vanity."pp. 27, 31-32.

Nuttall, Geoffrey F., "The Heart of The Pilgrim's Progress." In Reformation Principle and Practice: Essays in Honour of Arthur Geoffrey Dickens, pp. 227-39. Edited by Peter Brooks. London: Scholar Press, 1980.

Believes that Bunyan's imaginative manner is "consistent metaphor, not a suc-

cession of similes." What he wrote was not "an outer varnish or an escape mechanism to conceal or to avoid what was real, it was real." Further holds that through Bunyan's artistry the figure of Christ is presented throughout The Pilgrim's Progress in a variety of ways, including through the sayings and actions of Jesus which Bunyan lifts for commentary within the structure of the allegory. Also hold that Christ is in some sense mystically present, especially in the lives of those whom Christian meets.
Emphasizes that the allegory is "a work of supreme imaginative genius; but its power is as a book of 'the way': the way to Christ, the way of Christ, and the way with Christ."

Ogden, James. "Bunyan's Idea of a 'Wide Field.'" Notes & Queries 28 no. 226 (February 1981): 51.

Continues the controversy on Bunyan's meaning of a "wide Field." Reminds the reader that Clifford Johnson argued that Bunyan made moutains out of molehills in referring to a 'wide field full of dark mountains' and that Sheila Jackson contested that Bunyan must have understood 'field' to mean an area big enough at least to have hills--if not mountains--in it. Suggests an examination of the recording of the word in OED and and a consideration of Langland's 'field ful of folk.'

Ogden, Merlene Ann. "Nathaniel Hawthorne and John Bunyan." Ph.D. dissertation. University of Nebraska, 1964.

Excellent in showing the tremendous influence of John Bunyan, especially The Pilgrim's Progress, on a major American author. Sees Bunyan's influence in the method of allegory, in the pilgrimage theme, and in his concern with subject of man's destiny in an evil world. Secondary themes from Bunyan are also influential: the

ANNOTATED BIBLIOGRAPHY

attempt of the pilgrim to find release from his burden, doubt and despair caused by guilt, and the false pilgrimage which leads to tragic-destruction. The influence also extends to dramatization of allegorical episodes and character depiction.

Pascal, Roy. Design and Truth in Autobiography, Cambridge, MA: Harvard University Press, 1960, pp. 33-43.

Entire book is helpful in understanding autobiography as a literary genre. Grace Abounding shows a candor and simplicity worthy of praise, but the work lacks range.

------. "The Present Tense in The Pilgrim's Progress." Modern Language Review 60 (January 1965): 13-16.

Demonstrates how exact an artist Bunyan is even in the minutiae of his text. Pascal insists that whenever the present tense occurs in The Pilgrim's Progress (in contrast to the usual preterite tense), it "recalls the basic structure of a myth, repeated in many tales, something familiar and expected."

Pauli, Ruth F. Janda. "The Plot of Pilgrimage: The Quest as Organization Pattern in Bunyan's Narrative." Ph.D. dissertation. University of Maryland, 1976.

Identifies three model quests representing separate points of view with three distinct patterns and movements in Grace Abounding and The Pilgrim's Progress, Parts One and Two. The first quest is the "pagan cyclical" pattern, characterized by "the hero's setting out, reaching his goal, and returning." The second quest is the spiritual quest pattern with an inward meeting with God and a movement of growth, "with three phases--the inner search for the Shadow, for the Anima," and the "integrating of Ego and Shadow into a new Self or God."

The third pattern is the romance quest with its "journey, conflict, and recognition." Argues that an analysis of the three works shows that Bunyan uses the quest to organize his narrative and to express the tension existing between the spiritual and pagan quests. Contends that Bunyan has mastered the art of narrative by using the organizing structure of the quest.

Pickering, Samuel. "E.E. Cummings' Pilgrim's Progress." Christianity and Literature 28 (1978): 17-31.

Discusses parallels between Cummings' The Enormous Room and The Pilgrim's Progress.

Pooley, Roger. "A Study of John Bunyan's Language and Milieu." Ph.D. dissertation. Cambridge University, 1976.

The thesis considers the problem of literary history in relation to Bunyan and how we may best see him in the context of the Restoration. A chapter on Grace Abounding leads to a more general discussion on Bunyan and the Puritan culture. Some attention focuses on the plain style in religious discourse.

Pooley devotes two linked chapters to a reading of The Pilgrim's Progress. The first takes the phrase, 'the wilderness of this world' to open the connections between Bunyan's conception of pilgrimage and his use of language and allegory. The core of the second chapter on the allegory adapts structuralist techniques to demonstrate "the close resemblance between Part I of The Pilgrim's Progress and folklore, characterizes the differences between the two parts of the book, and describes the patterns of help and opposition that the pilgrims experience."

Two short chapters draw the study together.

------. "The Wilderness of this World--Bunyan's

ANNOTATED BIBLIOGRAPHY

Pilgrim's Progress." <u>Baptist Quarterly</u> 27 no. 7 (July 1978): 290-99.

Discusses the medieval tradition of the wilderness motif. Studies biblical background to the opening section of <u>The Pilgrim's Progress</u> to show the interconnection between the nature of Christian's journey and the "mode and perception of each place and incident."

Puzon, M. Bridget. "The Archetype of the Journey: Studies in Bunyan, Smollet, and Conrad." Ph.D. dissertation. Harvard University, 1973.

Studies <u>The Pilgrim's Progress</u> as a particular appearance of the journey archetype, "the primal model of process in the hero quest." The pilgrim's world takes its boundaries from the specific religious ideology which informs it, but despite its specificity, the allegory resembles other literary works of the journey. The informing source and power of <u>The Pilgrim's Progress</u> is the Bible.

Quilligan, Maureen. <u>The Language of Allegory</u>. Ithaca and London: Cornell University Press, 1979.

Challenges traditional definitions of allegory and defines the genre in terms of the text, the pretext, the context, and the reader. Contends also that allegory appeals to readers "as readers of a system of signs." Believes that the language of the pretext is so privileged in Bunyan's allegory that it threatens the autonomy of the narrative. Yet, Bunyan maintains a "suprarealist" attitude and he writes an alleogry of enduring art which is "of a piece with the Puritan aesthetic which suspects the abilities of man's own language unaided by scripture to speak the truth."

Reeves, Paschal. "<u>The Pilgrim's Progress</u> as a

Precursor of the Novel." <u>Georgia Review</u> 20 no. 1 (Spring 1966): 64-71.

    Asserts that since Bunyan left his literary successors new insights on narrative, setting, dialogue, and characterization, he cannot be ignored in any study of the development of the novel.

Reuter, John Edward. "A Quiet Habitation: The Spiritual Autobiography and the Development of the English Novel." Ph.D. dissertation. University of Rochester, 1968.

    Asserts that the spiritual autobiography is a central influence on "the structure, themes, and imagery of the early English novel." Concentrating on Bunyan, the study attempts to show the movement from spiritual autobiography through allegory to fiction. Traces his coinciding "spiritual and literary development from controversialist, to spiritual autobiographer, to interpretive allegorist to narrative allegorist." Holds that <u>The Pilgrim's Progress</u> is the first great English novel, which resulted "from Bunyan's need to universalize his private spiritual search and from his integrated spiritual and aesthetic consciousness."

Rexroth, Kenneth. "Classics Revisited: <u>The Pilgrim's Progress</u>." <u>Saturday Review</u> 49 (13 August 1966): 20.

    Declares that Bunyan's allegory presents a vision of life and contains the structure of the inner life.

Robinson, David. "Bunyan's House of the Interpreter and the Structure of <u>The Pilgrim's Progress</u>." <u>Dutch Quarterly Review of Anglo-American Letters</u> 7 (1976): 101-113.

    Argues that the Interpreter's emblems demonstrate a focus on the past, present and future. The sequence of this ordering, how-

ANNOTATED BIBLIOGRAPHY

ever, primarily shows insight into Bunyan's covenant theology rather than his methodology.

Roppen, George, and Sommer, Richard. Strangers and Pilgrims. An Essay on the Metaphor of the Journey. Oslo: Norwegian Universities Press, 1964, pp. 102-108.

    Examines the metaphor of the journey and focuses on Bunyan primarily in relation to the Apology to The Pilgrim's Progress.

Rosenwasser, David. "The Idea of Enclosure: Prisons and Havens at the Rise of the Novel." Ph.D. dissertation. University of Virginia, 1985.

    Asserts that ever since the exile from Eden thrust men into earthly captivity, they have invested "confined space with ambivalent meaning." Holds that enclosures are doubly ambiguous structures, for they can function as "either prisons or havens; and these settings can be primarily realistic or symbolic." Demonstrates the significance of such settings to the generic development of the novel. The Pilgrim's Progress, for example, originates in the jail "where the narrator dreams the book; and it follows Christian through the prisons and havens of 'the way' before delivering him to 'the desired haven' across the River Death." Further contends that where Christian struggles against the "entanglements of the flesh, Bunyan struggles against the realistic limitation of his art." Sees a connection between this conclusion and Bunyan's own words: "My dark and cloudy words they do but hold/ The Truth as Cabinets inclose the Gold."

Roulston, C. Robert. "Hawthorne's Use of Bunyan's Symbols in The Celestial Railroad." Kentucky Philological Association Bulletin (1975): 17-24.

AN OVERVIEW

Hawthorne appropriates Bunyan's symbols in The Pilgrim's Progress in order to attack Unitarianism and other nineteenth-century philosophies.

Sadler, Lynn Veach. John Bunyan. Boston: Twayne English Authors Series, 1979, pp. 32-64, 92-111.

Chapter two offers an analysis of the genre, the psychology, the "people" and style of Grace Abounding. Chapter three carefully studies the pilgrimage of The Pilgrim's Progress, the meaning of the allegory, and the language, style and themes. Chapter six focuses on Part Two and explains differences between the two parts.

Sams, Horace, Jr. "Temptation in Imaginative Literature of Milton and Bunyan: Two Faces of the Puritan Persona." Ph.D. dissertation. University of South Florida, 1985.

Compares the treatments of the temptation theme by Bunyan and Milton. Through an analysis of selected portions of imaginative writings seeks to show that Bunyan (and Milton) wrote out of a rich tradition of "Temptation, Fall, and Pilgrimage literature." Holds that Bunyan in writing of the pilgrimage of the soul to the Celestial City is most comfortable with the popular medieval allegory and the dream vision literary framework.

Santa Maria, Felixberto C. "An Audience Analysis of John Bunyan's Pilgrim's Progress." Ph.D dissertation. Michigan State University, 1962.

Attempts to describe the audience of the allegory since its publication in 1678, to relate the various categories of readers to their social milieu, and to analyze how changing social, economic, and religious conditions have influenced the readership. Claims that Bunyan's high credibility helped to enlarge the audience along with the simplicity of style, lucidity of language and the universality of the theme of the allegory. Also suggests that the use of allegorical form, replete with adventurous episodes, appeals to some readers. Holds that the popularity of the work has been related to the characteristics of the times: the allegory was more popular "during congenial times, and less popular during less congenial times." Concludes that relationships among source, message, and audience are highly complex.

Schnieder, Mabel, D.J. "John Bunyan's The Pilgrim's Progress in the Tradition of the Medieval Dream Visions." Ph.D. dissertation. University of Nebraska, 1970.

 Studies The Pilgrim's Progress against the tradition of the literary allegorical dreams, particularly those of fourteenth-century England. Dreams of the century are ultimately didactic in nature and seek to discover and impart divine truth. They also employ the form of the dream that overreaches the limits of time and space and that releases the soul from the confines of the body. In each the dreamer is also a main actor within the dream-work and is taught and assisted by guides. Sometimes the dreamer is fairly passive, but often participates in the action. Allegories prior to The Pilgrim's Progress are expressed "through a highly conventionalized 'symbolic language.'"
 The Pilgrim's Progress in comparison with the medieval dream visions displays the "breadth, complexity, and consistency of Bunyan's understanding of the relationship between God and man." Further holds that Bunyan's dream vision resembles its medieval predecessors in "content and in its use of conventionalized symbolic language." His dream vision, as his predecessors, depends on a concept of an "orderly universe ruled by absolutes, in which the disruptive con-

flict instigated by man's sinfulness is ultimately resolved in the harmonious union of man with God."

Seed, David. "Dialogue and Debate in *The Pilgrim's Progress*." In *The Pilgrim's Progress: Critical and Historical Views*, pp. 69-90. Edited by Vincent Newey. Liverpool: Liverpool University Press, 1980.

    Asserts that the allegory consists mostly of dialogue, and Bunyan is particularly adept at capturing different levels of discourse which correspond to certain characters. Believes that Bunyan is no mere tinker. His art distills the very essence of genuine regional dialects.

Sharrock, Roger, ed. Introduction to *The Pilgrim's Progress*, pp. 7-26. Harmondsworth, Middlesex: Penguin Books, 1965.

    Claims that *The Pilgrim's Progress* is a creation of myth, yet much of the book's appeal lies in its strong sense of realism. Asserts that the allegory has a theological structure grounded in a religious vision. The journey of Christiana differs from that of Christian's in its social milieu and in its pace.

------. *John Bunyan: The Pilgrim's Progress*. Studies in English Literature, no. 27, London: Edward Arnold, 1966.

    Studies the genre of *The Pilgrim's Progress*, shows that there is a mixture of genres in the allegory, thoughtfully discusses the verse "Apology," relates the allegory to *Grace Abounding*, and gives a critical reading of the action. Exclusive literary criteria fail to release a full appreciation of Bunyan, according to Sharrock.

------. *John Bunyan*. 1954; revised London: Macmillan, 1968.

ANNOTATED BIBLIOGRAPHY

A reliable and compact treatment of the man Bunyan and his background. Devotes chapters to each of his major works, including Grace Abounding and The Pilgrim's Progress.

------, ed., Bunyan: "The Pilgrim's Progress": A Casebook. Casebook Series. London: Macmillan, 1976.

Excellent introductory section on the reputation of The Pilgrim's Progress since its publication until the present time. Gives a brief survey of critical studies on Grace Abounding and The Pilgrim's Progress. Includes representative critical opinions from Bunyan's "Prefatory Verses" to the contemporary essay by John R. Knott, Jr., "Bunyan's Gospel Day: A Reading of The Pilgrim's Progress."

------. "John Bunyan in English Literature." The John Bunyan Lectures 1978. To Mark the 350th Anniversary of the Birth of John Bunyan and the Tercentenary of the Publication of 'The Pilgrim's Progress.' Bedfordshire Education Service, pp. 1-13.

Contends that Bunyan did not think of himself as a creative writer in the modern sense, but paradoxically, this seventeenth century sectarian has a world-wide audience. Claims that The Pilgrim's Progress and other writings of Bunyan are similar and holds that the wide appeal of the allegory is due primarily to the archetypal nature of the quest motif.

------. "Life and Story in The Pilgrim's Progress." In The Pilgrim's Progress: Critical and Historical Views, pp. 49-68. Edited by Vincent Newey. Liverpool: Liverpool University Press, 1980.

Rejects the Coleridgean view that Bunyan the artist triumphed over Bunyan the preacher. Something of the formal structure of sermons is carried over into the allegory. Explains that *The Pilgrim's Progress* is as universal as the folk tale.

Shenk, Robert. "John Bunyan: Puritan or Pilgrim?" *Cithara* 14 no. 1 (December 1974): 77-93.

    Questions whether *The Pilgrim's Progress* is even a Puritan work, since the idea of pilgrimage (as suggested by the title) is alien to the Puritan spirit. Bunyan's Christian, according to Shenk, comes to an understanding of God through his encounters with specific events and particular persons in the natural world. In brief, Christian attains union with the supernatural through the natural; furthermore, the allegory embraces "the collective adventure of pilgrimage" rather than the salvation of an individual, thus displaying a "poetic imagination" closer to Chaucer than to the Puritans.

Shrimpton, Nick. "Bunyan's Military Metaphor." In *The Pilgrim's Progress: Critical and Historical Views*, pp. 205-224. Edited by Vincent Newey. Liverpool: Liverpool University Press, 1980.

    Claims that Bunyan's military imagery gives internal coherence to the allegory. Also addresses the question as to whether *The Pilgrim's Progress* is indeed a progress. Argues that the work is static and progress painfully slow until at the House Beautiful, Christian is armed. Henceforth, he will be a warrior.

Smith, David E. "*The Enormous Room* and *The Pilgrim's Progress*." *Twentieth Century Literature* 11 no. 2 (July 1965): 67-75.

    Claims that Cummings appropriates Bunyan's allegory as the organizing structure of his parable, but restates some of Bunyan's embodied truths about man to a sinful world.

Smith, Herbert W. "Bunyan and Dante: A Comparison." Durham University Journal 69 no. 1 (December 1976): 5-13.

    Provocative examination of similarities and differences between The Pilgrim's Progress and The Divine Comedy which show the purpose to be similar and their structures not entirely dissimilar, particularly when Part Two of Bunyan's allegory is compared with the structure of The Purgatorio. Also, the primary source of each is the "Word of God."

Snyder, Susan. "The Left Hand of God: Despair in Medieval and Renaissance Tradition." Studies in the Renaissance 12 (1965): 18-59.

    Helpful in explanation of episodes such as Doubting Castle and others that deal with the subject of despair. Discusses relationship between despair and suicide as seen by a medieval theologian like Augustine and the changes in the view held by later theologians.

Spear, Jeffrey L. "Ruskin as a Prejudiced Reader." ELH 49 no. 1 (Spring 1982): 73-98.

    The focus is not entirely on Bunyan but rather on an examination of the religious context of Ruskin's definition of himself as an interpreter. The procedure is with Gadamer's analysis of the process of interpretation in mind--not itself a method, but an understanding of method. Investigates Ruskin's claim that his own special function was that "of the Interpreter only in The Pilgrim's Progress." Then, asserts that Interpreter deals in images, "the visible forms of eternal things, explaining to Christian, and later to Christiana, the latent meanings of paintings, dream visions, and allegorical tableaux, and teaching them to interpret on their own." The Interpreter links images to scriptural texts and Christian doctrines. Images and interpretation alike are conveyed by Bunyan's prose. Bunyan's Interpreter links image, Scripture and doctrine with absolute certainty; Ruskin, the Evangelical, found it impossible to link with certainty his own "canoned texts" and the art and landscape of Modern Painters.

Spengemann, Walter A. The Forms of Autobiography, pp. 44-51. New Haven: Yale University Press, 1980.

Salient features of Grace Abounding appear as "exacerbations of the formal difference" between Augustine's Confessions and Dante's La Vita Nuova. The autobiography continues "the drift, so noticeable in Dante's narrative, away from Augustine's emphasis upon the static design of known truth towards a concentration upon the dynamic process of experience of individuals rather than to doctrines which authorize that experience." Doctrines that explain Augustine and life "lay outside of life in a theological system"; Dante based the informing pattern of La Vita Nuova upon established Christian symbiology, but Bunyan's "idiosyncratic" reading of Scripture seemed to be experiences in their own rights rather than "doctrinally authorized interpretation" of experience.

Stokes, E.E., Jr. "Bernard Shaw's Debt to John Bunyan." Shaw Review 8 (1965): 42-51.

Shows the appeal which Bunyan's didactic motives had for Shaw.

Stranahan, Brainerd P. "Bunyan and the Bible: Use of Biblical Materials in the Imaginative structure of The Pilgrim's Progress." Ph.D. dissertation. Harvard University, 1965.

Analyzes the use of Biblical materials in the imaginative structure of The Pil-

ANNOTATED BIBLIOGRAPHY

grim's Progress in an attempt to provide means of appreciating Bunyan's literary art by showing how Biblical sources have become a part of his extended allegory. Applies the word "allegory" in two senses to The Pilgrim's Progress: as a species of trope--a mode of speech employed in the book and as a genre of which this trope is a characteristic device. Also considers influences that have combined with or supplemented Biblical material.

------. "Bunyan's Special Talent: Biblical Texts as 'Events" in Grace Abounding and The Pilgrim's Progress." English Literary Renaissance 11 no. 3 (1981): 329-43.

 Opposes the view that Bunyan's "aural orientation toward the Word, with the Scripture a Voice for the inner ear" is consonant with the Puritan conception of meditation as inner oratory, "in which the voice was not necessarily that of Scripture but might be that of the spiritual or rational self expostulating with the sensuous nature." Stranahan, however, suggests that Bunyan's "inner ear" appears "attuned almost exclusively to direct and unhidden Scriptural quotation." In Bunyan's autobiography and allegory, biblical passages explode on the narrator's mind like a "spiritual event." These biblical texts, which confront Bunyan like prophetic revelations, always have an appropriateness to the crisis at hand. Furthermore, the scriptural connotations and allusions in The Pilgrim's Progress underscore the presence of the biblical texts in the author's mind during the process of composition.

------. "Bunyan and the Epistle to the Hebrews: His Source for the Idea of Pilgrimage in The Pilgrim's Progress." Studies in Philology 79 (1982): 279-96.

 Introduces his study by asking the question, "Where did John Bunyan get the idea for his great allegory depicting his life as a pilgrimage?" Several possibilities are offered as partial influences, but the interpretation of the Old Testament story of the Exodus saga in the Book of Hebrews, which views the patriarchs as "strangers and pilgrims" journeying to a "continuing city," definitely encouraged an allegorical reading.

Sutherland, James. <u>English Literature of the Late Seventeenth Century</u>. Vol. 6: <u>The Oxford History of English Literature</u>, pp. 314-36. Edited by Bonamy Dobrée and Norman Davis. Oxford: Clarendon Press, 1969.

Shows the similarity between <u>Grace Abounding</u> and <u>The Pilgrim's Progress</u> and holds that even the method in <u>The Pilgrim's Progress</u> was not dissimilar to <u>Grace Abounding</u>, for in the autobiography there is evidence of the "visualizing quality of his mind."

Talon, Henri A. "Space and the Hero in <u>The Pilgrim's Progress</u>." <u>Études Anglaises</u> 14 no. 2 (1961): 124-30.

Contends that out of the symbolic vision natural to Puritans there grew for John Bunyan a literary vision, "just as the dreamer of <u>The Pilgrim's Progress</u> grew out of the dreams on which he fed daily for years." The real country of the allegory then is "just precisely this dream land which Bunyan created with that energy of vision and of faith which is one of the characteristics of genius." For Talon, the pilgrim must be considered in relation to the country "which is the projection of his inward landscape and the manifestation in space of his sense of values." After Evangelist becomes his guide, Christian shows himself to be a man with values, particularly seen in the fusion of belief and behavior.

ANNOTATED BIBLIOGRAPHY

------. John Bunyan. Writers and their Works no. 73, 1956; Reprint ed., London: Longmans, Green & Co., 1964; Reprint (with revision in bibliography) London: Longmans, Green & Co. for the British Council and the National Book League, 1972.

    Comments on subject of sincerity in Grace Abounding and offers insight on variety of tone in The Pilgrim's Progress.

------. John Bunyan, The Man and His Works. Folcroft, Pa: Folcroft Library Editions, Norwood, Pa: Norwood Editions, 1951; Reprint ed. 1976, 1977, 1980.

    Excellent study of Grace Abounding in chapter one and of The Pilgrim's Progress in chapter three. Careful attention to structure, characters, and symbolism.

Taylor, Dennis. "Some Strategies of Religious Autobiography." Renascence 27 no. 1 (Autumn 1974): 40-44.

    Contends that Bunyan places "the flux and refluxes of his will" within biblical patterns in order to overcome his willfulness.

Thickstun, Margaret Olofson. "Fictions of the Feminine: Puritan Doctrine and the Representative of Women." Ph.D. dissertation. Cornell University, 1984.

    Traces what she calls a "recurrent pattern in the literary presentation of women" in English allegorical narratives during the seventeenth century, including The Pilgrim's Progress. Argues that male protagonists displaced females from positive roles that women traditionally held and came to personify virtues that women conventionally represented. Contends that in The Pilgrim's Progress, the "displacement of women from the spiritual realm" becomes fully expressed structurally. Illustrates her thesis with

Standfast of Part Two. He, who is the "male perfection of female virtue, usurps Christiana's role as heroine and Bride; the type of 'higher chastity'; he is subsumed into the Godhead." Believes that the pattern derives from the Pauline interpretation of Christianity which greatly influenced Puritan attitudes.

------. "The Preface to Bunyan's <u>Grace Abounding</u> as Pauline Epistle." <u>Notes and Queries</u> 32 (June 1985): 180-182.

    Contends that Bunyan adapts the Apostle Paul's phrasing and epistle format to comfort and encourage his congregation, and to "introduce his spiritual history to the world." Amid Pauline references to remembrance of spiritual converts, Bunyan introduces the "spiritual benefits of remembering the workings of God's grace" upon the soul. In the "benediction" of <u>Grace Abounding</u>, Bunyan expresses the seventeenth-century motif of the Church Militant, "extrapolated from Paul's metaphor of the soldier of Christ."

Thompson, E.P. <u>The Making of the English Working Class</u>. London: Victor Gollancz, 1963, pp. 31-35, 40, 50, 52, 108, 184, 194, 408, 471.

    Considers <u>The Pilgrim's Progress</u> to be a "foundation text" of the working-class movement in England. The world of the allegory is that of the poor man, constantly under oppression from the powerful yet finding comfort in the belief of an afterlife.

Thorpe, James, ed. Introduction to <u>The Pilgrim's Progress and Grace Abounding</u>. Riverside Editions. Boston: Houghton Mifflin Co., 1969, pp. VII-XXI.

    The introduction analyzes <u>Grace Abounding</u> and contends that the work strongly influences subsequent works that deals with the role of the conscience in human conduct.

Succinct and careful examination of the structure, allegory, narrative methods, characters, and style of The Pilgrim's Progress. Contrasts Part one and Part Two.

Thurland, M.J. "John Bunyan: A Theological Approach to Grace Abounding and The Pilgrim's Progress." Ph.D. dissertation. University of Leeds, 1973-74.

The declared purpose of the dissertation is to read Bunyan's two major literary works in the light of his theology.
The study is divided into four chapters. The first chapter examines various approaches taken by selected critics and then shows that there is a place for a theological approach. Chapter two investigates the nature of Bunyan's theology and establishes him in a particular theological tradition; chapters three and four offer a reading of Grace Abounding and The Pilgrim's Progress from a theological point of view.

Tindall, William York. John Bunyan: Mechanick Preacher. 1934; reprint ed. New York: Russell & Russell, 1964.

Claims that Bunyan was a typical mechanick preacher, that Grace Abounding is similar to numerous other autobiographies, and that Bunyan's participation in religious controversy is an influence on The Pilgrim's Progress. Ignorance, whom he labels a Latitudinarian, is illustrative of the effect of Bunyan's polemical encounters.

Trull, Joe E. "The Ethics of John Bunyan." Ph.D. dissertation. Southwestern Baptist Theological Seminary, 1965.

Focuses on factors which influenced Bunyan's ethic. Explores his "ethical message" and gives evaluation of his "ethical system." Contends that The Pilgrim's Progress depicts "that individualism characteristic of Puritan thought which gives to Bunyan a deep conviction about personal ethical responsibility."

Turner, James. "Bunyan's Sense of Place." In The Pilgrim's Progress: Critical and Historical Views, pp. 91-110. Edited by Vincent Newey. Liverpool: Liverpool University Press, 1980.

Claims that Bunyan's places in the allegory are associated with a "generalized concept of the world." "The pilgrims' use of space while on the road is vocational ... in the palaces and vineyards ... it is recreational."

Tuve, Rosemond. Allegorical Imagery. Some Medieval Books and Their Posterity. Princeton: Princeton University Press, 1966, pp. 145-218.

Not especially helpful as a critical study of Bunyan's allegory, but Chapter III entitled "Guillaume's Pilgrimage" might be enlightening in considering the possible sources of Bunyan's pilgrimage. However, the author attempts to show that the work is an "unlikely" source, for the allegory in Guillaume is "more truly figurative, more subtle and closer to ancient ways of pursuing enigmatic truths, however much it may lack Bunyan's moving simplicity."

Van Dyke, Carolynn. The Fiction of Truth, Structure of Meaning in Narrative and Dramatic Allegory. Ithaca: Cornell University Press, 1985.

Proposes a definition of allegory that identifies a semiotic code that distinguishes allegorical works and the ways in which Prudentius uses that code. In subsequent pages the author suggests ways "in which other writers use and therefore alter that code, until it can no longer usefully be regarded as the same code." Argues that some critics' views of

Bunyan's allegory rest on the short-sighted assumption "that certain overt or inferable generalizations constitute the nonnegotiable meanings of allegory and that incompatible meanings must therefore be inadvertent or subversive." Such thinking fails to do justice to Bunyan's "particular kind of inconsistencies," which are "not so much conflicts as equivocations." For Bunyan readers an option remains: "to assume that the equivocations all serve some kind of semiotic unity."

Thinks of Bunyan's integration "of allegorical vision and empirical realism" as an unique achievement.

The first chapter shows the thrust of the book. The chapter entitled "Allegory and Experience: The Pilgrim's Progress," pp. 156-97, has particular relevance to Part One and Part Two of Bunyan's allegory.

Walch, Gunter. "John Bunyan--Dichter der Plebejischen Fraktion Revolutionarer Puritanismus und Allegorie." Zeitschuft fur Anlistik and Amerikanestik 27 (1979): 197-207.

Argues that the Marxist interpretation of Bunyan is still at its beginnings even though Jack Lindsay and Alice West are writers of some worth in understanding what Bunyan really wrote. Claims that the opening of The Pilgrim's Progress is fed by Bunyan's Plebian religious revolutionary experience and above all this experience is the all-encompassing structure of his allegory.

Walton, George William. "The Function of Proverbs in Certain Works by John Bunyan." Ph.D. dissertation. Texas Tech. University, 1976.

States that the highest incidence of proverbs in Bunyan's writings occurs in The Pilgrim's Progress, Parts One and Two. In both parts, the proverb becomes central to Bunyan's major allegorical devices, including "brief didactic episodes; pivotal emblems in the Interpreter's house; and significant characters such as Hopeful, Talkative, By-ends, and Ignorance."

Watkins, Owen C. The Puritan Experience. London: Routledge & Kegan Paul, 1972, pp. 101-120.

 Compares Grace Abounding to other autobiographies and praises its unity of presentation. Argues for the authenticity of Grace Abounding and contradicts critics who deny its validity.

Watson, Melvin R. "The Drama of Grace Abounding." English Studies 46 no. 6 (1965): 471-82.

 Claims that Bunyan deliberately treats time impressionistically, deliberately attempting to enable the reader to feel the drama of time.

Webber, Joan. The Eloquent "I." Style and Self in Seventeenth-Century Prose. Madison: University of Wisconsin Press, 1968, pp. 15-52.

 Compares and contrasts Donne's Devotions and Bunyan's Grace Abounding as demonstrating the styles of the Anglican and Puritan faiths. Donne's prose is complex, witty, analytical, meditative, and the "I" tends to make Donne the "object of contemplation"; Bunyan's prose is repetorial, objective, taking place in public, and the "I" invites the reader to see him as an "instrument of use."

Weidhorn, Manfred. Dreams in Seventeenth-Century Literature. The Hague: Mouton, 1970, pp. 7, 82-88, 123-24, 156-57.

 Shows the dream not only as framework of The Pilgrim's Progress but also as part of its theme and content.

Wenzel, Seigfried. "The Pilgrimage of Life as a Late Medieval Genre." Medieval Studies 35 (1973): 370-388.

ANNOTATED BIBLIOGRAPHY

Argues that the "pilgrimage of life" is a late medieval genre, different not only from genres that portray a journey to heaven or hell but also distinct from morality plays. He selects The Pilgrim's Progress (and Deguilevilles's allegory) as a particular example of the genre and then shows features which characterize this late literary type.

Wright, Elizabeth. "The Pilgrim's Progress" Chapter Notes and Criticism. New York: American R.D.M. Corporation, 1977.

Concentrates on Part One and Part Two of The Pilgrim's Progress and gives brief analysis of some characters. Provides summary of story and an appraisal. Includes a reprint of Henri Talon's "Space and Hero in The Pilgrim's Progress" and adds a list of study topics and a brief bibliography.

Wyke, Clement Horatio. "John Bunyan and the Puritan Metaphor of Conflict." Ph.D. dissertation. University of Toronto, 1970.

Examines how Bunyan uses metaphor which describes the various kinds of conflict characteristic of Puritan religious experience in the seventeenth century:"God against Satan, the flesh against the spirit, the Christian against his persecutors, the soul against temptation, the inner promptings of conscience against sin and such like." Thinks of the term, metaphor, as "figurative language involving a transference of some kind from one domain of significance to another." Contends that Bunyan's early period of Biblical exegesis is primarily dominated by a literal-historical interpretaion of the text, a practice which "concurs with his appeal to concrete and literal experiences in constructing the metaphor of conflict in Grace Abounding." Demonstrates a figurative balance in The Pilgrim's Progress. Also examines the dream tradition in the allegory.

INDEX

The index includes the names of critics and their works included in this study. When there is more than one study by a given author, titles are arranged according to the chronological date of publication. References to authors and works appearing in footnotes are placed in parentheses. Short titles are used for some studies.

Adeney, Elizabeth, "Bunyan: A Unified Vision?" 43-44, 175
Adrian, Daryl B., "Introduction to The Pilgrim's Progress" 175
Alpaugh, David J., "Emblem and Interpretation in The Pilgrim's Progress 41-42, 175
Alter, Robert, "Mirrors for Immortality" 175

Bacon, Ernest W., John Bunyan, Pilgrim and Dreamer 176
Baird, Charles W., John Bunyan. A Study in Narrative Technique 176
Bartell, Shirley Miller, "Uncertainty in Bunyan Versus Assurance in Fox" 176
Batson, E. Beatrice, "Bunyan as Creative Artist" 177, Allegory and Imagination 177, "John Bunyan: Conscious Artist" 177, "Teaching The Pilgrim's Progress" 177, John Bunyan: The Pilgrim's Progress 178
Beal, Rebecca S., Grace Abounding to the Chief of Sinners: John Bunyan's Pauline Epistle" 13-15, 65-83, 178, "Bunyan in Prison" 178
Beatty, Bernard, "Rival Fables: The Pilgrim's Progress and Dryden's The Hind and the Panther 178
Bell, Robert, "Metamorphosis of Spiritual Autobiography" 3-4, 179
Bellamy, Joan, "John Bunyan and the Democratic Tradition" 179
Bennett, Rachel, "Punch Versus Christian in The Old Curiosity Shop" 179
Bizzell, Patricia Lynn, "Willfull Simplicity: the Charm of John Bunyan's Poetry" 179-80
Bloom, Morton W. "Allegory as Interpretation" 180
Bridges, Margaret, "The Sense of an Ending: The Case of the Dream Vision" 180
Brink, Andrew, "Bunyan's Pilgrim's Progress and the Secular Reader: A Psychological Approach" 180-181
Brittain, Vera, "Literary Testaments" 181
Broes, Arthur T., "Journey into Moral Darkness" 181
Bruss, Elizabeth W., Autobiographical Acts 182-83
Bzowski, Frances, "A Continuation of the Tradition of the

Irony of Death" 182

Campbell, Gordon, "The Theology of The Pilgrim's Progress" 45, (153), 182
Cantarow, Ellen, "A Wilderness of Opinions Confounded" 182
Carlton, Peter J. "Bunyan: Language, Convention, Authority" 10-13, 182-83
Clifford, Gay. The Transformations of Allegory 183.
Cobau, William Weinschenk, "Historical Modes in The Pilgrim's Progress 183-84
Cowan, Michael, City of the West 184
Curley, Thomas M., "The Spiritual Journey Moralized in Rasselas" 184

Damrosch, Leopold Jr., "Experience and Allegory in Bunyan" 35-37, 56-57, God's Plot and Man's Stories 184
Daniells, Roy, Milton, Mannerism and Baroque 184-85
Davie, Donald, A Gathered Church 185
Davis, Nick, "The Problem of Misfortune in The Pilgrim's Progress, 26-28, 185
Delaney, Paul, British Autobiography in the Seventeenth Century 185, "Bleak House and Doubting Castle" 185-86
Donaldson, Ian, "Bartholomew Fair and The Pilgrim's Progress" 186
Dutton, A. Richard, "'Interesting but tough': Reading The Pilgrim's Progress" 186

Ebner, Dean, Autobiography in Seventeenth Century England 186
Edwards, Philip, "The Journey in The Pilgrim's Progress" 22-24, 186-87
El-Gabalawry, Saad, "The Pilgrimage: George Herbert's Favorite Allegorical Technique" 187

Finch, Geoffrey, "The Puritan Imagination of John Bunyan" 44-45, 187
Fish, Stanley, "Progress in The Pilgrim's Progress" 17-20, 187-88, Surprised by Sin 187, Self-Consuming Artifacts 188
Fitch, Robert Elliot, "Odyssey of the Self-Centered Self" 188
Fletcher, Angus, Allegory: The Theory of Symbolic Mode 188-89
Forrest, James F., "How Grace Abounded" 189, "Ignorance as White Devil: a Bunyan Debt to Thomas Adams" 189, "Ready-to-halt's Dance and the Promises" 189, "Bunyan's Ignorance and the Flatterer" 47, 189, "Mercy with her Mirror" 59, 189-90, "Some Spiritual Symbols in Puritan Literature" 190, "Bunyan's Threatening Hill" 190, "Patristic Tradition and Psychological Image in Bunyan's Three Shining Ones" 190, "Vision, Form, and the Imagination in the Second Part" 54-55, 172-74, 190-191, "The Pilgrim's Progress, A Dream that Endures," 191
Frye, Northrop, The Secular Scripture 191
Frye, Roland Mushat, God, Man and Satan 191-92
Furlong, Monica, Puritan's Progress 192

Gilbert, Sandra M., "Plain Jane's Progress" 192
Gillie, Christopher, Character

in English Literature 192-93
Greaves, Richard L., "John Bunyan and Covenant Thought in the Seventeenth Century" (81), 193, John Bunyan (153), 193, "Bunyan Through the Centuries" 61-62, 193
Greene, Donald, "On The Pilgrim's Progress 193-94
Guibbory, Achsah, The Map of Time 194
Guilzo, Allen C. "John Bunyan's Christian at Three Hundred" 194

Haferkamp, Berta, Bunyan als Kunstler 194
Halewood, William H., The Poetry of Grace 194-95
Hammond, Brean S., The Pilgrim's Progress: Satire and Social Comment 195
Hardin, Richard F., "Bunyan, Mr. Ignorance, and the Quakers" 48, 195
Harding, M. Esther, "The 'I' and the 'Not I'" 195
Hardison, O.B. Jr., "Criticism and the Search for Pattern" 196
Harrison, G.B., John Bunyan: A Study in Personality 196
Haskin, Dayton, "The Light Within" 196, "Bunyan, Luther, and the Struggle with Belatedness" 4-5, 196-97, "The Burden of Interpretations" 163, 197
Hawkins, Anne, "Archetypes in the Spiritual Autobiographies of Augustine, John Bunyan, and Thomas Merton" 197-98, "The Double Conversion in Grace Abounding" 5-7, 160-62, 198
Henson, Gail Clark Ritchie, "A Holy Desperation" 198-99
Hinds, Carol Louise, "The Implication of Puritan Principle" 199
Honig, Edwin, Dark Conceit 199
Hough, Graham, An Essay on Criticism 199
Howell, Elmo, "Bunyan's Two Valley's" 48, 199-200
Hunter, J. Paul, The Reluctant Pilgrim 200

Inglis, Fred, An Essential Discipline 200
Iser, Wolfgang, "Bunyan's Pilgrim's Progress" 24-26, 85-124, The Implied Reader 200-201

James, Canon Eric, "The Significance of John Bunyan Today" 201
Johnson, Barbara Ann, "From Piers Plowman to Pilgrim's Progress 201-202
Johnston, Eleanor Isabel, "Puritan Poetics" 202

Kaufmann, U. Milo, The Pilgrim's Progress and Traditions in Puritan Meditation 15-17, 57-58, (154), (156), (168), 202-203
Keeble, N.H. The Pilgrim's Progress: A Puritan Fiction" 46-47, 203, "The Way and the Ways of Puritan Story: Biblical Patterns in Bunyan and his Contemporaries" 49-53, 204-205, "Christiana's Key: The Unity of the Pilgrim's Progress" 53-54, (152), 203, "Richard Baxter, Puritan Man of Letters" 203, "Introduction" The Pilgrim's Progress 168-71, 204, The Literary Culture of Nonconformity in Later Seventeenth Century England 205

Kelly, Balmer H., "Pilgrim's Existence" 205
Kelman, John, The Road 206
Knott, John R., Jr., "Bunyan's Gospel Day" 20-21, 166-67, 206, "Bunyan and the Holy Community" 55, 125-57, The Sword of the Spirit 206-207, (227)
Kornblum, Peter Edward, "The Neighborhoos of Reason" 207-208
Knox, R. Buick, "John Bunyan and His Pilgrim's Progress 207
Kuder, Stephen R. "The Literature of Conversion" 208

Lacassagne, Claude, "De Bernard à Bunyan, du Berger Fidèle à Evangélistse" 208-209
Leavis, F.R., "Afterword to The Pilgrim's Progress 209
Levin, Harry, "Paradises, Heavenly and Earthly" 209
Lewalski, Barbara Kiefer, "Typological Symbolism and the 'Progress of the Soul' in Seventeenth-Century Literature" 209
Lewis, C.S., "The Vison of John Bunyan" 209-10
Lindsay, Jack, John Bunyan, Maker of Myths 210
Lyons, John O., The Invention of Self 210

MacCaffrey, Isabel G., Spenser's Allegory 210-211
MacDonald, Ruth K., "The Case for The Pilgrim's Progress" 211
MacNeice, Louis, Varieties of Parable 211
Mandel, Barret John, The Autobiographer's Art 211-12m "Bunyan and the Autobiographer's Artistic Purpose" 8-9, (79, 80), 211-12
Manlove, C.N. "The Image of the Journey in Pilgrim's Progress" 212
Marohl, Joseph William Jr., Argument and Narrative Technique in John Bunyan's Autobiography 212
Mills, David, "The Dreams of Bunyan and Langland" 212-13
Monk, Samuel Holt, Introductions to Selections from Grace Abounding and The Pilgrim's Progress 213
Morris, John N., "John Bunyan and the Head of Goliath" 213, "The Example of John Bunyan" 213-14

Nakano, Nancy Yashiko, "The Authority of Narrative" 214
Nellist, Brian, "The Pilgrim's Progress and Allegory" 37-38, 214-15
Nevo, Ruth, The Dial of Virtue 215
Newey, Vincent, The Pilgrim's Progress: Critical and Historical Views 22, (153), 215-16, "Bunyan and the Confines of the Mind" 215, Dorothea's Awakening" 216
Newman, S.J., "Bunyan's Solidness" 58, (152), 216-17
Nussbaum, Felicity A., 'By These Words I was Sustained', Bunyan's Grace Abounding" 9-10, 163-64, 217
Nuttall, A.D., Two Concepts of Allegory 217
Nuttall, Geoffrey F., "The Heart of The Pilgrim's Progress" 217-18

Ogden, James, "Bunyan's Idea of a 'Wide Field'" 218
Ogden, Marlene Ann, "Nathaniel

Hawthorne and John Bunyan" 218-19

Pascal, Roy, Design and Truth in Autobiography 219, "The Present Tense in The Pilgrim's Progress" 219
Pauli, Ruth F. Janda, "The Plot of Pilgrimage" 219-20
Pickering, Samuel, "E.E. Cummings Pilgrim's Progress" 61, 220
Pooley, Roger, A Study of John Bunyan's Language and Milieu 220, "The Wilderness of this World" 220-21
Puzon, M. Bridget, "The Archetype of the Journey" 221

Quilligan, Maureen, The Language of Allegory 28-34, 221

Reeves, Paschal, "The Pilgrim's Progress as a Precursor of the Novel" 221
Reuter, John Edward, "A Quiet Habitation" 222
Rexroth, Kenneth, "Classics Revisited" 222
Robinson, David, "Bunyan's House of the Interpreter and the Structure of The Pilgrim's Progress" 222
Roppen, George, and Sommer, Richard, Strangers and Pilgrims 222
Rosenwasser, David, "The Idea of Enclosure" 223
Roulston, C. Robert, "Hawthorne's Use of Bunyan's Symbols in The Celestial Railroad" 223

Sadler, Lynn Veach, John Bunyan (154), 224
Sams, Horace Jr., "Temptation in Imaginative Literature" 224

Santa Maria, Felixberto C. "An Audience Analysis of John Bunyan's The Pilgrim's Progress" 225
Schneider, Mabel D.J., "John Bunyan's The Pilgrim's Progress 225
Seed, David, "Dialogue and Debate in The Pilgrim's Progress 42-43, 55-56, 226
Sharrock, Roger, "Introduction to The Pilgrim's Progress 227, John Bunyan: The Pilgrim's Progress 227, John Bunyan (154-55), (157) "The Pilgrim's Progress": A Casebook 228, "John Bunyan in English Literature" 228, "Life and Story in The Pilgrim's Progress 39-41, (152), 228
Shenk, Robert, "John Bunyan: Puritan or Pilgrim?" 228
Shrimpton, Nick, "Bunyan's Military Metaphor" 22, 228
Smith, David, "The Enormous Room and The Pilgrim's Progress" 228-29
Smith, Herbert W. "Bunyan and Dante" 229
Snyder, Susan, "The Left Hand of God" 229
Spear, Jeffrey L., "Ruskin as a Prejudiced Reader" 229-30
Spengemann, Walter A., The Forms of Autobiography 230
Stranahan, Brainerd P., "Bunyan's Special Talent" 231, "Bunyan and the Bible" 230-231, "Bunyan and the Epistle to the Hebrews" 231-32
Stokes, E.E. Jr., "Bernard Shaw's Debt to John Bunyan" 230
Sutherland, James, English Literature of the Late Seventeenth Century 232

Talon, Henri, 54, "Space and the Hero in The Pilgrim's Progress 232, (239), John Bunyan. Writers and their Works
Taylor, Dennis, "Some Strategies of Religious Autobiography" 233
Thickstun, Margaret Olofson, "Fictions of the Feminine" 233-34, "The Preface to Bunyan's Grace Abounding as Pauline Epistle" 234
Thompson, James, ed., Introduction to The Pilgrim's Progress and Grace Abounding 234,
Thurland, M.J., "John Bunyan: A Theological Approach to Grace Abounding and The Pilgrim's Progress 235
Tindall, William York, John Bunyan: Mechanick Preacher (209), 235
Trull, Joe E., "The Ethics of John Bunyan" 235
Turner, James, "Bunyan's Sense of Place" 48, 236
Tuve, Rosemond, Allegorical Imagery 236

Van Dyke, Carolynn, "The Fiction of Truth" 236-37

Walch, Gunter, "John Bunyan" 237
Walton, George William, "The Function of Proverbs in Certain Works by John Bunyan" 237-38
Watkins, Owen C., "The Puritan Experience" 238
Watson, Melvin, "The Drama of Grace Abounding" 7-8, (79), 238
Webber, Joan, The Eloquent "I" 238
Weidhorn, Manfred, Dreams in Seventeenth-Century Literature 238
Wenzel, Siegfried, "The Pilgrimage of Life as a Late Medieval Genre" 238-39
Wright, Elizabeth, "The Pilgrim's Progress" 239
Wyke, Clement Horatio, "John Bunyan and the Puritan Metaphor of Conflict" 239